Spring Awakening

VIKING
Penguin India

WILLIAM RAEPER
MARTIN HOFTUN

SPRING AWAKENING

An account of the 1990 Revolution in Nepal

VIKING

VIKING

Penguin Books India (P) Ltd., B4/246, Safdarjang Enclave, New Delhi 110 029, India

Penguin Books Ltd., 27, Wrights Lane, London W8 5TZ, UK

Penguin Books USA Inc., 375 Hudson Street, New York, NY 10014, U.S.A.

Penguin Books Australia Ltd., Ringwood, Victoria, Australia

Penguin Books Canada Ltd., 10, Alcorn Avenue, Suite 300, Toronto, Ontario M4V 382, Canada

Penguin Books (N.Z.) Ltd., 182-190 Wairau Road, Auckland 10, New Zealand

First published in VIKING by Penguin Books India (P) Ltd. 1992

Copyright © the estate of William Raeper & Martin Hoftun 1992

Typeset in Times Roman by The New Concept Consultancy Services, New Delhi

Made and printed in India by Ananda Offset Private Ltd., Calcutta *for*

Mina Maharjan

Contents

Preface

Living in Kathmandu in late 1989 and early 1990 one could not but become involved in what was happening politically. The Indian Trade Embargo had hardened public opinion. There was a clear feeling that the Panchayat government could not last and that significant events were about to take place. The result was a political revolution.

By 18 February 1990 when the first demonstrators took to the streets to be met with police brutality there seemed no option but to record what was happening. In this way the book slowly started to take form. At first we intended to write a short, chronological description of the seven week revolution, but the book grew in depth and scope to take in the introduction of the new constitution and the democratic elections in May 1991.

The interviews on which much of the book is based were conducted partly in Nepali and partly in English and recorded on tape. The politicians willingly spared the time though it was not always easy to contact them given the political situation.

The writing of this book was completed between June and November 1991. Both of us spent the autumn of 1991 in Kathmandu in order to finish the book. Given our method of working it is hard to say who did what and in its final form the book is the product of a joint effort.

We are aware that we have concentrated on only sixteen months in Nepal's modern political life. Moreover, much of what we have written has been confined to the Kathmandu valley. This is because the decisive events did take place there, but it is also due to the limitations of geography and communications which Nepal imposes. Reports from the districts were notoriously difficult to verify. Even in the Kathmandu valley we often had to steer our way carefully through contradictory statements.

We have chosen to write now while the events of the revolution are still fresh. As much as possible we hope that the voices of those we have spoken to, who represent the hopes and aspirations in Nepal today, are expressed fully in this book.

Gjeving, Oxford, Kathmandu   *William Raeper*
1992.   *Martin Hoftun*

Acknowledgements

This book would never have been written without the generosity and enthusiasm of a large group of individuals. Some of these individuals have been so central to the project that their names deserve to be listed on the front cover.

Foremost among these are Krishna Raj Ghimire and Gautam Nepaune. From the beginning Krishna worked full-time on the project, filling every role from secretary to driver to translator and political informant. He has done all this with an unflagging commitment. Gautam worked as a research assistant from early February 1991 until May 1992. He was our main informant writing daily reports on the latest political developments. He was also instrumental in organizing most of the interviews.

Another close friend and valuable informant was Nar Bahadur Gurung. Uttam Kumar Bajrecharya must also be mentioned. He gave us inside information about the uprising in Patan and at a later stage worked full-time to obtain photographs for the book.

Warm and sincere thanks must be given to all the interviewees. They made this book possible. Without even one of them the book would have been the less. Space does not permit all of them to be mentioned here. However, special thanks must be given to Krishna Prasad Bhattarai, Narayan Man Bijukche (Comrade Rohit), Padma Ratna Tuladhar and Ghore Bahadur Khapangi.

We are also tremendously grateful to NORAD (Norwegian Agency for Development Cooperation) who provided the necessary funds for us to turn this material into a published book. We would like to make special mention of Ane Haaland who helped make these funds available.

All the interviews had to be transcribed and many had to be translated. We would like to thank the following for undertaking this time-consuming work: Tullis Hoftun, Ishwori Ghimire, Prakash Ghimire and Bård Arne Olsen.

Shanti Mishra read through our manuscript before it was sent to the publisher. We are grateful for her constructive comments and suggestions.

Most of the photographs in this book were provided by the following people free of cost: Prakash Kaphley, Sushil Pyakural, Phil Grabsky, Merete Lindstad, Håkon Lislerund, Bjørn Ødegaard, and Kristian Løvås. Some of the photographs came from individuals in Kathmandu whom we were unable to identify. We express our thanks and apologize for our inability to mention them by name. During the period of research in Nepal a number of friends provided practical assistance and encouragement. Among these were Ellen Merete Wilkens, Else Braut, Astrid Hovengen, Neil Whittaker, Sue Pennington, Dhanalal Maharjan, Kristian Løvås and Odd Hoftun.

Lastly, we would like to thank all those who contributed in some way towards this book and whose names have not been mentioned.

It is thanks to the people of Nepal that this book came into being. More than anything this book is theirs.

ONE

The Historical And Cultural Setting

The modern nation of Nepal dates back to 1768 when King Prithvi Narayan Shah, from the small kingdom of Gorkha in the central hills of Nepal, conquered the Kathmandu valley. Prior to this, the Kathmandu valley, one of the most fertile valleys in the world, had been in the hands of the Newaris, who were known particularly for their mercantile skills and crafts and were expert creators of the magnificent temples and pagodas which still grace the Kathmandu valley. The Newaris, a Tibeto-Burmese people, have the oldest literary tradition in Nepal and possess their own language. With their complex mixture of Hindu, Buddhist and Tantric rituals and beliefs, they have maintained cultural and religious traditions which have long since disappeared from other parts of Asia.

King Prithvi Narayan Shah's achievements were numerous. He expanded his tiny kingdom ten-fold and built up a highly centralized state. His strategy was simple, but effective. Following the old ideals of a Hindu warrior, Prithvi Narayan Shah was able to establish his suzerainty over the rulers of the central Himalayas. In doing so he carved out a kingdom for himself twice the size of modern Nepal. In order to keep the different ethnic and religious groups under his command in check, he relied on the imposition of Hindu rituals from above.

With more than thirty different languages and a hundred different ethnic groups and castes, Nepal has remained a vivid mosaic of cultures. This astonishing diversity is largely due to Nepal being at the meeting point between the two main cultures and races in Asia— namely the Aryan-Indian and Mongolian-Chinese. The Tibeto-Burmese peoples of Nepal and the Hindu high castes live mainly in the Himalayan and central hill regions. In contrast, Nepalis of Indian origin and other indigenous groups live in the Terai, the flat, lush plains to the south, which border India.

Prithvi Narayan Shah's small empire did not flourish long. Although the House of the Gorkhas continued to expand after his death, a war in 1814 with the British East India Company soon put paid to its growing power. Initially the outcome of the war was uncertain. The Gorkha soldiers were noted fighters and accustomed to mountain warfare. Finally, however, the British forces proved superior and the Gorkhas were forced to accept a humiliating defeat. In the Peace of Segauli in 1816, the territory of Nepal was trimmed down and its borders fixed more or less along present lines.

After the defeat by the British, the ruling class in Nepal underwent a profound change. Instead of embarking on a policy of military expansion, the ruling class was introspective and an era of deadly court intrigues began. Politics became a game played by the few high caste families who mainly belonged to the Gorkha area. Much blood was shed before a strong, single ruler finally emerged. It was during these treacherous years that the king lost his *de facto* powers and the influence of the Prime Minister grew in importance.

This state of affairs was institutionalized by Jang Bahadur Rana in the middle of the nineteenth century. He was probably the most remarkable politician in the history of modern Nepal after Prithvi Narayan Shah.

Jang Bahadur Rana began his political career with the murder of his uncle. From then on he was in the forefront of the struggle for power, and violence, intrigue and deceit were his hallmarks. The climax came with the Kot massacre in 1846. In a bloodbath in the royal courtyard in the centre of Kathmandu, Jang Bahadur Rana eliminated all his possible competitors. As a result, he became the most powerful person in Nepal and succeeded in making the post of Prime Minister hereditary to his own family. His family now took the name Rana which was a royal title.

Jang Bahadur Rana became popular with the British in India after he sent soldiers from Nepal to help curb the Revolt in 1857. He was invited to Britain by Queen Victoria in gratitude, becoming the first native ruler from the Indian subcontinent to visit Europe.

A century of Rana rule had now begun in earnest—and it is this period which comes to the minds of most Nepalis when they talk about the 'hard old days'. The Ranas lived in extravagant, despotic luxury and ruthlessly suppressed the Nepali people. The country remained in the grip of a family oligarchy which was obsessed with real or imaginary threats to its position of absolute power. Remnants of these days are the airy, white palaces scattered all over modern Kathmandu built in a pseudo-classical western style. These palaces appear to have been colonial buildings in a country which was never a colony. They remind the modern onlooker of a time when no distinction was made between the Maharaja's privy purse and the country's treasury. The Ranas lived insulated lives. They did not want to be associated with their own people or their own culture. They wanted to be as European as possible, but at the same time they tried to fend off all foreign influence from the rest of the population. Their measures for ensuring this were extreme.

In all towns there was regular curfew at night which started at five or six in the evening after which no one was allowed to venture out. Development work of any kind was seen as a political threat. Education for anyone other than the Ranas was discouraged. All organized social and cultural activities were illegal and people were jailed even for circulating popular Hindu religious texts.

The people who had to bear the brunt of the regime's injustices were the farmers. They carried the load of taxation. Whenever the Maharaja wished to increase his own allowance, he simply announced new taxes.

The Ranas employed some clever means to ensure that their autocratic rule continued. Most important was the *Pajani* system which helped maintain the loyalty of all government servants to the ruler. According to this, all civil servants could hold a post no longer than a year. They were transferred from job to job making it impossible to build up any individual power-base. There was also a complex system of rituals in which officials in government service regularly had to show their loyalty and obedience to the ruler.

The Ranas were able to keep the country isolated because of the Himalayas to the north and the dense jungles to the south. Within the country they preserved their power through the imposition of a Hindu social order. What had begun in the days of Prithvi Narayan Shah with the promulgation of a few ritual laws now developed into an all-encompassing social code called the *Muluki Ain,* or the Law of the Nation. Through this code all the country's ethnic groups and castes were organized in a hierarchical system of four social classes and thirty-six castes. Each individual's daily life was regulated according to rituals which varied depending on which caste one belonged to. Various revised versions of this code existed as the only written constitution of Nepal until 1959.

In this way the Ranas were propped up by isolation and by maintaining the status quo. These two aspects were inter-related. Subsequently, the rule of the Ranas came to an end when the country finally opened up its borders as a result of the revolution in 1951.

Even so, during the last years of Rana rule it was impossible to carry on a policy of isolation. The Gorkha recruits, for example, who had been recruited into the British army and who fought in the First and Second World War, brought information about the outside world back to their mountain villages. Within Kathmandu itself, the opening of Trichandra College, a small college of further education in 1923, had helped foster a small intellectual élite. This group was to play an important role subsequently. Although they belonged to the high caste élite, they were barred from high positions within the regime because they were not part of the Rana family. Their frustration led to a few forming the first political party in 1935, called the Praja Parishad. The main aim of this party, which met underground for two years, was the overthrow of the Rana government. But by 1937 the government had executed three of the party members and the remaining members were all given life imprisonment. By swift action the Ranas had managed to put down internal dissent, but they were not able to prevent liberal ideas from influencing members of their own rank. In 1948 the new Maharaja Padma Shumshere took the unprecedented step of announcing a new constitution.

Though the constitution did not provide for full parliamentary democracy, it was enough to put the Ranas on the defensive. Padma Shumshere suffered a predictable fate. He was exiled from the country and replaced by the last Maharaja, the hardliner, Mohun Shumshere.

At this moment, however, external events began to overtake the Ranas. With the end of British rule in India, the Ranas lost their most important ally. The new Indian leadership did not support the Ranas and viewed them as, at best, an anachronism which would soon disappear under the floodtide of a popular revolt. Meanwhile, a politically active group of Nepalis had formed and strengthened itself in India. They were nationalists and most of them had been involved in Mahatma Gandhi's Quit India movement. They believed that the overthrow of the Rana government in Nepal was simply a logical continuation of the fight against colonial rule in India.

In 1947 the Nepali National Congress Party was formed at Varanasi. A few months later they joined forces with a group of exiled Ranas in Calcutta and changed their name to the Nepali Congress Party. It did not take the new party long to act. The party organized a strike in the jute mills, just inside the Nepali border. These mills were the only industry in Nepal. The Nepali Congress tried to follow the strike with an unsuccessful movement of civil disobedience against the government.

It was, however, King Tribhuvan of Nepal who took the first, vital step. He had been virtually a detainee of the Maharaja and had shown no inclination to alter his position. Having received the Maharaja's permission to go on a hunting trip, the King left the palace with his family in early November 1950. Much to everybody's surprise, the party made no pretence at going shooting, but drove straight to the Indian Embassy in Kathmandu. There the King requested political asylum. A few days later the King flew to New Delhi. Meanwhile, a small rebel army led by the Nepali Congress made inroads into Nepal's border in the south.

The insurrection was prematurely called off. The moment King Tribhuvan arrived in New Delhi, the Indians took the lead. Superseding King Tribhuvan and the Nepali Congress, the leaders in New Delhi forced a compromise. As a result, a coalition government of Ranas and the Nepali Congress came to power. Finally, on 18 February 1951, King Tribhuvan, who had now become a symbol of democracy, was reinstated as ruler.

The revolution forced open the borders of Nepal, but first in was the Indian government. Jawaharlal Nehru, then Prime Minister of India, talked about a 'special relationship', but in practice this meant that the Indians took control of all Nepali decisions. During the first two years after the revolution, Nepali leaders visited New Delhi thrice to solve domestic problems. The Indian ambassador in Kathmandu, C.P.N. Singh, was rumoured to be more powerful than the Prime Minister. Indian experts were quickly put in charge of reorganizing the Nepali army and the civil service.

Political instability spread through Nepal as King Tribhuvan kept delaying the announcement of elections for a constituent assembly. Dozens of political parties sprang up and claimed that they spoke for the majority. There were two coup attempts. The government in Kathmandu exercised little jurisdiction over what went on in the district. On one occasion they even had to call in the Indian army to crush a rebellion in eastern Nepal.

Six months after it assumed office, the Rana-Congress coalition collapsed. From then on the King installed and dismissed governments as he wished. As the only force of political stability within the country, King Tribhuvan's position grew steadily in importance. He remained popular, and appointed a party-based government in 1952, but his accommodating attitude towards the Indians led to increasing unrest.

Yet there was no national-level leader to take over in Nepal. In 1951 the literacy rate was still less than two per cent and there was no means or tradition for any form of political participation. The revolution of 1951 was, therefore, instigated by the Palace and merely replaced one élite with another. Political life in the years following 1951 consisted of personal feuds and rivalry among a small, influential clique.

The political mood changed radically with the death of King Tribhuvan in 1955. In contrast to his father, King Mahendra was a strong man with an iron will and solid experience to back him. His manipulative abilities became apparent very quickly and he resorted to all kinds of exotic methods to keep his finger on the pulse of public opinion—including allegedly dressing up as a poor farmer to walk the streets of Kathmandu. More than anything, King Mahendra was an ardent nationalist. His first priority seemed to be to extract Nepal from India's tightening grip.

In order to pursue his independent line, the king appointed Tanka Prasad Acharya as Prime Minister in 1956. Acharya was well-known for his stand against India and during his term of office made the first official contacts with China. Possibly reacting to Indian demands, the King dismissed Acharya in mid-1957, but in an act of cool political manoeuvre, asked the former rebel leader, K.I. Singh, to form the new government. To everyone's surprise, the new Prime Minister displayed a friendly attitude towards India. This prompted King Mahendra to dismiss him after only five months in office. Thereafter, Mahendra took power into his own hands.

The first few years of Mahendra's rule marked a noticeable shift in Nepal's foreign policy. India was unable to dominate Nepali politics as it had done under King Tribhuvan. Contacts were established with China and diplomatic links were forged with the US and France. Nepal became a member of the UN and began to receive aid from many countries. Finally, after being cut off from the world for so long, Nepal became a member of the international community of nations.

The 1950s represent the beginning of the modern period in Nepal's history. With the arrival of the first tourists and aid workers, the old isolation was broken for ever—and the country was open to foreign influences. Nepali culture and politics received a boost in the country and a political élite formed where politics previously had amounted to little more than the personal whims of the ruler.

The end of the 1950s brought two major surprises. On 12 February 1959 King Mahendra made a momentous announcement. He proclaimed a new democratic constitution and declared that free elections would be held shortly. Even though the constitution had been given by the King and not by an elected assembly, most politicians welcomed this move which came at a time when many of them had given up any idea of democratic reform.

The second surprise was the overwhelming victory for the Congress Party in the elections held during February and March. Due to the terrain and problems of communication, the election was a month-long affair. When the results finally came in, Bisheswor Prasad Koirala, the leader of the Nepali Congress Party, became the first elected Prime Minister of Nepal. Koirala's government was efficient and stable and swiftly started to implement radical reforms. The most controversial of these was the Land Reform Act. This act abolished all the tax-free *Birtha* lands held by rich landowners. The legislation drew a strong reaction from segments of the rural élite. King Mahendra watched the government's actions and was not satisfied.

During the short reign of this government, law and order posed a problem in some parts of country. In Gorkha, a part of the population rebelled and the situation seemed to get out of hand. This was the excuse King Mahendra had been waiting for. Invoking emergency powers granted to him by the constitution (which he himself had drawn up), Mahendra dismissed the Koirala government on 15 December 1960. The members of parliament and the cabinet were taken into custody. King Mahendra declared that the elected government had failed in its democratic duties.

Koirala and King Mahendra symbolized the major conflict in Nepali politics during the modern period. Both were accomplished leaders and statesmen. Koirala represented popular power, while the King was seen as a symbol of the status quo. In contrast to the King,

B.P. Koirala was educated abroad. Like many others, he was part of Gandhi's non-violent movement and became the leader of the Nepali Congress from its inception. He was an idealist and a committed socialist. Many of his ideas were set out in his novels and short stories. At the same time he was both uncompromising and pragmatic. King Mahendra's royal coup was, therefore, a victory for traditional power.

King Mahendra defended his actions by stating that Nepal was not yet ready for multi-party democracy. Instead, a democratic system more suited to the needs of Nepal would be introduced. With this in mind, the King announced the Panchayat constitution on 16 December 1962. This constitution remained in force in Nepal until the revolution of 1990.

The word 'Panchayat' refers to the village council which was supposed to be the basis of the system. The masses were to rule directly through their local panchayats ensuring a grassroots democracy. Power was to flow from the people directly to government—bypassing any need for political parties which, in any case, only served the interests of a few. Members of village and city councils were elected directly. From these councils, representatives were elected to the district panchayats, which again elected members of the Rashtriya Panchayat, the parliament. The elected government was, therefore, a kind of pyramid with the village councils at the bottom and the parliament at the top.

The Panchayat constitution was not based on any central governing principle. In it, the old idea of a Hindu kingdom was combined with a modern one-party or no-party state. At the centre of the Panchayat system, however, was the King. He was all-powerful.

The Panchayat constitution strengthened the King's position. Article 21 stated that the Nepali people only constituted a nation 'united by the common bond of allegiance to the crown'. Twenty per cent of the seats in the parliament were reserved for royal nominees. Mahendra also had other, more effective, ways of enforcing his will. Inside the Palace, the Raj Sabha, the Palace Assembly, the King's Council, the Raj Parishad, and the Palace Secretariat operated as a kind of shadow government.

The overweening bureaucracy made decisions difficult to trace and often no one wanted to claim responsibility for political actions. The cabinet often found itself in an awkward middle position. Chosen by the King, but responsible to the public, it was manipulated ruthlessly by the Palace.

King Mahendra, in fact, set up several parallel structures within the Panchayat system. One important feature was the Class Organizations. They were set up ostensibly to represent different classes of people in the country, including workers, peasants, youth, women, ex-servicemen and students. These Class Organizations played an important role in the Panchayat system and had their own separate representation in the Rashtriya Panchayat, the parliament.

Nepal was further divided into fourteen zones and each had a zonal commissioner with wide-ranging powers, appointed by the King. These commissioners were the King's men, receiving their orders directly from the palace and even being able to control local elections.

A few years after the introduction of the Panchayat system, the King introduced the 'Back to the Village National Campaign'. Inspired by the Cultural Revolution in China, the campaign was intended to educate and mobilize the masses by sending academics and students out into the villages. In effect, the 'Back to the Village National Campaign' soon became another institution through which the King was able to control events in the districts. The committees set up by the campaign came to be referred to as the 'politburo' of Nepal.

The Panchayat system served to revive old political traditions. Elements from the Rana regime were preserved and even developed further. Instead of the direct flow of power from the masses upwards as was claimed, the Panchayat system was a tool whereby the King exercised supreme power. The main principles of the Rana regime were left intact. Power was exercised from above and all government servants had to show personal loyalty to their superiors. In the day-to-day functioning of the bureaucracy even minor decisions had to be referred above. The decrees and directives the King issued, often took no account of the plans of the administration.

Hinduism was central to the Panchayat system just as it had been central to the Rana regime. But the Hinduism of the Panchayat system contained important differences. With the abolition of the caste laws and the declaration in the constitution that Nepal was a Hindu kingdom, Hinduism was no longer the fabric of the social order, it became a state religion.

Two of the objectives of the Panchayat system were the neutralization of the political élite and the prevention of ethnic politics. But ironically, the political system created an élite stronger than the previous one. And, with no political parties, elections became focused on communal and ethnic distinctions. The Panchayat system failed, however, for other reasons. In the end, it was unable to sustain the wishes of the people.

Opposition to the Panchayat government dated right back to its beginnings. After King Mahendra dissolved the Koirala government, the then-banned Nepali Congress Party and Communist Party mounted a steady campaign against the new regime in Kathmandu. At times opposition became violent. However, King Mahendra's repressive policies, lack of foreign support, and the inability of the banned parties to mobilize for a mass uprising, meant that the opposition had little or no effect. During the 1960s many former party politicians found their way into the Panchayat system and old political conflicts were somehow absorbed and disappeared.

Fresh hopes for reform surfaced with the death of King Mahendra in February 1972. The new king, Birendra, had been educated abroad. He was known to be liberal-minded, and to have a genuine wish for the development of the country. Even before the coronation several organizations had petitioned the new King for reforms. To everyone's disappointment, however, the second amendment to the constitution in 1975 lacked any substantial change. On the contrary, the dreaded 'Back to the Village National Campaign' was actually brought into the constitution. Many thought this reactionary turn was connected with the sudden introduction of martial law in India; others felt the King to be reacting against the terrorist activities of the extreme leftist group, the Naxalites, in eastern Nepal.

It was at this moment that the former Prime Minister and leader of Nepali Congress Party, B.P. Koirala, decided to change his political tactics. In his own words he changed his party's policy from that of, 'confrontation to that of reconciliation'. In 1977 King Birendra granted Koirala an amnesty and a little later gave him an audience. New events, however, meant that this new strategy of the Nepali Congress Party was unable to bear any fruit.

On 6 April 1979 the students in Kathmandu organized a massive demonstration. They were protesting against the assassination of President Zulfikar Ali Bhutto in Pakistan and pressing for educational reforms. The demonstration was crushed mercilessly by the police. Unrest spread to other parts of the country sparking off strikes and protests. The demands became political and the masses joined the students in their struggle for democratic reforms. The movement swelled and culminated in a major demonstration in Kathmandu on 23 May. The crowd reached the royal palace, setting fire to several government buildings on the way.

Unexpectedly and dramatically, King Birendra announced a national referendum the following morning over Radio Nepal. He stated that the people should be given the choice of either a reformed Panchayat system or a return to multi-party democracy. Both the opposition and the government were taken completely by surprise by the news. The King's decision can only be explained as his own spontaneous reaction to the demonstration of the previous day.

What followed the royal announcement was a year of political freedom. The ban on the major political parties was lifted, they organized meetings and rallies, and campaigned for multi-party democracy. Censorship was lifted and political writing flourished. Having been forced underground for more than twenty years, however, the political parties lacked an organizational base. The party leaders, on their release from jail, had to fight the well-organized propaganda machine of the government—and the government was determined that the Panchayat system should continue. With the government being in an advantageous position, the referendum campaign became a futile exercise.

The vote was taken on 2 May 1980. The Panchayat government won with a small margin of 54.7 per cent of the votes, compared to 45.2 per cent who voted for the reintroduction of multi-party democracy.

The Panchayat system had survived its first major crisis. Yet its victory had been far from convincing and the political system's continued survival was no longer certain.

Nepal In Crisis

Any hopes of political change in Nepal in 1980 were dashed when the results of the referendum were announced. The leaders of the multi-party coalition were thrown into confusion as none of them had actually admitted the possibility that their side might lose. Alongside the initial shock and disappointment in the ranks of the opposition, there was a sense of bewilderment in the country as a whole. With the prospect of the return of multi-party democracy defeated, no one knew what the King had meant by his promise to reform the Panchayat system.

In a speech given six months before the referendum the King had made certain public declarations. He had stated that whatever the result of the referendum, he would introduce direct elections to the parliament and the cabinet would be elected by and be responsible to the parliament. No one was confident that these reforms would actually be implemented. Rather the reverse—there was a widespread fear that the referendum results would only be seen by the present government as a symbol of the existing order.

On 15 December 1980, King Birendra announced the Third Amendment to the Constitution. This was a moment of irony, for it came exactly twenty years after his father, King Mahendra, had dissolved the first and only democratic government in the country in 1960.

Although the King refused to lift the ban on political parties, the amendment seemed to have brought about some reforms. A degree of democracy was introduced into the Panchayat system. The parliament, the Rashtriya Panchayat, was to be elected on the basis of adult franchise for the first time. The cabinet was to be elected by, and be responsible to, the parliament. But, in the final analysis, little had changed. The constitution had been merely given a face-lift as the King still held on to absolute power and could interfere in government affairs. Members of the opposition were still effectively barred from standing for parliament, as, in order to be eligible, they had to be members of the Panchayat Class Organizations.

Worse, still, was the creation of a new and powerful committee—the Panchayat Policy and Evaluation Committee. Ironically, this committee was set up to reform the Panchayat system as the King had promised. But in effect this body replaced the 'Back to the Village National Campaign'. The committee was invested with sweeping powers to check any member of parliament and keep them within the strict limits of Panchayat democracy. Members were nominated personally by the King and the chairman of the committee was also the chairman of the Rashtriya Panchayat. By abolishing the tight local structures of the 'Back to the Village National Campaign' this new, toned-down version of what had been dubbed 'Nepal's politburo' might have proved more acceptable to the country as a whole. But the opposite was the case. The Panchayat Policy and Evaluation Committee was independent of parliamentary control and powerful. It was a sinister and efficient tool in the hands of the power élite around the palace and was used frequently to control the government.

While the King's Third Amendment to the Constitution seemed liberal in principle, the practice was very different. If anything, reactionary power in the country grew stronger. If the Panchayat Policy and Evaluation Committee functioned as a kind of 'politburo'—the National Sports Council, though under an innocuous name, organized and trained the storm-troopers who maintained the force of the Panchayat system.

In the long run the referendum did not bring about reforms, rather the contrary—the clock was turned back. Reactionary elements used constitutional and non-constitutional bodies to exercise their power.

The closer to the King they were, the greater their power, but the degree to which the King controlled their activities remains an open question. The power clique remained hidden behind closed doors. Yet in the years after the 1980 referendum it became a part of the popular understanding. In hushed voices the clique would be referred to by different names—names such as 'Bhumigat Giroha' (which literally means 'Underground Elements'), 'the Palace' or even 'the Mandales'. The Mandales were originally the members of the Nepal Rashtriya Swatantra Vidhyarthi Mandal (which enjoyed the support of the Panchayat government)—but throughout the 1980s the term came to be used for any conservative or reactionary member of the political system.

Meanwhile disillusion had set in among the opposition. Even so, the political parties began to reorganize themselves very quickly and tried hard to adapt to the new situation. Though they were banned once again, their position was very different than was the case prior to the 1979 uprising. Now if the parties accepted the 'banned label' and restricted their activities to the minimum, there was no interference. Large public meetings were declared illegal, but the parties were allowed to keep their organizations intact. Signboards were pulled down all over Kathmandu, but the parties were allowed to keep their offices. The press was given a substantial degree of autonomy (something which was unthinkable before) as long as they put the words 'banned' in brackets before the party's name.

After the referendum, however, the government very quickly reintroduced press censorship. But, just like the treatment of the political parties, press censorship was very haphazard. When the government crack-down was initiated against the press, whole editions of newspapers would be seized and editors or journalists arrested. Even so, other publications were allowed to criticize the government as long as they did not write anything against the King. The situation was confusing and the methods used by the government were crude. One common way of silencing a newspaper was for the government to buy it. This was hardly effective as the same newspapers sprang up barely a week later under different names with much the same kind of critical articles as before. The government's erratic treatment of the opposition was what characterized the early part of the 1980s.

After the Third Amendment to the Constitution there was some careful optimism towards the Panchayat government among broad segments of the population. These people pointed out that some reforms had been implemented even if they were not significant or far-reaching. They hoped for a kind of evolutionary democracy within the Panchayat system.

The first real test of the genuineness of the reforms after the 1980 referendum came with the elections to the Rashtriya Panchayat, in 1981. These (the first direct elections since 1959) were boycotted by the banned political parties. Despite the boycott voter turnout was higher than expected. Since political parties could not take part, the election campaign tended to be fought along ethnic and caste lines. In the event, Surya Bahadur Thapa was re-elected as Prime Minister by a majority of the parliament. Thapa therefore became the first Prime Minister to lead a properly elected government within the Panchayat system. This apparent strength, however, led to the government's downfall. Thapa's government enjoyed more power than the Palace clique could tolerate and he was ousted. Describing how he was finally dismissed as Prime Minister, Surya Bahadur Thapa said: 'There was some intrigue and a voice of No Confidence was raised in the parliament. The members whose support I had were badly pressed by the Palace to vote against me. I naturally did not want to put any pressure on my friends and I resigned.' Afterwards it was discovered that all members of parliament had received phone calls from the Palace ordering them to vote against Thapa. In this way the old guard of the Panchayat government secured another victory and the Third Amendment to the Constitution lost all practical relevance.

With Thapa gone, Lokendra Bahadur Chand became Prime Minister in mid-1983. The power élite in the Palace thought that Chand was a safe choice, but soon even he proved too independent for them. It was only after the second direct election to parliament in 1986 that the Palace succeeded in installing a puppet Prime Minister with Marich

Man Singh Shrestha. Shrestha came to power in much the same way as Lokendra Bahadur Chand—with the help of a majority vote in parliament. Even so, everybody knew that the majority were really behind Rajeshwor Devkota, the other Prime Ministerial candidate.

The proceedings of the Rashtriya Panchayat had little influence on the day-to-day life of the people of Nepal. Everyone knew that it had little *de facto* power. People ignored it—at least until the middle of the 1980s when a series of corruption scandals shook the government.

A few ministers were forced out of their posts, but it was widely believed that corruption was more rampant than the government dared to admit. Rumours were rife around Kathmandu and articles in certain banned newspapers suggested that the royal family itself was implicated in smuggling drugs and gold. These rumours gained strength as important official posts were handed out to members of the royal family. The King's brothers, whose reputations were at best shady, were given the chairmanships of several important trusts. More importantly, the Queen was made head of the newly-established Social Services National Commission. The Queen had become a public figure in her own right and it did not help alleviate suspicion that she came from Rana stock. All aid money from private agencies was to be channelled through the Social Services National Commission and it was feared that a substantial amount of cash would disappear into Palace pockets.

During this period one person more than anybody else managed to uncover the truth about the rumours concerning corruption and abuse of power at the top levels of government. This man, an experienced politician and journalist named Padam Thakurathi, said: 'My main political goal was to attack the power élite. As a journalist, I wanted to expose the activities of the so-called "unconstitutional elements", this gang of hooligans and smugglers in the Palace, who actually run the politics of Nepal. So I made investigations and uncovered one story after another about the activities and dealings of these people—both in money and in politics. They mainly wanted to control politics in order to continue their dubious businesses undisturbed. I also brought the illegal acts of the royal family to light knowing that I broke the law in doing so'. After a long series of threats there was an attempt on Thakurathi's life in the summer of late 1984. 'It was a warm night,' he recalled, 'so my wife and I slept just under the open window in our bedroom. In the middle of the night my wife was woken by a gunshot.' Pointing to a deep hollow in his forehead and damaged right eye, Thakurathi said: 'The bullet hit me here. They thought they had killed me, but amazingly I survived.'

The attempted murder of Padam Thakurathi led to one of the most spectacular court cases in the history of Nepal in 1987. Several top officials were convicted of the crime in a military court including top police and government officials. Also convicted was Bharat Gurung, the ADC of the king's brother, Prince Direndra. The accused were all given severe prison sentences. Shortly after, Prince Direndra left the country after renouncing his royal title and privileges.

This top-level reshuffle by the regime came as a surprise to everybody. But it came too late to swing public opinion in favour of the government. Rather, the trial confirmed popular suspicions about corruption and some people even claimed that worse crimes had been committed and gone undetected. Had the court case come up immediately after the attempted murder of Padam Thakurathi the situation might have been different. But several incidents strengthened the opposition's hand and feelings grew against both the government and the Palace. The most important of these incidents was the series of bomb explosions in 1985.

On the afternoon of 20 June 1985 five bombs went off simultaneously at various places around the Royal Palace in Kathmandu. Two days later more bombs went off in other parts of the country. Seven people were killed and dozens were injured. These incidents sent shock waves throughout Nepal. Consequently, the Nepali Congress called off their Satyagraha against the government which they had launched only a few weeks previously.

Subsequently, a politician belonging to the opposition and living in exile in India, Ram Raja Prasad Singh, claimed responsibility. Two months later he was sentenced to death. Almost immediately after Singh's confession, however, rumours began to circulate in Kathmandu that those really responsible for the bombs were safe inside the Palace—including another of the King's brothers, Prince Gyanendra. Rumour had it that Prince Gyanendra and his henchmen had been intent on stopping the Nepali Congress Satyagraha campaign and that they had paid Singh 300,000 rupees to take the blame. What bolstered these rumours was the mysterious murder of Bhadya Nath Gupta, a close associate of Ram Raja Prasad Singh, just two days after Singh's confession. It was said that Gupta knew that Singh was not guilty. The case of the bomb explosions has still not been satisfactorily solved. At the time, however, these bombs gave a new gravity to the political situation in Nepal.

Towards the end of the 1980s the political struggle in Nepal intensified. The banned political parties increased their activities and the government crack-down was severe. In the 1986 elections for the parliament, the communist parties encouraged their members to stand as candidates for the first time. Several of them including the populist leader in Kathmandu, Padma Ratna Tuladhar, won resounding victories. These communists spent their time in the National Legislature, openly opposing the prevalent political system. As a result, they shuttled back and forth from prison to parliament. The Nepali Congress took its cue from the communists and entered the local elections of 1987—but with a lesser degree of success. Nepali Congress candidates did become Mayor and Assistant Mayor in Kathmandu, but the Mayor's term of office was short-lived. He refused to take part in the official celebrations of Constitution Day and was promptly dismissed.

In 1987 Amnesty International published a special report on Nepal. All at once the world's attention was focused on the grave human rights offences in the country. Quietly, but inexorably, political suppression had been on the increase since the early 1980s. Yet when a mass boycott was mounted against seemingly contaminated milk powder and the government was confronted with a large scale public protest, its position appeared to be weak.

The weakness of the Shrestha government became even more apparent in 1988. That year was characterized by two disasters, both of which developed into political scandals. There was a stampede at the main sports stadium in Kathmandu in March because of a hailstorm in which around a hundred people were killed. According to rumours, the National Sports Council carried much of the blame for the injuries. Instead of a proper investigation, government response was to reshuffle the cabinet slightly.

Then, on 21 August, a major earthquake hit eastern Nepal. In the Kathmandu valley only the city of Bhaktapur was affected. An official in Bhaktapur called Hyoju was accused of misappropriating funds meant for earthquake victims and was lynched by an angry mob five days later. Most of the opposition leaders in Bhaktapur were arrested and charged with the murder, including the top communist leader, Comrade Rohit, who had not even been present at the site of the incident. Charges were trumped up and all those arrested received severe prison sentences.

In response to the increased government repression, former minister Rishikesh Shaha founded the Human Rights Organization of Nepal in December 1988. The government banned it immediately, but that did nothing to hinder its rapidly increasing membership. In just a few months it became one of the largest organizations opposing government policies.

Although opposition grew towards the government during the late 1980s, the 1990 revolution might never have taken place had it not been for the unexpected events of 1989. What weakened the Panchayat government more than anything and strengthened the opposition was the Indian Trade Embargo imposed on Nepal during the spring of 1989.

Nepal is a landlocked country and the vast majority of its imports come from India or at least have to pass through India. In an aggressive show of political strength, when the Trade and Transit Treaty between the two countries expired on 23 March, the government in New Delhi brought trade between the two countries to a halt. Furthermore, the Indian government did everything in its power to make the transit through India of goods to Nepal from third countries difficult. In just a few weeks traffic dropped by half in Kathmandu because of the fuel shortage and endless queues of Nepalis sprang up all over the capital, waiting patiently for their weekly ration of kerosene.

What probably came as a surprise to the authorities in New Delhi was the Nepali government's resolve. A massive propaganda campaign was launched to make the international community aware of Nepal's position. This campaign especially emphasized the danger to Nepal's environment, already on the verge of ecological catastrophe. Strict austerity measures were announced inside the country and a new economic policy was launched to diversify Nepal's business and make the country less dependent on India.

At first the crisis seemed to strengthen the Panchayat regime. The government declared the situation a national crisis and all Nepalis were called on to unite patriotically to resist the foreign aggressor. Yet, when the students protested against India in Kathmandu, the government violently crushed the demonstrations. In the aftermath, the universities were shut down and the students sent home.

But as the crisis continued without any apparent solution and as prices went up, attitudes began to harden against the government. The people started to lose patience and show discontent. The opposition, which had been quiet, as no one wanted to be seen supporting India, began to criticize the government more boldly. Anger that had been directed solely against India was turned closer to home. Finally, on the anniversary of the death of their former leader, B.P. Koirala, the Nepali Congress organized a widespread campaign which resulted in the arrests of scores of party workers. Furthermore, during the early autumn of 1989, the Nepali Congress and the communists began to form tentative links with the prospect of joining forces against the Panchayat government. This was a remarkable move.

Opposition to the Shrestha government and its handling of the Indian Trade Embargo did not only come from the banned political parties. Criticism within the Panchayat system grew louder and more bitter as the year progressed. Votes of No Confidence against Shrestha were squashed and this only added to the frustration. Describing the last of these No Confidence motions one member of parliament, Shree Bhadra Sharma, said: 'In the last session of the Rashtriya Panchayat, we, 53 members, passed a resolution that the Prime Minister should resign. But we were not allowed even to discuss the resolution. We were told during the parliamentary crises that the King did not want to change the Prime Minister. This just shows that the Constitution has never had a fair trial.' The disaffected members of the Panchayat system simply wanted the Constitution to adhere to its own principles. They also wanted new reforms to be implemented within the framework of the existing constitution.

The end of 1989 saw more and more open rallies organized by members of this opposition. Many of these politicians had been victims of the Panchayat system in some way, including the former Prime Minister Surya Bahadur Thapa, and the Prime Ministerial candidate Rajeshwor Devkota. This opposition from within the Panchayat system condemned both the government and the party-led opposition. The government was warned that unless it found a speedy remedy to the crisis with India it would play straight into the hands of the anti-Panchayat groups. The government found itself wedged between growing criticism from within and outside the Panchayat system. It was clear that something would have to change. What really prepared the ground for the 1990 revolution, when it did come, was not one isolated incident, but a latent discontent among the population which climaxed with the Indian Trade Embargo.

The educated middle classes in the cities were vocal in their condemnation of the prevailing state of affairs. One university professor as early as February 1988 complained: 'There is a national crisis in Nepal of immense proportions. It is political, economic, moral and cultural. I see no solution. Our people are suffering a collective psychological crisis. We are totally confused, and the responsibility for our confusion rests with our political leaders.' Other voices joined the swelling chorus of complaint. One engineer stated: 'In many ways the government has already missed the chance of developing the country. Thanks to its shortsightedness, the government has lost the overall aim of development.... The situation has not changed since the Rana regime of the 1930s. The role of a government officer is still to maximize his income from the land and the people. With such officials in charge, the king cannot handle the present situation....' People pointed out that while bureaucracy was on the increase, efficiency was declining. Moreover, corruption was spreading.

Most people seemed to agree that development in Nepal had failed owing to a lack of political rights and freedom. A teacher of history at the university put it succinctly: 'Since 1960 we have had economic modernisation without political modernisation. This is like fitting a square peg in a round hole, and is the crux of Nepal's problem. We have exposed the country to the modern world in every area except that of democratic politics. That is the only instrument which would show what people wanted and what they did not... Only with political modernisation would the people be in control of society and be able to decide what kind of development they want. We need the fundamental principles of democracy: human rights, freedom of speech, freedom of association, and equality before the law. These are fundamental human rights and cannot be dismissed out of hand simply by calling them Western.' Many people remarked that Nepal's Panchayat politics had had a detrimental effect on the ethics of Nepali society as a whole. An administrative officer said boldly: 'Our whole society is sick. To be moral is only a disadvantage. Corruption is widespread and nobody really seems to care.'

At the root of the moral crisis was another—a religious crisis. Several critics pointed out that Hinduism, which ought to exist to provide the people with moral guidance, had become a political tool in the hands of the governing élite. King Birendra stood at the head of his country as an incarnation of the Hindu god Vishnu—but faith in his divinity and in his character was on the decline. There was disorder everywhere—education lagged behind and the university was in the doldrums. Literature and art seemed to be on the wane, constricted and warped by the difficult political situation.

Some poets, however, claimed that honest opinions could be expressed in their work and that often the government was too stupid to understand what they were actually doing: 'The government has not been able to stop us writing poetry....It is through our poetry that we Nepalis manage to express our true feelings and honest opinions. More and more people are now able to read what we write, and they understand what the government misses.'

In the spring of 1989 there was a feeling of crisis everywhere, but this feeling was mingled with the strong conviction that political change would come. Nearly everybody hailed change, but did not know what kind of change they wanted. Most, however, seemed to agree on the following: 'The only hope for Nepal is to have a popular democratic government. Our society has been through a bad time. The politics of the past twenty years have only caused us grievous injury. It is high time to change this. The process will, of course, be a long and difficult one, but it has to start soon....'

That autumn, people in Kathmandu could follow the changes in Eastern Europe as they appeared on television, introduced to Nepal only five years earlier. The altered political situation in parts of Eastern Europe and access to popular Indian television programmes had a deep impact on the people's consciousness.

The stage was set for change in the existing political order but the strategy to be adopted to affect such change was yet to be worked out and the major political parties and leaders were not making any long-term commitments.

Constitution Day and King Mahendra Memorial Day, on the first of the Nepali month of Poush and in the Nepali year of 2046, fell on 16 December 1989. People hoped that King Birendra would announce reforms. This seemed to be his last chance to save the Panchayat system. The festival day was celebrated in the usual way with processions and speeches, but as the King saluted the status-quo he was non-committal about any far-reaching changes. No reforms of any kind were announced. And the people began to talk of revolution rather than reform.

The People Who Brought Democracy

The 1990 revolution in Nepal lasted only seven weeks from 18 February until 9 April. The struggle for democracy, however, had been continuing for more than fifty years, to which many important leaders had contributed. There were the veterans of the 1951 revolution who had persevered through decades of repression; there were also the younger communist leaders whose ideals had been formed in the wake of the Cultural Revolution in China and the Naxalite movement in India in the early 1970s; finally, there were the 'panchas', members of the Panchayat regime. They were either pragmatic idealists, opportunists, or hardliners. Some 'panchas' were genuine liberals, while others were managed by the Palace clique. In addition there was a more indefinable group of reactionaries whose outlook stemmed from the days of the Ranas and who were staunch nationalists.

Besides the politicians, Nepal's new group of politicized intellectuals also played a major role during the revolution. These were people who had grown weary of the Panchayat system. They were convinced that their own personal aspirations could not be fulfilled by Panchayat politics and they longed for change. They were sympathetic to the political parties, but were not necessarily members.

Veteran politicians were to be found both in the Nepali Congress Party and in the moderate communist parties. They were the first generation of politicians in Nepal in the modern sense of the word. Though aged, they were still very highly respected and important members of the pro-Democracy movement. Though these politicians had opted for either one party or the other, their backgrounds were similar and they shared a broad political outlook.

This old guard had come together in the 1940s. Most of them had been educated and had become politically active in India. Even those who stayed in Nepal had been influenced mainly by political ideas from India. Their ideology had been shaped by Mahatma Gandhi's Quit India movement. Even in 1990, Gandhian principles of non-violence played an important role in their political behaviour. They had also been influenced to some degree by socialism or communism. These ideas, too, harked back to the 1940s and 1950s when Nehru's socialist outlook had played a dominant role in India. Consequently, these leaders sought to introduce in Nepal democracy based on the Indian principles. Their own personal affinity with Indian politics and politicians was unquestionable.

These politicians had enjoyed a brief period of freedom in the 1950s. Some had been a part of the government in 1959–60. For a large part of their lives, however, they had been persecuted and suppressed either by the British, the Ranas or the Panchayat system. Many had been in and out of prison, some for as long as fifteen years. Many had also spent long periods of exile in India or had been forced to go underground in Nepal. Yet faith in the possibility of political change was undiminished.

Several of them were motivated by strong Hindu or Buddhist convictions. The frugal lifestyles of these politicians added to their popularity both before and after the revolution.

The history of the Nepali Congress Party was linked largely to the person of B.P. Koirala. He remained the leading figure of the party for thirty-five years, and to a majority of the people B.P. Koirala and the Nepali Congress Party were synonymous. Koirala had established the Nepali Congress Party in Varanasi (Benares) in 1947. He became the party's first democratically elected Prime Minister in 1959. When he died in 1982 the Nepali Congress Party did not only lose a leader, it lost its greatest ideologue, policy maker and statesman. The veterans left holding power after Koirala's death were: Ganesh Man Singh, Krishna Prasad Bhattarai and Girija Prasad Koirala (B.P. Koirala's younger brother).

Of these three, Ganesh Man Singh was the oldest. At the time of the revolution in 1990 he was 75. He was not only leader of the Nepali Congress, but supreme leader of the pro-Democracy movement. He admonished the King and Panchayat leaders in strong, straight-forward language. Along with his wife, Mangala Devi, he symbolized loyalty, and perseverance. Their old Rana-style house in Kathmandu became the headquarters of the pro-Democracy movement.

What he lacked in education and sophistication he made up for with his long record of struggle for freedom and democracy. He was born in Kathmandu in 1915. Like so many others of his generation he went to India to be educated. There he became aware of the opposition to Rana rule within Nepal, and in 1939 he went back to Kathmandu to join the Praja Parishad. Singh was arrested and sentenced to life imprisonment. In fact, he faced the death sentence three times—in 1939, 1950 and 1989.

Ganesh Man Singh escaped from prison after four years and made his way back to India. There he joined forces with B.P. Koirala to found the Nepali National Congress. With Koirala, he played a major part in the 1951 revolution and afterwards became Minister for Industry in the Rana-Congress coalition government. He later served as Minister for Works and Transport in the B.P. Koirala government of 1959.

After King Mahendra's royal coup, Ganesh Man Singh spent eight years in jail before returning to India in exile. He came back to Nepal in 1976 and inherited Koirala's mantle as leader of the Nepali Congress on Koirala's death in 1982. By this time Ganesh Man Singh had become an internationally acclaimed political figure. He campaigned for multi-party democracy in Nepal and in 1990 had emerged as one of the leading lights of the country's struggle for democracy.

Concerning his own role, Ganesh Man Singh said: 'I've been in politics for the last fifty years and I have had to undergo many hardships. If the people give me the title of National Leader because of this contribution I will be pleased to receive that reward. But I don't think I am at all worthy of the award. I still have to go many miles to become a true National Leader.'

The link between personal and political beliefs was a strong one for these politicians. The person known for his integrity in this respect was Krishna Prasad Bhattarai. He was President of the party and later Prime Minister of the interim government after the revolution. Bhattarai had spent fifteen years in jail and, consequently, had never been able to marry. He had devoted his life to bringing democracy and freedom to Nepal. Sitting with his bare feet curled up in a chair, Bhattarai loved telling jokes and stories, but one soon realized that he had a sharp analytical mind and was a sophisticated politician.

Krishna Prasad Bhattarai's determination to fight corruption in government was evident from his own lifestyle. He lived frugally while he was the country's Prime Minister and led by example.

Krishna Prasad Bhattarai's grandfather was the royal priest exiled to Varanasi in India in connection with Jang Bahadur Rana's 'massacre' in 1846. His own political career began when he was a student in Varanasi in the 1940s and had participated in the Quit India movement in 1942. During the revolution of 1951 he served as a general in the rebel forces against the Rana regime. Later, during the short phase of democratic government from 1959–60, he was the Speaker in the parliament. During much of the Panchayat period, Bhattarai was in jail, though he remained central in organizing party activity.

Long before the 1990 revolution, Bhattarai had repeatedly stressed his commitment to a British-style democracy with a constitutional monarch in Nepal. In an interview in May 1989, eight months before the revolution, he was confident that political change was imminent: 'We will very soon force the King to become a constitutional monarch,' he had declared.

There were veterans amongst the communists as well as in the Nepali Congress Party. These leaders were moderates and were instrumental in forming the United Left Front on 10 January 1990. They had entered politics at the same time as the Congress veterans and some of them had even been former members of the Nepali Congress Party. All of them felt that the Nepali Congress Party was not radical enough on the issue of social reform.

The founder of the Nepal Communist Party in 1949 was Pushpa Lal Shrestha. He was the main leader of the party until his death in 1978. He could have held a similar position in the Communist Party as B.P. Koirala in the Nepali Congress, but he was not able to prevent the communists from splitting. The communists had a history of internal dissent. Their disputes related either to organizational matters or concerned future communist strategy inside Nepal. By 1989 the communists in Nepal had split into at least fifteen parties or factions.

One of the most influential of the communist veterans was Sahana Pradhan. She played a leading role in the 1990 revolution and was president of the newly-established United Left Front. As widow of Pushpa Lal Shrestha and leader of the Nepal Communist Party (Marxist), which she had led since her husband's death, Sahana Pradhan was widely respected.

Her political career had begun before she married in 1954. She described how she had begun her involvement in politics. 'When I was still in my early teens in Kathmandu, there was the independence movement in India. I was very impressed by this and I was very interested in studying the Soviet revolution and movements in other countries. I had to get pamphlets and other reading material very secretly—one couldn't get them in public. My friends and brothers used to smuggle things in and so I got interested. I was also enthused by the political freedom fighters of Nepal, those who were called the martyrs. In my early childhood I read books about them and, you know, this was a real thing that inspired me. In 1948 there was the first civil rights movement in Nepal. I was sixteen. My sister and I took part in the movement and I was arrested and put into the barracks for sixteen days. They could not put women in the jail.'

Sahana Pradhan's political involvement grew out of her desire to be educated. She was born in Burma where she went to school. Her parents moved back to Kathmandu in 1945 and she was not able to continue her education. 'When I came to Nepal as a twelve-year-old', she said, 'I was debarred from education. There were many traditional customs and I couldn't go anywhere. I was almost in purdah. So a sort of resentment, a revolt, came into my mind to get education.'

Sahana Pradhan studied with her sister at home. In 1949 her parents acted against family pressure and allowed her to go to college in India. In 1953 she was the first woman in Nepal to receive a Bachelor's degree. As there was no recognized university in Nepal in those days, she received her degree from Patna University.

Sahana Pradhan was active in the Communist Party in the early 1950s, but left politics to pursue a full-time academic career. She was the first woman involved with the new university in Nepal. She was reprimanded several times for her links with the banned Communist Party.

Sahana Pradhan was unanimously elected leader of the United Left Front. A calm, assured woman, she was not a controversial figure and could show a long record of loyalty and commitment to the communist cause. Her marriage to Pushpa Lal Shrestha did play a role in her appointment, but more important was her ability to reason clearly in the midst of chaos. Later in the interim government after the revolution she became the Minister for Industry and Commerce. 'My subject was economics, you know' she said. 'Before I used to teach; now,' she laughed, 'I have to practice.' About suddenly becoming a member of government she said: 'Every job is challenging in the beginning. But I soon understood the job and then it became a little easier.'

Throughout the 1960s the communist leaders, most of whom lived in exile in India, debated over their strategy towards the Panchayat system. Their common goal was the creation of a classless, communist state and the abolition of the Panchayat. However, they could not agree as to how this was to be achieved. Some communists believed in working within the Panchayat system while others went as far as to propose armed revolt against the government. A third, more moderate view was that it would be possible to transform the existing Panchayat system into a communist one. These varying opinions led to the many splits within the communist movement during the 1960s and 1970s. By the 1970s there emerged a new generation of activists in Nepal. These leaders were highly motivated to fight against what they perceived as economic and political exploitation of the country.

The first organized movement of this kind surfaced with the Jhapali movement in the far-eastern Terai region. The Jhapali movement was influenced by Mao's Cultural Revolution and was linked directly to the Naxalite movement just across the border in north-west Bengal. The Naxalites were well-known for their guerrilla tactics, and posed a serious threat to law and order. The Jhapali movement was just as extreme, but not as sophisticated. The movement took up the cause of the peasantry and called for the implementation of the Land Reform Act, recently passed by the Panchayat government. The activists educated the villagers about their rights and pressurized the rural aristocracy to adopt a conciliatory attitude with regard to the problems of the rural folk. But the government took a tough stand, and carried out mass arrests, which forced the movement to go underground.

After the announcement of the National Referendum in 1979, Jhapali activists resurfaced and founded the Nepal Communist Party (Marxist-Leninist). They had used the interim period to rework their strategy and strengthen the organizational base. Though they favoured peasant rights and the implementation of the Land Reform Act, the call for armed insurrection was given up and emphasis was laid on mass support. Their radical and fiery speeches had popular appeal within the communist movement.

The Marxist-Leninists soon became one of the largest communist parties in Nepal. Their support was vital to the success of the pro-Democracy movement. Yet during the revolution they followed double standards. Whereas within the United Left Front they advocated moderate policies, in actuality their slogans were radical, often bordering on the extreme.

The most important leaders of both the Jhapali movement and the subsequent Marxist-Leninist group were the Mainali brothers. The more popular of the two was the younger brother, Chandra Prakash. He had achieved fame because of his escape from Nakhu Jail near Kathmandu. He spent weeks digging a secret tunnel which he concealed from the authorities by throwing the stones and earth he piled up into a nearby canal. He finally succeeded in escaping one night before any of the guards discovered him.

During the 1990 revolution his elder brother, Radha Krishna Mainali, was the only leader of the United Left Front who avoided imprisonment and was able to lead the movement *in absentia.*

Radha Krishna Mainali described how he had spent his entire life opposing the Panchayat regime: 'In those days we were young and we were driven by an almost supernatural force and vitality. We wanted to do something about the injustice we saw around us. And we understood that we had to fight. Later on we realised that we also did many stupid things, but still our cause was just!'

He explained further: 'I got involved in politics while I was still at High School in the late sixties when I joined the illegal All-Nepal Free Student Union. But my political career only got going after the announcement of the Land Reform Act when I joined groups fighting for peasant rights inspired by what I had read about Marxist thought. We first started to pressure the landowners to give away land to their tenants. After a while when the landowners and the police formed an alliance using guns against us we realised that we could not continue to fight bare-handed. Towards the end of 1972 we started our armed revolution armed with home-made weapons and knives and we attacked the land holders and our group killed eight of them. At that time the police had already tried to arrest me at home and I tried to go underground. The police continued their violent movement to arrest us and first they managed to take around ten of our group. Eight or nine of this first group were killed by the police while they were transferred from one jail to another. Fortunately I was only arrested in the second batch in 1973. I was given a ten-year sentence and immediately after I was released in 1983 they re-arrested me under the Public Security Act with a four year sentence. I was finally released in 1986 and since then I've been arrested only twice for short periods lasting up to one year. So altogether I have spent sixteen years in jail.'

Radha Krishna described his years in jail: 'My first years in jail were spent in the "death cells". Several of us were kept in a cage six by five feet with only a hole in the corner for a toilet. We were given 700 grams of bad quality rice a day as well as 60 paisa to buy whatever other necessities we needed. That was not enough even for a few vegetables. Seven of our friends died in these conditions from tuberculosis in just two years. It was only after the Referendum that I was allowed to join the other detainees, but I was still not allowed to read newspapers or books or receive visitors. The story of my years in jail is a painful one.'

He emphasized the need for a consensus and was in full agreement that the Congress and other communist parties had to work together to bring about democracy in Nepal. He said: 'You must understand that Communism is about change. One needs to adapt to every new situation. That is what dialectical thought is all about. Of course our activities in the early 70s were extreme and we made many mistakes, but you must understand that the situation then was different. The dictatorship in Nepal was much harsher then. At that time I was not even allowed to express my political opinions in private to a foreigner. What we want now is a free democratic society where people are free to express their views. We are against monarchy in principle, but we must accept that the majority still wants the King. What we want is a society where the political struggle does not deal with ideology or dogma, but where we can deal with real issues—the position of the peasants, the workers and the poor in Nepali society.'

Fifteen years of suppression had brought the once feared Jhapali movement into the mainstream of Nepali politics. But not all the communist groups were moderate. Some refused to join the United Left Front. The best known of these was the extreme left Mashal Communist Party. The Mashals still proclaimed an armed revolution and the Dictatorship of the Proletariat. Though they did not officially join the United Left Front, they did take part in the demonstrations.

The best known amongst these extreme communists was Mohan Bikram Singh. He was one of the veterans of the communist movement and had always followed a radical line within the party. He had built up a strong following in his home area, the Piuthan District in western Nepal, so that it was now called 'Mashal country.' Most of the other radical communists were younger—men like Babu Ram Bhattarai. He headed the United National People's Movement, a combined front of the five most doctrinaire communist parties which did not join the United Left Front.

Bhattarai was a Brahmin intellectual from Gorkha and possessed all the advantages of his privileged background. He first became interested in Marxism during the late 1970s while he was studying for a Ph.D at Jawaharlal Nehru University, New Delhi. Intense and articulate, he shrugged off all accusations of extremism. He showed himself to be singularly adept at using political language. 'We are the true democrats,' he insisted. 'We don't want only the old kind of democracy which gives power only to rich people, the capitalists and the feudals. We want real new democracy which gives power to the oppressed, the peasantry and the poorest of the poor living in the villages. How then can people say that we are against democracy and that we are terrorists? Only, if the government tries to resist democracy with arms we are duty bound to do the same. We don't use arms on our own, but we do retaliate. Terrorists are those who do not believe in the people's power.'

Babu Ram Bhattarai went on to state that the 1990 revolution was only the first step. It was the necessary capitalist revolution coming before the people's revolution and the final establishment of true democracy in Nepal. When questioned as to what true democracy actually consisted of and what methods his party would use to achieve it, Bhattarai became vague and evasive. Finally he said: 'We will organise the people and then we will snatch power. Then we will redistribute property and hold free and fair elections. Finally we will create a real democracy.'

Bhattarai admitted that the time was not yet ripe for people's revolution. Until the appointed time he and his party would respect the new constitution and continue their work within the present system. In general, however, he was pessimistic as regards the revolution, though he was willing to give the new leaders a fair chance.

The revolution of 1990, however, was not only run by Brahmins from Gorkha, members of the Mashal Party, or survivors of the Jhapali movement from the eastern Terai—though they all contributed. The revolution was also a popular uprising which began in the Kathmandu valley. Many of those taking part and most of those killed were

Newaris. The vast majority had never taken part in any political activity before and were not members of any political party. They were leaders who were less dogmatic than of old and more practical. Several of them were communists but they were communists of a Nepali or a Newari hue. They had built up local support by dint of their integrity and driving personalities.

Narayan Man Bijukche, popularly known as Comrade Rohit, was one of the most popular leaders in Nepal. He was an unlikely man to be a populist leader. Short, middle aged and with a soft voice and warm smile, it was hard to believe that he had posed such a dire threat to the Panchayat government. He had spent his entire life avoiding arrest. Even so, he had spent many years in jail and bore the marks of torture. Two fingers of his right hand had been damaged for life. When he spoke, he spoke simply and to the point. This was part of his appeal to the people of Bhaktapur, a town still largely inhabited by peasants and artisans. He described how he and his colleagues had worked tirelessly among the inhabitants of Bhaktapur and made gradual progress: 'We educated the people in hygiene and morals. We helped them fight alcoholism and sin in general. We even taught them about religion. We preached how men could become good and righteous and how they could become real human beings. We served the people and educated them. And we became their friends, not their gods.'

Comrade Rohit's brand of politics was influenced by religion and ethics. His mother's influence had been profound. 'I learned from her example,' he recalled. 'An urge to help the poor was also formed in us children.' It was only in the late 1950s and early 1960s as a student that he was introduced to socialism. Socialism, Comrade Rohit believed, fell naturally into line with his earlier Buddhist values. In socialism he finally found a collective ideology for his own personal beliefs. He also studied the Chinese peasant revolution and even visited China in 1959–60. Through this he came to understand that even the peasants were able to revolt.

Politics, however, was not his only love. He was strongly influenced by literary traditions abroad and began writing at an early age. 'Some of us came together and organised a literary forum where we presented our own poems every week. They were about the plight of the poor and social injustice. We also read classical and romantic literature like Shakespeare, Byron and others. I became interested in French literature and, of course, the Russian writers like Tolstoy and Chekhov.'

After the Panchayat system had been introduced, Comrade Rohit worked for the implementation of the Land Reform Act. He was sympathetic to the demands and aspirations of the Jhapalis and advocated non-violent methods for their achievement.

The Land Reform Act was supposed to guarantee the peasant two-thirds of his crop. Previously the peasant's share had only amounted to one-third with two-thirds being the share of the landowner. The passing of the act changed nothing in practice. 'In this conflict with the landowners,' Comrade Rohit stated, 'the peasants always lost. We started to organise mass meetings saying that the new Land Reform Act should be implemented. We organised several court cases for peasants to claim their rights from the landowners, but even in court the peasants lost. Most of the lawyers had been bribed by the landowners. On the land which the landowners unrighteously called theirs, we helped the peasants harvest the crop and bring it to their houses. On such occasions the police came and arrested us, accusing us of theft.'

This peasant campaign soon spread to other districts. It was organized both within and outside the Panchayat system.

As Comrade Rohit explained: 'The Communist Party was banned so we worked inside the Panchayat system. I was even elected to the Nagar Panchayat (the town Panchayat) in Bhaktapur. We were members of the Panchayat Peasant Organisation and our own illegal peasant organisation. We followed the words of Lenin saying that one should work for the benefit of the poor even inside the reactionaries' organisations.' Rohit's political activity meant that he was constantly harassed by the police. 'Warrants were issued and many of my friends were arrested. I went from village to village and during the day I continued to read Marxist literature underground. The government had already blocked two attempts of mine to earn a living—first as a schoolteacher, then as a writer. Because I couldn't get out during the day it was impossible for me to marry.'

The peasant movement, Comrade Rohit stated, grew to become the Nepal Peasants' and Workers' Organization. 'We now understood that launching this social movement was not enough. We had to get involved in politics. We needed to launch a revolution to topple the government, so we went to India where all the Nepali communist leaders lived in exile and said that it was necessary to mobilise the peasants inside Nepal to launch a revolution. We continued our struggle to implement the Land Reform Act, and at the same time organised underground communist groups in various places.'

Comrade Rohit believed that a peasant revolt based on the Chinese model could be carried on in Nepal. However, by 1990 his views had changed, but he was still confident that economic equality could only be achieved by the government taking over the means of production. His form of communism, however, was open to reform. He claimed that he had consciously tried to shed old dogmas and practices which he thought were bad. 'We have learned that in a one-party system governed by the idea of a dictatorship of the proletariat there can be no development. There must be fundamental freedoms—freedom of speech and so on. There has to be a multi-party system, the freedom of religion and the freedom to criticise. A country must not be ruled by the gun.'

There was more, however, than ideology to Comrade Rohit. Much of his support had come as a result of his stand on local issues and the Newari cause. He was the direct descendant of the Commander-in-Chief for the last Malla king of Bhaktapur who had ruled the principality until it had been invaded by King Prithvi Narayan Shah in 1768. Subsequently, Comrade Rohit's family had been persecuted and ruined. He now saw his own family history linked to the destiny of his community: 'The Newaris of Bhaktapur have been oppressed for 200 years. The peasants were not allowed to sow their rice before the Nepali-speaking police and military officers had sown theirs. If their normal daily wage was 30 rupees, the Newaris would only get 20. We were second class citizens in our own territory.'

Comrade Rohit went on to express his deep love for the Newari language and culture which had been discouraged by Nepali officialdom for so long.

Comrade Rohit shared a deep sense of affinity towards Newari language and culture with Padma Ratna Tuladhar. Tuladhar had first started out as a journalist on a Newari daily called *Bhasa Patrika* . He was also a writer of Newari literature and was active in the Nepal Basha Manka Khala, an organization set up to promote the Newari language. It was this interest in language which led him into politics. In 1979, just after the King had announced the referendum, Tuladhar criticized the monarch for making the announcement only in Nepali, for which he was arrested. While in prison, he resolved to fight for human rights. 'I realised,' he said, 'that none of the political prisoners were supported from outside by newspapers and so on. So, when I was released, I started a committee for the release of political prisoners and through this I also came into contact with the politicians.'

Tuladhar's political pragmatism was similar to that of Comrade Rohit's. Like Rohit, he was an individualist. He was not a member of any political party, and yet his influence was such that he played an important role as a mediator between the communists and the Nepali Congress prior to the launch of the pro-Democracy movement. While Comrade Rohit's activities were confined to Bhaktapur, Tuladhar was a politician of national standing. Furthermore, he was a representative of the new intellectuals who were pressing for reform. Regarding his involvement in Newari culture and language, he said: 'I'm a nationalist, but I'm not a communalist.' This stance was borne out by the support he received from Brahmins, Chetris and many others besides Newaris.

Tuladhar became popular while he was a member of the Rashtriya Panchayat. He was elected as an independent in 1985 from a constituency in Kathmandu and immediately began to oppose the Panchayat system. He made it clear right from the beginning that he had only gone into parliament to voice his opposition to the system. About his tenure as parliamentarian he said: 'It was a dual kind of participation. I was fighting for democracy from the bench of the

Rashtriya Panchayat. At the same time I also participated in programmes outside campaigning for the multi-party system. Although I was arrested many times, twelve times in all, during that period, I believe it was worthwhile.'

By the time the 1990 revolution began, Padma Ratna Tuladhar had become the most popular politician in Kathmandu. He was respected by politicians of all shades. Even the Palace thought highly of him and Lokendra Bahadur Chand, during his brief two-week spell as Prime Minister, towards the end of the 1990 revolution, asked him to initiate negotiations between the government and the opposition.

Tuladhar became a symbol of defiance during the revolution, and his arrest, together with communist leader Tulsi Lal Amatya during a demonstration, was seen as a virtuous display of non-violence. Tuladhar was also an important spokesman for the intellectuals in Kathmandu—those who helped topple the old regime, but who did not feel fully satisfied within any of the political parties. Perhaps for this reason Tuladhar was keen to launch a new party when the revolution ended.

Many of the politicized intellectuals in Kathmandu and other towns played a significant role during the revolution. Some were members of the Nepali Congress party or one of the communist parties, but the main political outlet for these people was not the political parties but the newly-established human rights organizations and professional associations. Besides the popular uprisings in the Kathmandu valley these groups were responsible for the revolution being a success.

Mathura Prasad Shrestha was another important political personality connected with the revolution who became Health Minister in K.P. Bhattarai's interim government. He was both Chairman of the Forum for the Protection of Human Rights and Professor of Community Medicine at the teaching hospital in Kathmandu. His hospital was where some of the first protests against Panchayat repression took place.

Mathura Prasad Shrestha was arrested twice during the seven-week long revolution. The first time was after he had had an audience with the Prime Minister. The second arrest came just as unexpectedly: 'The police came early in the morning into our bedroom. Both I and my wife were forced to dress in front of them. They took me off to the police station where I was interrogated every ten or fifteen minutes and asked silly questions, never allowed to rest in between. But I was not tortured like the students or other young prisoners.'

This white haired, finely featured man was clearly ill-at-ease in his large office as Health Minister in the interim government. He confessed as much: 'I feel guilty,' he said, 'about being a member of government while my people still suffer and while injustice is still being practised.' He went on to say that he had first been drawn to politics in the mid-fifties, while he had been a student. It was the Communist Party which had attracted him. He had been punished for his views even then and, after finishing his medical studies in India, had decided to devote himself completely to his profession and gave up politics. His main priority, he believed, should be to help improve the health of his nation. Even though he was no longer politically active, the Panchayat government made sure that he was transferred from job to job because of his deeply-held communist beliefs. Finally, he came to the conclusion, 'that the health of the people was very much dependent on the health of the country and that the health of the country could not improve unless the political system changed.' This view led Shrestha to contribute towards human rights and paved the way for his political appointment.

Like many others, Shrestha did not believe in democratic politics as an end in itself—rather democracy and freedom were a necessary framework within which people could discharge their duties most effectively. He was certain that once democracy was firmly in place in Nepal he would leave politics to the politicians and return to medicine once more.

After the revolution, Ganesh Man Singh, Supreme Leader of the pro-Democracy movement, and Krishna Prasad Bhattarai, the new Prime Minister, found themselves to be the focus of media attention. By this time the revolution was visualized as the saga of a courageous struggle against evil, but vague, powers. The word 'pancha' had become a derogatory term overnight.

The panchas could be divided into liberals and hardliners. It was also known that it was pancha dissension as much as anything else which had contributed to the fall of the old regime.

The dubious triumvirate of the Prime Minister, Marich Man Singh Shrestha, the Home Minister, Nirenjan Thapa, and the Chairman of the Rashtriya Panchayat and Panchayat Policy and Evaluation Committee, Nava Raj Subhedi were the three officially responsible for the suppression of the democratic forces during the revolution. They quickly took on the guise of cartoon monsters in the popular mind, but the questions remain: were these men ruthless power brokers or merely puppets worked from behind the political scenes?

Marich Man Singh Shrestha was believed to be the weakest of these three. He was described as being entirely in the grip of the Palace and did not have any decision-making powers. After the revolution he was put under surveillance and placed under house arrest.

He began his career as a Newari high school teacher from the western Salyan district of Nepal and rose to become Prime Minister. Shrestha said that he had become disillusioned with politics in the 1950s while he was still young. Politicians, he believed, were only interested in power and had no principles. In his disillusion, only the King had appeared to Shrestha as a saviour—the one man who truly understood Nepal's situation and who could unify the country successfully. Shrestha believed in the Panchayat system, therefore, and became involved at the local level while he was still a teacher. He had risen gradually to become a member of the Rashtriya Panchayat, Speaker of Parliament, and, finally, Prime Minister. Shrestha's loyalty to the King and belief in the King's role as central to governing Nepal was absolute: 'The only hope for this country is the active leadership of the King. He is the only one who can unify the country and assert its position in front of our powerful neighbour whose intentions are total hegemony.'

Marich Man Singh Shrestha described his political goals as, 'The unification of the country and the strengthening of national independence and identity.' Shrestha's own nationalist views were evident in his belief that the pro-Democracy movement had been engineered by outside forces. It appeared as though he had been in fact, a victim rather than a suppressor.

Both Marich Man Singh Shrestha and Nirenjan Thapa came from poor, ordinary backgrounds. They saw their own rise as an example of the equality to be found within the Panchayat system. 'In what multi-party democracy could this really happen?' challenged Marich Man Singh Shrestha. 'Look at neighbouring India where political power can only be bought through money or family connections.'

However, background was all that Nirenjan Thapa had in common with Shrestha. He was said to have been responsible for the police firing and butchering of ordinary citizens during the revolution. After the revolution he appeared to be cool, confident and completely in control of the situation. He was also eager to justify his actions. 'They have made a big charge against me,' he complained. 'Because I suppressed the people. I ordered that the people should be killed. Some have even said that I shot at people from a helicopter. But honestly I can tell you that the Panchayat system has had no more of a democratic Home Minister than me.' Thapa pointed out that certain liberal measures had been introduced while he had been Home Minister. The period of detention under the National Security Act had been shortened, the use of handcuffs for torture had been banned and hanging had been abolished as a form of capital punishment. When confronted with the police killings, Thapa vehemently defended himself, saying that he had only been obeying the law. 'You must remember that opposition to the constitution was illegal. I only did what I had to do.' He also pointed out that some of the reprisals during the revolution such as in Bhaktapur and Patan had been the decisions of the local administration and nathis. He denied the allegations that the military had been used during his tenure as Home Minister. 'But even so,' he said, 'I was seen as the villain. I think it is an international phenomenon that Home Ministers are seen as the villains. Because of their position they are never the people who come with good news. Even so, I think that few Home Ministers have been as misrepresented as me! After having served as a loyal Home Minister for two years, loyal to the King and the constitution, I'm not even allowed to call myself an ex-minister now. Every time the newspapers refer to me they only write Nirenjan Thapa.'

Thapa had been the youngest ever Home Minister in Nepal's history. Wearing western leisure clothes, running shoes and loose cotton trousers he sat in his new four storey brick house in Kathmandu and related how he had become involved in Panchayat politics. He was a poor man's son from the mid-Terai. He had become involved in Panchayat politics as a schoolboy and later as a student had been one of the founder members of the Nepal Vidyarthi Mandal, the Panchayat student association founded in the early seventies. He was still a member of the Mandal in 1979 when the referendum had been announced and, as he had just finished his law studies, he took time off to tour the country and canvassed in support of the Panchayat system. His efforts were noticed by the King who nominated him and some other active members of the Mandal to the Rashtriya Panchayat after the referendum in 1980. In all, Thapa was nominated three times by the King—once to the Rashtriya Panchayat and twice to the cabinet. Subsequently he became the elected member to the Rashtriya Panchayat from his home constituency. Finally, two years before the revolution, Marich Man Singh Shrestha appointed Thapa as his Home Minister. 'I was driven by my love for the nation,' he declared, 'and my deep respect for the King.'

Thapa still believed in Panchayat democracy and insisted it was the only system whereby people could move up in the political hierarchy in a fair manner. He was disillusioned with politicians, however, and saw them all as engaged in one long power struggle: 'All 140 members of the Rashtriya Panchayat wanted to become the Prime Minister, but of course this was impossible.' Thapa firmly believed that the Panchayat system was the only means of keeping the country united and sovereign.

Nava Raj Subhedi was the ideological force behind the Panchayat system and one of the most powerful members of the old regime. During the revolution he was forced to go underground, but he retained an undented belief in the Panchayat system. 'I really believed in the Panchayat system,' he said, 'that is why I joined it. And I still actually believe that it was the best political system for Nepal, having its base right down to the local village ward and, more importantly, the leadership of the King. Nepal lacks leaders that the whole population will respect and therefore the King is the only leader who can unify all the different groups and castes in the country.'

Subhedi's main complaint after the revolution was that he was misrepresented as a hardliner. He pointed out that he had always been seen as a liberal before the revolution and had gone so far as to propose a Fourth Amendment to the Constitution just the previous year. He was fearless, however, concerning the new regime: 'There is nothing to punish me for.'

The partyless Panchayat system, as many of its opponents pointed out, had actually split into many factions by the end of the revolution. The monolithic system forced all personal ambition and aspiration, ethnic, class and caste conflicts into one simmering cauldron. As a result some said that there were as many political factions as members in the Rashtriya Panchayat. Politics became personalized, which enabled the Panchayat system to survive. It was only in the last years of the Panchayat system that a united opposition to it emerged. When it did, it hastened its demise, by shaking the Panchayat regime to its roots.

The main pancha opposition leader, vocal in his criticism of Marich Man Singh Shrestha's government, was Rajeshwor Devkota. While his liberal credentials could have been doubtful, no one doubted his abilities as a politician. Many claimed that his evident ability had actually hampered his career. The King seemed rather intimidated by him and appointed Marich Man Singh Shrestha as Prime Minister, superseding Devkota. Thus his life's ambition to reach the highest office was never fulfilled.

Rajeshwor Devkota belonged to the old generation of Nepali politicians. He had become politically active as a student at the Sanskrit Vidyalaya, the Ranas' Sanskrit School in Kathmandu. He had joined the Congress and communist veterans to demand a wider range of subjects in the school's curricula. He was exiled to India for his efforts and joined the Indian freedom movement and later the Nepali Congress. Two years later, after the 1951 revolution which brought Rana rule to an end, Devkota returned to Nepal and founded his own party. This party lasted until King Mahendra introduced the Panchayat system. Devkota actively supported the system from the very beginning and worked his way up through the ranks. As he himself pointed out: 'I did not really climb quickly inside the system. Many people went past me.'

Even though he never became Prime Minister, Rajeshwor Devkota was an influential figure and one of the outstanding members of the Panchayat government, having a mind of his own. Certainly, the way he repeatedly lifted the receiver of his telephone to give orders to his political colleagues showed that he was used to being in charge. When asked about the pro-Democracy movement, he said that the movement had come as no surprise. Such a conflict was inevitable, he said. That was why he had called for reforms in the months leading up to the revolution. He had wished to retain some features of the old regime but could not muster enough support. His view was that the failure to compromise and the subsequent violence had come about because the western idea of a multi-party system had taken root firmly among the members of the opposition. After the revolution, Devkota was critical of the new interim government. He did not believe they were capable of running the country and he feared a sell-out to India. Reflecting on the position after the revolution, he said: 'I do not on any account feel like a political outcast after the recent revolution. I knew that the revolution would come and I had for a long time advocated the establishment of a constitutional monarchy even as early as eight months before the movement....My main objective now is to strengthen the development of a multi-party democracy.'

Another member of the pancha opposition, but a very different character from Rajeshwor Devkota, was Keshar Bahadur Bista. Bista had lectured in political science at the university in Kathmandu and had also studied in the US. He represented the typical modernized liberal pancha—the kind of person who made it impossible for the Panchayat system to be categorized purely as a totalitarian dictatorship. Like so many others, he became involved in politics while he was still a student and his full-time activity started in 1972 when he gave up his job to take part in local elections. Bista eventually ended up as Minister of Education and Culture. He believed in the evolutionary character of the Panchayat system and was always quick to criticize it when he thought necessary reforms were not forthcoming. His views took him to prison in the late seventies when he called for changes in the electoral system. The reforms he had worked for finally came with the Third Amendment to the Constitution after the referendum in 1980. Keshar Bahadur Bista commented, 'These reforms were really radical.' He blamed reactionary forces within the country for hindering the passage of these reforms from legislation into practice. 'You must remember that these people, the underground elements whom they now call the Mandales—it was us, the panchas, who first exposed and criticised them.'

By the time the pro-Democracy movement began, Keshar Bahadur Bista was disillusioned with the Panchayat system. But he still hoped that some form of compromise was possible. That was why he had joined the opposition within the Panchayat ranks. Popular participation in the revolution did not come as a surprise, he claimed, but he was horrified at the use of violence. He insisted that he had pleaded with the government to begin negotiations and end the bloodbath. He had also, on one occasion, mediated between the police and the crowds in his home constituency of Patan. He had contacted the zonal commissioner, the Anchaladhis, directly and threatened that unless he called the police off, he himself, their local Panchayat representative, would join the movement.

Given this scenario, why did he not resign and join the movement? To this question Keshar Bahadur Bista's reply was evasive. He merely stated that events had occurred too quickly and that he had retained some loyalty towards his opposition colleagues within the Rashtriya Panchayat. He was hopeful of returning to active politics in due course.

'People's Movement?' the man thundered. 'No, there was never a People's Movement! What we can call the recent political happening in Nepal is a national rape by foreigners!'

These were the strong words of Grishma Bahadur Devkota immediately after the revolution. He was a supporter of the old school; a scribe and Brahmin intellectual from the days of the Ranas. He was also a member of the influential Raj Sabha, the Palace Assembly. Some people believed that this council had more power than the parliament itself. While his opinions might appear extreme, Grishma Bahadur Devkota represented a strong traditionalist element within Nepal which still wielded significant political influence. Nepalis like him were intent on retaining Nepal's national identity along with its culture and traditions—including Kingship and Hinduism. What these people feared most was foreign domination, particularly Indian domination. Grishma Bahadur's suspicions were, therefore, that the pro-Democracy movement had been engineered by India following the Trade Embargo. The Nepali Congress and communist parties, in his opinion, were full of Indian agents whose main aim was to create internal dissension in Nepal. Even the foreign press had been duped. They had supported India's stand and claimed as many as 1,000 people had been killed when the true number was not even a tenth of that. And who was killed? Grishma Bahadur Devkota demanded. None of the opposition leaders. He frowned and maintained that a true movement should be like Gandhi's movement in India. He led the way and the masses followed. Nothing like that had happened in Nepal.

Grishma Bahadur Devkota's own opinion of the Panchayat system was that: 'After the political system of Great Britain the Panchayat system was the very best that existed in the world. This I can prove. From every group of a hundred households there would be appointed one political leader. In parliamentary systems of government only those who are members of a party can play a role.'

Grishma Bahadur Devkota explained that in a parliamentary system parties could rule even when they did not have the support of the majority of the people. In Nepal, however, even the old constitutions of the Rana government, the *Muluki Ain*, the caste laws, had been written with an understanding of the whole people in mind. Laws in parliament were decided only by members of parliament, not by the people in general.

A central figure caught in the cross-currents of all the conflicting groups during the revolution was the Foreign Minister in the Marich Man Singh Shrestha government, Shailendra Kumar Upadhyaya. He was an influential liberal in the hardline camp and tried to convince the Panchayat establishment and the King to agree to a compromise. He was, however, denied an audience with the King during the crucial period. Shailendra Kumar Upadhyaya was both a nationalist and pragmatist. He had been responsible for negotiating with India during the difficult period of the Trade Embargo and had found himself caught between an arrogant Indian government in Delhi and a stubborn royal palace at home. Upadhyaya's strength was that he was a non-conformist who held to his own ideals and principles. He was quite prepared to sacrifice party membership, leadership or a seat in government if that was the price to be paid for maintaining his beliefs.

Like so many other veteran politicians in Nepal, Upadhyaya's political education had begun in India, where his family lived in exile, and Upadhyaya became involved with the Indian independence movement while he was still a schoolboy. He took part in the Quit India Movement in 1942 and his first job had been as a messenger boy. He was a young but enthusiastic participant and described his enthusiasm thus : 'I was only a young boy of fifteen or sixteen when all these things happened. Things started to grow around you and you felt a part of it, although only a very small part.'

Upadhyaya's political zeal led him to join the Nepali National Congress and then the communist movement. He threw in his lot with the communists because he believed they were the only people who could effectively counter the stark social inequalities existing in Nepal. He was, therefore, one of the founder members of the Nepal Communist Party in 1949 and one of the first to lead the fledging communist movement. Yet a few years later Upadhyaya's opinions changed again. Like many other communists at that time he was shocked by Nikita Khrushchev's denunciation of Josef Stalin's atrocities in the Soviet Union. Upadhyaya explained: 'Seeing the destruction of this father-figure of ours was very painful. And I came to the conclusion that Stalin's atrocities could not only be the result of one evil individual, but had to say something about Communist society as a whole. As you know, Communist thought only sees the individual as a product of society. I thought that in producing a figure like Stalin there had to be something wrong with the whole Communist system. In this way I came into conflict with my party colleagues.' The event which finally forced Upadhyaya to break irreconcilably with the Communist Party was the Soviet invasion of Hungary in 1956. Upadhyaya's party colleagues did not agree with his stand in supporting the people of Hungary and he had to resign from the primary membership of the party. Now his sympathies lay with the Nepali Congress, but he did not join them and during the elected government of 1959 he took his seat in parliament as an independent.

This, however, did not mean that he could be in the good books of King Mahendra. During the royal coup of 1960, Upadhyaya was rounded up and imprisoned with the others. After his release, however, King Mahendra softened his stand and successfully convinced Upadhyaya to support his plan for partyless democracy. 'After all,' Upadhyaya explained, 'if you really wanted to introduce a national democratic system with social justice, something I have been fighting for all my life, why not give the King a chance?'

Disillusionment with King Mahendra's Panchayat system set in long before the launching of the pro-Democracy movement of 1990 and Upadhyaya found himself isolated due to his liberal views.

Upadhyaya was convinced of King Birendra's good intentions, however, and hoped that the King would announce gradual reforms leading to full democracy in the country. Upadhyaya argued vigorously for implementation of reforms especially during the last years of the Panchayat system—but when King Birendra left for Pokhara just before the revolution started Upadhyaya was no longer able to advise him.

Upadhyaya's own position during the revolution became clear when he resigned as Foreign Minister by the end of March. His resignation led to the downfall of the Shrestha government just a week later and was probably a significant factor in allowing the democratic forces to gain such a total victory. Asked after the revolution about his tenure as Foreign Minister, Upadhyaya gave the impression that he had tried to make the best of an unhappy situation. 'I really didn't want to serve under this Prime Minister,' he said, 'but I felt I had to when I heard the King wanted me to join the ministry. I found I was working with the wrong person. He had no concept at all of politics, of diplomacy or of economics. He was a very narrow-minded person.'

Upadhyaya confessed that he had wanted to resign after only four months, but circumstances had persuaded him to remain in office for four years. The South Asia Regional Conference was to be held in Kathmandu in 1987 and Upadhyaya felt responsible for helping to organize it and the Indian Trade Embargo and the pro-Democracy movement followed soon after. His main regret was that he did not resign earlier. 'If I had known the King wouldn't change his mind; if I had known nobody would listen to me, but would rather pursue this path of violence, I would rather have resigned at the very beginning of the revolution.' He was sober now about his political future after the revolution: 'It would be very difficult for any political party to accept me as I have worked in the Panchayat system for many years. I have to accept this and face the consequences.'

Shailendra Kumar Upadhyaya was not the only person who found himself caught between opposing groups and ideologies. If anything, his position shows that the labels of pancha, Congress and communist do not adequately define the complex situation which unfolded in Nepal during the first few months of 1990. The conflict as such was between individual personalities who represented a wide range of political ideas and experience. The key to understanding what happened lies with who among these leaders had the ear for the masses and was able to bring them out on to the streets.

TWO

Diary Of A Revolution

As the 1980s drew to a close it was evident that the Panchayat regime could not sustain itself for long. Dissension had split its ranks and the government was continually harassed by the outlawed political parties. Change of some kind was now inevitable.

The first few months of 1990 witnessed a complete turn-around in the politics of Nepal; the Panchayat regime had given way to an interim government, which was committed to the introduction of multi-party democracy. King Birendra, who for so long had been an absolute ruler, had to pave the way for a popularly elected government and became a constitutional monarch. As the revolution reached its climax, day-to-day events moved at such a rapid pace that the end result seemed far from certain. There were rallies, arrests and torture. Opinion was divided—and the ordinary citizens of Kathmandu, where most of the major incidents of the revolution took place, often were left with little or no information about the progress of events.

The revolution when it actually occurred, had not been sudden and did not take place in a political vacuum. It had been carefully planned in terms of strategy. The opposition's final triumph was due partly to its unity, but also to the unexpected and overwhelming support it received from the masses. This support, particularly in the urban areas, cut across all caste, class and ethnic groupings—and included all age groups.

From early December 1989 rumours began to circulate in Kathmandu that the banned political parties had issued an ultimatum to the King. Either he was to introduce major political reforms before 18 January 1990 or else passive resistance would begin. The opposition called for sweeping changes. These were the restoration of the multi-party democratic system and the formation of a broad-based interim cabinet to guide Nepal towards free and fair elections. The fact that these demands had been issued jointly by the Nepali Congress Party and the communists created an atmosphere of expectation and suspense in Kathmandu. The Nepali Congress Party and the communists had for long been at loggerheads as far as their political goals were concerned. But on the question of multi-party democracy and elections, they had been able to arrive at a consensus and forged an effective union to challenge the status-quo. Expectations were fuelled further by the realization that the Panchayat regime was moving towards an irrevocable split. Daily meetings and mass rallies were organized by important Panchayat politicians who demanded the resignation of the Prime Minister, Marich Man Singh Shrestha. Meanwhile, the government controlled newspapers continued to praise the achievements of the Panchayat system. Yet the louder these newspapers praised, the deeper suspicion and expectation grew amongst the population as a whole. At last the country held its breath. Most believed that something was about to happen—though no one was sure exactly what.

The opposition had been quiet since the referendum of 1980 which had endorsed the Panchayat system. Now the political parties began to openly criticize the government. As a result, a joint co-ordination committee was formed with representatives from both the banned Nepali Congress Party and the banned communist parties, towards the end of December 1989 at Kathmandu, to lead the movement. On 10 January, seven communist parties joined forces to create the United Left Front under the leadership of Sahana Pradhan and declared their commitment to the restoration of democracy and the re-introduction of a multi-party system.

Finally, on 18 January, the day which had been fixed as the deadline for the King, the Nepali Congress began its convention in Kathmandu, the impact of which was significant. This was the first political meeting held in Nepal for ten years. Although the law constrained mass gatherings, several thousand people including liberal Panchayat politicians, representatives from the communist parties and foreign politicians gathered outside the home of the Congress leader Ganesh Man Singh. While this open and large-scale defiance of Panchayat authority was shocking enough, the sensation of the convention was undoubtedly the speech given by Chandra Shekhar, leader of the Janata Dal in India. An astute politician (and later India's Prime Minister in 1990-91), Chandra Shekhar openly voiced his support for Nepal's struggle for democracy. He added that this was not just his opinion, but the opinion of all the major Indian political leaders. Though Chandra Shekhar stirred up controversy, the police did not interfere. Instead, the government responded promptly through its own media. Radio Nepal repeatedly condemned 'aggressive foreign elements' and 'terrorists inside the country' who wanted to destroy 'our glorious King, and Panchayat system'.

The Nepali Congress Convention ended on 21 January 1990 with the pledge that unless the King met the opposition's demands within a month, the pro-Democracy movement would be launched on 18 February. This date was chosen to coincide with the official celebrations of 'Democracy Day'. Democracy Day had been instituted to mark the anniversary of King Tribhuvan's triumphant return from India in 1951 which marked the fall of the old Rana regime. Democracy Day, however, had been turned into a farce, being little more than a propaganda ceremony for the Panchayat regime.

In response to such a clear political challenge from the Nepali Congress, the government responded by organizing a series of public meetings all over Nepal. These culminated in a mass rally in Kathmandu. The government hoped to draft in enough supporters to voice their belief in the Panchayat system and help quell the rising opposition. In fact many of those who attended the rally in Kathmandu were paid two hundred rupees and provided conveyance from outlying districts. While the government claimed that more than 100,000 people had taken part in this rally, probably less than 10,000 actually attended and the event was deemed a failure. Thus the Panchayat government had failed to demonstrate that it commanded the support it had claimed for itself.

The entire cabinet was present at the rally. Several prominent politicians including the Prime Minister, expressed their views condemning the 'anti-nationalist elements' and praised 'true democracy'—that is, Panchayat democracy—in the country. However, important panchas who had openly criticized the government such as former Prime Minister Surya Bahadur Thapa and Rajeshwor Devkota, were conspicuous by their absence.

The government was clearly worried that the opposition would mobilize the people. The first signs of anti-government stirrings could be seen on 4 February, when the Tribhuvan University began a new term. The students openly declared their support for the pro-Democracy movement. Slogans declaring 'Live or Die for Democracy' appeared everywhere at university campuses in Kathmandu. The students were joined by the University Teachers' Association and the Bar Association, which ensured widespread support for it among the professionals.

The government's first response to this challenge was to close down the two most important independent newspapers in Nepal—*Bimarsa* and *Nepali Awaj*. Worried that the government might be about to crack down hard, the *Samalochana Daily* was surreptitiously handed out to pedestrians on the streets of the Kathmandu bazaar before it could be confiscated. This newspaper, issued on 11 February, announced the two-point programme for the planned uprising which had been agreed upon by the Nepali Congress and the United Left Front. The paper stated that the Nepali Congress would be responsible for the demonstration on 18 February, Democracy Day, against the Panchayat regime and for a general strike on 19 February. After that the United Left Front would organize a 'black day' on 25 February, and a second general strike on 2 March.

Behind the scenes, it was rumoured, the government was actively expanding the capacity of the jails in preparation for a large number of political arrests.

On 14 February, Sahana Pradhan, president of the newly formed United Left Front, was arrested and all telephone lines of the top leaders of the pro-Democracy movement were cut and three days later the veteran leaders of the Nepali Congress Party, Ganesh Man Singh, Krishna Prasad Bhattarai, and Girija Prasad Koirala, were placed under house arrest. Singh had just rejected a proposal from the Panchayat regime by declaring there was no longer room for compromise. The Panchayat system had to go, he said, and though the government had resorted to its time-tested tactics to stall the opposition, its efforts had little effect on the political goings-on in the country. The pro-Democracy movement was now poised to begin and the events about to take place in the country in the coming two months were to bring major political changes.

As Democracy Day began, Kathmandu was full of riot police armed to prevent the spread of political meetings and gatherings. The heaviest concentration of police was found around the open parade grounds in the city centre, close to the Palace. Police officers spent most of the morning tearing down democratic slogans and party flags which had appeared in profusion in the dead of night.

The Panchayat government was determined to show its strength and announced that this year's celebration of 'National Democracy Day and King Tribhuvan Memorial Day' was to be the biggest ever. The annual procession through the city had accordingly been made compulsory for all government employees in order to marshal support. However, that same morning the opposition was provoked further. The King's speech, broadcast on Radio Nepal, made no mention of the much awaited reforms. Instead the King wanted the Nepali people to respect the 'verdict of the majority' given to the Panchayat system in the referendum ten years earlier.

That same afternoon, a large, excited crowd began to collect outside the RNAC (Royal Nepal Airline Corporation) building in the city centre. The people tried to spill into the parade grounds, but were prevented by the police. About 10,000 people carried party flags, shouted slogans, and distributed leaflets to bystanders. Suddenly, white puffs of tear gas rose and began to drift into the thick of the crowd as police tried to head off the demonstrators. A fierce body blow of batons was unleashed. Several people were injured, but the police were outnumbered and could not disperse the crowd. Every time they beat the front row back, waves of new people emerged from side streets to take their place. While this was going on, the demonstrators collided with the official Democracy Day procession. Skirmishes broke out in which the government group disintegrated.

For the rest of the day clashes between police and demonstrators erupted all over the capital. That evening Radio Nepal reported that 'extremists' had tried to disrupt the Democracy Day celebrations, not only in Kathmandu, but all over the country. There had been a few injuries. In the town of Hetaura, a policeman had died.

The opposition's intention was that the protest on 18 February, should be followed by a general strike the following day. On 19 February all shops in Kathmandu were closed, and traffic was minimal. Later that same day reports of a serious and spontaneous uprising in Bhaktapur reached Kathmandu. Bhaktapur, near Kathmandu, is a town of narrow streets and striking temples, populated almost entirely by Newaris. Eyewitnesses claimed that police had opened fire on a crowd, killing six and injuring twenty-five people. Clashes broke out between the people and the government forces in which almost the entire population, including women and children, took part actively. Later it became public that the police had used dum dum bullets in Bhaktapur—a weapon illegal in Europe since the First World War—banned because these bullets can cause a slow, agonizing death. This was what later provoked the Medical Association to actively criticize the government.

There were also serious clashes in Kirtipur, another Newari town in the Kathmandu valley, and violence broke out in southern Nepal, in the Terai region. Demonstrations actually took place in most of the major towns in the Terai. At Janakpur, close to the Indian border, Radio Nepal claimed that three people had been killed and seven wounded when a 'mob of anti-social elements' attacked the local police force. Independent sources the next day claimed that five people had been killed and twenty wounded.

This violent outburst had come as a direct challenge to the government, but a greater threat to the government's authority was posed by the professional organizations in Kathmandu. The Lawyers' Association called a nationwide strike on 20 February. On 23 February the whole staff of the Maharajganj Teaching Hospital organized a strike to protest at government excesses. One eyewitness reported: '...the police were stealing dead bodies from the hospitals.... So the medical staff at least took photographs of those people who were admitted and preserved them.... The bodies of three persons who died after they had been brought to the hospital were put in the mortuary. About two or three hundred police arrived to steal the bodies from the mortuary. The nurses came first and lay down on the ground in front of the cars carrying the dead bodies, and the doctors, and even the patients and their relatives surrounded the police vehicles. So the police were forced to negotiate.' He went on to say: 'The police used to bring the wounded, and as soon as they were treated they would take them to the jail. So we doctors and nurses made them escape from the hospital grounds. We made them stop taking the injured away and we hid the injured in the community.'

Meanwhile in Kathmandu the university went on strike and illegal party flags could be seen flying outside all the campuses in the Kathmandu valley. Tension ran so high that soldiers practising salutes on the parade grounds in Kathmandu caused people to flee and shops to close. The whole city was on edge.

The political turmoil in Nepal did not go unnoticed outside Nepal. The Indian government expressed concern over reports that the Nepali government had used the military to crush the popular uprising in Bhaktapur. In an interview with the BBC, the Minister of Home Affairs, Nirenjan Thapa, claimed, however, that Nepal respected all fundamental human rights. He swept aside all objections, and stated that the demonstrators had left the police no option but to open fire.

By 22 February the movement seemed to have spread to the remotest parts of the country. Further protests were organized in Kathmandu including demonstrations by women in Kathmandu and

Biratnagar in the eastern Terai region. Forty members of the Rashtriya Panchayat, strongly condemned the use of violence by the government, while prisoners, just released in Kathmandu and Chitwan, told of torture in Nepali jails. These revelations fuelled public concern. The following Saturday, a delegation of human rights activists led by Dr Mathura Prasad Shrestha, had a two-hour-long audience with the Prime Minister. They demanded the immediate end of government repression and political arrests. They then asked for a list of persons killed and detained since the movement started. Shrestha recalled the meeting: 'The Prime Minister first refused to talk to us. Then after he agreed we gave him our evidence of human rights violations and ultimately he agreed that he would investigate, and he said that no one would be arrested. They didn't arrest us, and I remember the Prime Minister came up to the gate to see all of us off. But they arrested me between ten-thirty and eleven the same night in my house.'

The previous evening had been Shiv Ratri, the night of Shiva. Kathmandu had been bulging with thousands of Indian pilgrims who had come to wash and purify themselves at Pashupatinath, one of the holiest of all Hindu shrines, on the banks of the Bhagmati river. That night, as ceremonial bonfires burned in the streets and vermillion powder was scattered in ritual, it seemed that Shiva, the god of creation and destruction, was waiting to strike. Yet, though the Panchayat government had been shaken it had still not fallen.

25 February had been dubbed 'black day'. Major demonstrations had been planned by the opposition and protestors carrying black flags were due to file through the centre of Kathmandu against government oppression. All supporters of the pro-Democracy movement had been asked to wear black arm bands. In the event, the government succeeded in quashing the planned demonstrations. Radio Nepal warned that taking part in any of the demonstrations would lead to 'serious repercussions'. The streets of Kathmandu swarmed with riot police who raided the centre of Kathmandu around New Road. Normally New Road is a bustling place full of shops and traffic and crowded with people. Now any pedestrian who even stopped and glanced round was arrested. Shops were closed and public transport suspended.

There had been some outbreak of violence in the Terai and in Kathmandu police had resorted to a lathi-charge to disperse a crowd of about a thousand people, west of the city centre. In all, about a thousand people were arrested, including Hari Bol Bhattarai and Padma Ratna Tuladhar.

About the police excesses Padma Ratna Tuladhar commented: 'In Kathmandu all the arrested students and youth leaders were tortured in police custody, but not people like me because of our status. I was not tortured in police custody or jail—though there was a kind of psychological torture. I was taken from place to place late at night, even outside Kathmandu.'

Black, in fact, summed up the mood of the opposition supporters by the end of the day. The 'black day' heralded a period of terror unprecedented in Nepal's modern history as the government tried to regain control of the country. Brutality and oppression were the order of the day and relations between the government and the opposition deteriorated. The political situation was very fluid and many came to fear that the fight for democracy would be a fight to the finish and that violence would overshadow the movement's peaceful ideals.

On 26 February the employees at Bir Hospital, Kathmandu, staged an hour-long strike. The following day, students protested all over the country and the opposition leaders were worried about the situation getting out of hand. Ganesh Man Singh urged the supporters of the pro-Democracy movement not to resort to violence as this would only strengthen the Panchayat camp.

If the 'black day' of 25 February had been a failure from the point of view of the opposition, the general strike on 2 March was deemed successful, as it spread beyond the Kathmandu valley. There were reports of clashes in Dharan, in eastern Nepal. Kathmandu itself was quiet, except for a few sporadic incidents of arson.

About two hundred doctors belonging to the Nepal Medical Association issued a joint statement condemning the government. They were especially critical of the police firing at Bhaktapur.

On 5 March, five hundred members of the Bar Association of Nepal organized a strike against the Panchayat system. In courts across Nepal, including the Supreme Court, barristers and solicitors carried black flags and banners demanding human rights. They offered their services, free of charge, to all political detainees.

That very day fifty of Nepal's most famous writers, led by Kedar Man Vyethit, former minister and chancellor of the Royal Nepal Academy, sent an open letter to the government asking for a review of human rights in Nepal. The Nepali Paramedical Association sent a similar petition.

It seemed that the government had not been too perturbed by the situation in the country, and appeared confident, when Radio Nepal broadcast that life was normal throughout the kingdom. But by now Nepalis had realized that the case was quite the opposite, and that life had been seriously disrupted throughout the length and breadth of the country.

The government responded to the opposition's activities quite predictably—with force. The behaviour of the Panchayat government appeared to be to impose itself on the rebellious Nepalis at all costs. In Kathmandu, people claimed that the government had drafted in several thousand 'Mandales'—thugs trained in different fighting techniques by the National Sports Council. These men, it was rumoured, were patrolling the streets in addition to the regular police force. Many of those in police uniform, it was suspected, were actually soldiers.

Bodies were found dumped in public places. These showed signs of severe beatings. Most people believe they were the corpses of political detainees—left to frighten the people. The government, however, claimed that they had been killed by the opposition.

Radio Nepal continued its propaganda campaign by reading out statements made by released prisoners. These statements declared that in view of the recent violence these prisoners had lost faith in the pro-Democracy movement. Unofficial sources, however, pointed out that the government was merely torturing people till they confessed to crimes they had not committed. Or else they were forced to sign statements condemning the present uprising.

On 9 March, Radio Nepal announced that the assistant minister, Keshab Kumar Budathoki, had been asked to resign from his post in the Shrestha administration on grounds of misconduct. The same broadcast also reported that D.P. Adhikari had been permitted to resign from his post in the Rashtriya Panchayat. He was the second royal nominee to resign as a protest against the actions of the government. These resignations gave the impression that the government was unable to handle the pressure.

Demonstrations continued all day and effigies of Panchayat leaders were burned in several places. In the Sunsari district of the Terai region, fighting broke out between police and demonstrators.

By 10 March, an uneasy truce had been reached. The pro-Democracy movement had been temporarily withdrawn in the face of police repression although support for the movement had grown slowly but surely.

Unrest finally spread among government employees. On 13 March workers at the Agricultural Development Bank organized a one-hour sit-in strike in favour of the pro-Democracy movement. Though it was not a prolonged affair, it did show how far dissent had spread. Again, Kathmandu was filled with police and again the strike was successful. This time there was little violence. A few buses were damaged by people throwing stones and police managed to prevent a crowd from setting fire to a bridge close to Biratnagar. While Radio Nepal announced that the strike had been a failure, the BBC World Service reported that, on the contrary, it had been a success.

The situation at the Palace, however, was uncertain. The King was inaccessible and was surrounded by a small group of his closest associates. In his first public message since he had been placed under house arrest, Krishna Prasad Bhattarai, the acting president of the Nepali Congress, told the King that he could maintain his own integrity and position and avoid further unrest by announcing reforms in his speech at the Panchayat rally in Pokhara on 16 March. However, the King made no use of this opportunity to announce reforms. King Birendra merely reiterated what he had said earlier. He referred back to the result of the 1980 referendum which had voted in favour of the Panchayat system and said that the Panchayat system had a firm democratic base within Nepal.

During the following two weeks tensions within the Panchayat system increased and even affected members of the government. Liberal panchas such as Shree Bhadra Sharma were criticized by hardliners for abusing their positions. More importantly, former minister Pashupati Shumshere Rana, an influential member of the opposition, openly criticized the government and urged the two sides to negotiate immediately.

As conflict grew within the Panchayat system, popular protests showed no signs of abating. Students, medical workers and industrial workers struck work all over the country. Teachers held a successful strike and even housewives planned their own demonstration outside the Padma Kanya College in Kathmandu. On 16 March, writers and artists again staged a demonstration in Kathmandu. More than 200 of Nepal's best-known writers and artists sat down outside Trichandra College in the city centre. They tied black scarves across their faces, in a silent demonstration, to symbolize how they had been gagged by the government. Reliable sources claimed that 158 people were arrested, but most were released later that day.

On 20 March a large meeting was held at the auditorium of Kirtipur University Campus in Kathmandu by some of Nepal's leading intellectuals, to discuss the political crisis. Half-way through the meeting there was a police raid and five hundred people were arrested.

While rallies in support of the Panchayat system continued to be organized in different parts of the country, pancha rhetoric was growing weary and events were rapidly moving towards a climax.

The University campuses continued to be racked by demonstrations. Some of these became more violent than before. The police resorted to tear gas and batons once again, while the students retaliated with stones and bricks. Many were arrested and injured, including some children who had been caught up in the fighting.

According to eyewitnesses, the police had pushed five students over the edge of the roof of Amrit Science College in the centre of Kathmandu while they stormed the building, and at Bhanu Bhakta Memorial High School in Kathmandu, demonstrators set fire to six government vehicles before police could disperse the crowd.

The government responded by closing down all university campuses without prior warning on 30 March.

By the end of March protest had spread further. The whole of Kathmandu and neighbouring areas were plunged into darkness periodically as a result of a voluntary blackout called for by the opposition. Between 7.00 and 7.30 p.m. the streets of Kathmandu echoed to the cries of youngsters running and shouting: 'Bhati Nibau—Panchayat vyavasta murdabad!' ('Turn off your lights—death to the Panchayat system!').

The next decisive stage in the revolution, however, took place in Patan, Kathmandu's twin city, across the other side of the Bhagmati river in the Kathmandu valley.

The other major Newari towns in the Kathmandu valley, Bhaktapur and Kirtipur, had already seen heavy clashes with the police while Patan had remained relatively quiet. Irritated by Patan's lack of resolve, rumours stated that Bhaktapur and Kirtipur had sent bracelets and necklaces to the population of Patan, implying that the people of Patan had only the courage of women. This possibly helped spark off a tense situation in Patan. Shops and offices closed and normal life came to a standstill. There were clashes with the police at several places and many people were reported killed.

Meanwhile, Radio Nepal reported that fifty people had been taken into custody for 'terrorist activity under the supervision of extreme communists' during the blackout the previous evening. Another 200 had been arrested in connection with the demonstrations the following day.

Ganesh Man Singh, who had been hospitalized, declared: 'We Nepalis will no longer accept slavery, not even under God Almighty.'

The following day, a fresh ultimatum was given by the government through Radio Nepal to all government employees in hospitals, post offices, the fire brigade and other community services saying that participation in any strikes or demonstrations would result in 'grave repercussions'.

Violence in Patan continued, however, and was now directed at the police. Nearly every household armed itself with knives and pitchforks. The police opened fire. Local people in Patan became angry at police action. The police arrested people and looted their houses. In response to this, the people organized themselves, block by block. They bought radios and tuned into the police frequencies so that they could warn people when the police were coming and where they were going to raid. Finally, the people of Patan drove the police back to the main temple square and penned them up there. One person involved in this incident says that there were 185 police involved. For the first day they were not allowed anything to eat or drink and were reduced to drinking sewerage. Afterwards they were allowed to drink and some people brought them food. It took three days, however, for all of them to be released safely.

Eyewitnesses claimed that more than 50,000 people turned out to demonstrate in Patan and slogans had appeared, not only against the Panchayat system, but also against the monarchy.

The Minister for Foreign Affairs, Shailendra Kumar Upadhyaya, resigned in protest against Prime Minister Shrestha's policy of repression. He called for immediate negotiations with the opposition. In a later interview describing this event, Upadhyaya revealed that the cabinet at that time had been divided on how to deal with the pro-Democracy movement: 'In the cabinet not only me, but some of my colleagues also supported me in wanting to know the actual numbers of casualties. The Home Minister said twenty-three was the actual figure—then we asked about the reports of torture we had been hearing. The Home Minister, Nirenjan Thapa, said that there was no torture. So we mentioned the Human Rights group which was chaired by a very senior advocate, Bashu Dev Dhungana, who is a Panchayat stalwart and not a member of the opposition. "Why don't you let him visit the prisoners and find out if they are being tortured," we asked? "They are not ready," Thapa answered. So everything started smelling of some conspiracy.... Had I known in the beginning that the King would not listen, or that he did not trust me and would not listen to me, I would have resigned much earlier. I thought he was listening to me and that he would take proper action at the proper moment.'

A couple of days later, on 3 April, Kedar Man Vyethit, resigned from his post in the Palace Assembly, the Raj Sabha. He did so in protest against the repressive policy of the government.

The Panchayat Policy and Evaluation Committee asked influential opposition panchas, including three former Prime Ministers, for advice on how to handle the crisis. There was unanimity on the fact that Prime Minister Shrestha should resign. Shortly afterwards the Committee announced a national panchayat convention to be held on 18 April.

In fact, there was a cabinet reshuffle on 1 April involving eighteen members of the cabinet and seven assistant ministers. Four new ministers refused to take the oath because of the existing political situation. Those left in the cabinet were all known to be loyal to the Prime Minister. This seemed to prove that Shrestha still enjoyed the confidence of the King. In other words, the government was unwilling to change its uncompromising attitude in the midst of the mounting crisis.

To add to its problems, the government lost complete control in Patan. On 1 April, 20,000 people gathered for a mass meeting in the centre of the city. By now the people had taken the law totally into their own hands by placing guards on every street corner. The lowest estimate was that four people had been killed and six seriously injured since the upsurge in Patan had begun.

On 2 April, yet another general strike was called. Kathmandu was once again full of police in riot gear. Medical staff all over the country continued to strike and RNAC employees launched a three-hour strike wearing black scarves in defiance of government threats.

Barricades now blocked the main entry points into Patan. As many as 80,000 people demonstrated and the police could no longer force their way into the city.

By 3 April Patan was totally cut off from the rest of the country. Trenches had been dug in all the streets leading to the centre of the city and local guards carrying khukri knives and spears, seized from the temples, barred the entry of the police.

At a mass meeting in central Patan, the leftist leader Siddilal Singh Shrestha and the Nepali Congress leader Omkar Lal Shrestha pointed out that the time had come for the King to declare himself:'Is he for us or against us?'

The next day, 4 April, crowds gathered at all the major Hindu and Buddhist shrines in the Kathmandu valley to mourn the dead and pray that their political leaders be granted wisdom. Police were present, but did not intervene. At Pashupatinath, the temple holy to Shiva, worshippers carried banners declaring 'Ram is truth, the Panchayat system is deceit' and were stopped just outside the temple area. At Swayambunath, the major Buddhist stupa in Kathmandu, worshippers were chased away by police just after prayer had ended.

Demonstrators blocked the main road into the Kathmandu valley and fighting lasted for more than four hours. The RNAC went on strike again and flights had to be cancelled. Kathmandu, Patan and Bhaktapur were devastated by riots.

Five former Prime Ministers declared that the National Panchayat Convention, planned for 18 April, was useless now and would not solve the crisis. If anything, the government had stirred up further anger with the killing of unarmed civilians.

The climax of the movement came between 6 and 9 April. On 6 April the most comprehensive strike of the campaign was launched all over the country, in which both government employees and the airport staff participated.

The King issued a royal proclamation broadcast by Radio Nepal, and announced the formation of a new cabinet headed by Lokendra

Bahadur Chand. This was a last ditch effort as Shrestha had failed to maintain law and order. According to the King, the main tasks of the new cabinet were to begin talks with the leaders of the banned parties, conduct an inquiry into the killings, and establish a constitutional amendment commission. After the King's speech, the people of Kathmandu, Kirtipur and Patan poured out into the streets. The crowd was estimated by many to be around half a million, the largest ever gathering in Nepal's history. They were confident of victory.

Though the town was full of police, they did not interfere, but let the demonstrators assemble peacefully for a mass meeting at Tundikhel in the centre of Kathmandu. The mood changed dramatically in the afternoon. Crowds began to move towards Durbar Marg, towards the Palace, chanting slogans against the King and Queen. Without warning, soldiers appeared and opened fire with machine guns.

Panic and confusion swept through the demonstrators. Some people were even gunned down in the back while running for shelter. The BBC reported in the evening that at least fifty had died as a result of this incident. This ruthless bloodbath turned the whole course of events.

After this massacre demonstrations broke out with new force all over the capital and the police opened fire in several instances. No one knew how many had been killed or injured that day. The jubilant mood had changed to one of horror and the voluntary blackout that evening seemed more an act of deep, crushing despair than defiance.

On the evening of 6 April curfew was imposed in Kathmandu and Patan which was extended the following morning into a twenty-four-hour total curfew.

The new Prime Minister, Lokendra Bahadur Chand, tried to consult Ganesh Man Singh, but Singh made it clear that he would only agree to talks after the Panchayat government had officially announced the introduction of a multi-party system. Padma Ratna Tuladhar described the events of that day: 'Finally on the 25th of Chaitra (7 April), the day after the massacre in Durbar Marg and in the middle of the curfew, I was brought from Chautara jail to the Prime Minister,

Lokendra Bahadur Chand's residence. I was asked to initiate negotiations between the government, the Nepali Congress and the Communists.' Tuladhar had to reassure the communist leaders, who were still under house arrest, that they could resume their political activities without fear of reprisal. This implied that the curfew was imposed by the government to bide its time before initiating any action—and also to see what severe pressure the Panchayat government was now under.

On 8 April, the curfew, which had now been extended to Bhaktapur and other cities in Nepal, was lifted in Kathmandu for two hours in the afternoon. People hurried out into the streets to queue for food and were subdued. They whispered nervously to one another. They were worried that the curfew might go on and on and that a political solution to the crisis was further away than ever.

One tourist had been killed during the massacre on 6 April. Many others who tried to leave the country afterwards, found that they could not and panicked.

The Prime Minister once again urged opposition leaders to meet round the table. However, they refused to negotiate with anyone except the King. Finally, the King relented and a meeting took place in strict secrecy.

Shortly before midnight on 6 April, Nepal TV announced that the King had lifted the ban on the political parties. This was a sudden turn-around. Pictures of the Congress leaders Krishna Prasad Bhattarai and Girija Prasad Koirala, together with communist leaders Sahana Pradhan and Radha Krishna Mainali flashed on the screens. Asked about the result of their audience with King Birendra, Bhattarai replied: 'Our demands have been met and our movement is clearly and categorically called off.' All the opposition leaders rallied in support and praise of the King. Bhattarai went on to say: 'He has a deep and sincere concern for the Nepali people.'

Six people were killed during the night while celebrating the news. They were shot in the streets by soldiers who had not been informed that the curfew and revolution were over.

The following morning, when the news was repeated on Radio Nepal, huge crowds immediately took to the streets, and the announcement was widely welcomed.

The crowds gathered at Tundikhel for a mass meeting where the Congress and communist leaders, just released from prison, addressed the people. The leaders declared that the door to democracy had now been opened, but there was still a long way to go to build a fully democratic society in Nepal. The real democracy movement was just beginning, though the first stage was now over. Koirala pointed out:'Our goals are the establishment of a constitutional monarchy and a constitution based on the will of the people. Our history is full of broken promises from the King, therefore we will now make sure the promises are fully implemented. Only through continued unity may we reach these goals.'

Koirala's rhetoric seemed to signal the end of the old regime. Yet, though the pro-Democracy movement had won in principle, it still had to put its victory into practice. Celebrations continued in Kathmandu and across the country for several days, but gradually the realization dawned that the introduction of multi-party democracy was far from ensured. All that the King had agreed to was the omission of a small paragraph in the Panchayat constitution, which meant that Panchayat politicians were unaffected. On 10 April the United National People's Movement held an open-air meeting at Tundikhel, criticizing the Nepali Congress and the United Left Front for giving up the struggle for democracy too quickly. The meeting was attended by about 10,000 people.

If anything, Ganesh Man Singh was in agreement with the communists. He complained that the democratization process was going too slowly. He further stated that if the King did not dissolve the Panchayat government and establish an interim government quickly, the people would soon be out on the streets again.

The following day on Radio Nepal the Prime Minister, Lokendra Bahadur Chand, announced the second round of talks with opposition leaders. The opposition politicians, however, clung to their position that they would negotiate with no one except the King. Pressure on the opposition leaders for a fresh initiative began to increase substantially. More and more groups demanded full-fledged democracy on the terms of the pro-Democracy movement. These included the human rights organization under the leadership of Mathura Prasad Shrestha, as well as the extreme 'Mashal' Communist group, and some within the United Left Front and the Nepali Congress. The leaders of the pro-Democracy movement realized that they had to act.

On 12 April the leaders of the United Left Front and the Nepali Congress held a meeting at the residence of Ganesh Man Singh. At a press conference after the meeting, the leaders explained that eight clear demands had been presented to the King. The most important of these were: the immediate establishment of an interim cabinet (including both Congress and communist members), the dissolution of the Panchayat system at all levels, and the release of all political prisoners.

The following day all remaining political prisoners were released. But still the King did not act. In his message for the Nepali New Year on 14 April he merely announced that he would establish a Commission for the Amendment of the Constitution with members from all political groups. Ganesh Man Singh complained bitterly:'The whole political situation of the country has changed, but the style of the King remains the same.'

What the opposition was invited to were talks organized by Prime Minister Lokendra Bahadur Chand. The political parties spent hours deciding whether they should attend. In the end they sent only minor leaders. The Panchayat government tried to follow suit by only sending ministers and liberals who had no real power. The Prime Minister did turn up, opened the proceedings, and tried to leave. However, the majority of the people who had gathered outside the Academy Hall where the talks were taking place, refused to allow the Prime Minister to leave. They even padlocked the entrances to the premises. From early in the afternoon until after midnight, thousands chanted outside the Academy Hall:'Give us what we ask for or resign!' The opposition leaders went out periodically to calm the crowd and the police did not interfere.

Talks continued until 3 a.m. Allowed out of the building by the remaining demonstrators, Prime Minister Chand drove straight to the Palace to hand in his resignation to the King. This spelled the final capitulation by the Panchayat regime.

The following morning a royal proclamation was broadcast by Radio Nepal. It was announced that the King, in consultation with the standing committee of the Raj Sabha, the Palace Assembly, and the steering committee of the Rashtriya Panchayat, the parliament, had dissolved the parliament, the Panchayat Policy and Evaluation Committee and the Class Organizations. In other words, the entire Panchayat system had been dismantled at one stroke. In addition, the King announced the removal of a few paragraphs from the constitution to make the formation of a new government easier.

Two weeks later, on 28 April, all village, town and district panchayats were dissolved. The two remaining institutions of the old regime, the National Sports Council and the fourteen zonal commissioners were formally abolished on 7 May.

The King asked Prime Minister Chand to continue in his post until an interim government could be formed. On the afternoon of the royal proclamation, the King met Ganesh Man Singh and asked him to head an interim government. Singh refused on health grounds, but suggested Krishna Prasad Bhattarai. The King also agreed at this meeting to give up his political position and become a constitutional monarch.

Returning from the Palace, Ganesh Man Singh immediately convened a meeting of the United Left Front and the Nepali Congress. At a press conference afterwards, Bhattarai announced that he had accepted the offer of heading the new interim government. This would consist of members of the Nepali Congress and the United Left Front. The priorities of the Government would be, first and foremost, to alleviate economic hardship in Nepal and, secondly, hold elections on the principle of one adult one vote from the age of eighteen and over. A third, but highly important, task for the interim government would be to solve the trade dispute with India which had been dragging on for over a year.

Bhattarai handed over his list of cabinet members to the King on 18 April, and the latter added two more of his own. The interim cabinet consisted of three members of the Nepali Congress, three members of the United Left Front, including its president Sahana Pradhan, two leading human rights activists, and two royal nominees.

This interim government was sworn in on the following day, 19 April, 1990. Breaking with protocol, only the Prime Minister took oath at the Palace. The rest of the cabinet were sworn in at a public meeting at Singha Durbar, the old Maharaja's palace in the centre of Kathmandu which was now the main government building.

Ganesh Man Singh was the main speaker during the swearing-in ceremony. He told the interim cabinet that the responsibility for implementing the pro-Democracy movement's eight demands now lay with them. The new government hoped to announce a new constitution within ninety days, and hold elections within a year. Now the interim cabinet had to begin to steer Nepal towards a new future.

The new government's first task was to re-establish law and order in the country. This meant more than clearing away the litter of revolution lying in the streets. The army was still loyal to the King and suspicious of the new political leaders. Furthermore, supporters of the old regime actively opposed the new government. In many places the people's own 'guards' still patrolled the streets instead of the police. The government first had to wrest confidence from the people, and then impose their authority.

A series of violent incidents rocked Kathmandu, bringing the city to the brink of emergency, but no one knew if they were wanton acts of hooliganism or a planned attempt at a 'counter-revolution' by disaffected reactionaries. This violence sent shock waves of uncertainty through the capital and showed how fragile the new interim government actually was.

One incident occurred on 16 April when a group of anti-social elements attacked the Biswojyoti Cinema Hall in Kathmandu and set fire to it. Several of these arsonists were recognized as 'Mandales'.

There were also reports of men in police uniforms carrying out acts of sabotage and burglary. People were afraid that sections of the old regime were trying to strike back with terror. Girija Prasad Koirala, General Secretary of the Nepali Congress, appealed to the public to form security committees to guard against extremist acts. One of these committees caught several important members of the National Sports Council a few days later on 22 April in the worst night of burglary, looting and theft in Kathmandu. This had come about after a spate of sleepless nights in Kathmandu when homes and shops had been attacked and plundered.

On 23 April, the leaders of the Nepali Congress met to discuss the difficult situation. By then the people had taken matters into their own hands. In Kalanki, another part of Kathmandu, five police officers without identity cards were taken into custody by a crowd. A few hours later, the Minister for Internal Affairs, Yog Prasad Upadhyaya and the Inspector-General of Police, arrived to try and secure the release of the officers. Rather than giving in, the crowd held the Inspector-General of Police prisoner also and led him in a procession to Tundikhel. In an open-air meeting, the Inspector-General of Police promised to dismiss all police personnel, who had been found abusing their position within a week.

Throughout the day, processionists walked through the centre of Kathmandu parading wounded and dead police officers and shouting slogans against the King. Tear-gas and batons were used to control them—ordered by the new interim government. In Hanuman Dhoka, the central temple square of Kathmandu, police standing on the roof of their headquarters opened fire and killed two of the demonstrators and wounded several more.

A rumour spread round Kathmandu that three cars full of armed men had tried to enter the government buildings at Singha Durbar at midday with the intention of kidnapping the members of the cabinet. However, they were turned away at the entrance.

Violence continued in the afternoon; a crowd gathered outside the office of the Bhagmati Zonal Commissioner and his office and some government vehicles were burnt. The police retaliated by opening fire. A crowd also set fire to the house of the Mandale leader, Sharad Chandra Shaha, in Dilli Bazar.

The new Prime Minister, Bhattarai, met the King and later that day made an appeal through Radio Nepal, for everyone to remain calm. He said that reactionary elements were plotting against the new interim government and that the people should fight back, but in a wise and careful manner. The people's demands would be met, but the government needed time, at least two months, to begin the democratization process in earnest.

Finally, on 25 April, in a message from the Palace, the King asked the people to give their full support to the new government. This was a clarification of the King's position and showed the police, the panchas and the military where the King's sympathies now lay. Many people believed that the King's announcement came as a result of Bhattarai's visit to the palace two days earlier. It was alleged that Bhattarai had threatened to resign if the King did not give his total commitment to the new interim government.

It was not until 6 May, however, that the General Secretary of the Nepali Congress, Girija Prasad Koirala, gave the King the following ultimatum: either the King had to transfer all his power to the new government or else the whole cabinet would resign. According to Radio Nepal, the King gave in gracefully and unconditionally to all of Koirala's demands.

This meeting was the turning-point. Though night curfews continued in Kathmandu for a short while and there were incidents of violence, the interim government had survived. The pro-Democracy leaders had consolidated their gains, had averted a possible 'counter-revolution' and were now in a more secure position from which to govern.

The First Awakening

As crowds poured out into the streets of Kathmandu in spring 1990 to demand civil liberties and political rights, the picture that many had of Nepal as a remote, isolated Himalayan kingdom was abruptly changed. This potent picture had been created and maintained for many years by tourists, anthropologists and foreign scholars. These westerners wanted to believe in Nepal as a society of peace-loving people living in one of the most stable societies in the world. It was true that poverty was part of this picture—but it was a gentle, persevering poverty—not a condition which would lead to violence and upheaval. Furthermore, poverty and hardship were often linked in westerners' minds with religion and an inner (and coveted) spiritual peace derived from Hinduism and Buddhism.

The main factor of social stability in Nepal was reckoned to be the caste system. The Chetris and Brahmins stood at the forefront of an elaborate and intricate social pattern which kept any possible conflicts at bay. In such a controlled society a political revolution in the traditional sense of the word was simply unthinkable. For this reason also, what happened in 1990 came to many as a shock.

For those familiar with Nepali society, the revolution should not have come as a surprise. Forty years had passed since Nepal had first opened its borders to the outside world and in that time Nepali society had changed drastically. Just a few kilometres from Kathmandu, the mountain villagers appeared to live in a timeless medieval era, but the country had, in fact, undergone a profound social revolution. Old social constraints had disappeared and ordinary Nepalis now had new horizons and new demands. They were also increasingly aware that these demands could not be met by an unyielding political system ruled by an absolute monarch. So, while the timing and extent of the revolution were unforeseen, it had already been clear for several years that some kind of political change would have to come. Under the Panchayat façade, forces and ideas had gradually developed which eventually undermined the whole regime. In effect, two impulses were at work: the sweeping democratic revolutions in Eastern Europe in 1989 which put Nepal on the road to democracy and a long cumulative process of discontent within Nepal itself.

The Panchayat regime had many faces. It is usually criticized on account of the limits it imposed on Nepali society. After all, the Panchayat system did restrict personal and political freedom. On the other hand there were other aspects of Panchayat policy. The Panchayat government advocated sweeping social and economic change and thus (perhaps unwittingly) engineered profound changes in Nepali society.

The most obvious and far-reaching of these changes was the enormous explosion in education. In 1951 the literacy rate in Nepal was only two per cent. By the late 1980s it had reached close to forty per cent. During that same period, the population of Nepal had risen from eight million to twenty million and yet education had more than kept pace with this colossal increase.

While education had been a priority with the pre-Panchayat governments of the 1950s, primary education had only really taken off in the 1970s after the Panchayat government had introduced the New Education Plan in 1971. This plan was a central part of the Panchayat government's strategy to develop Nepal. Nepali was made the official language, the curriculum was standardized in the country's schools, and subjects relating to national culture and history were introduced. The aim of this was to further integration among Nepal's diverse inhabitants. Practical skills, not theoretical knowledge, were emphasized, as aids to development.

Many of the principles of the New Education Plan were never put into practice and after a short while the whole plan was deemed a failure. Even so, primary education flourished. Many pointed out that this growth was quantitative and not qualitative, but the fact remains that by 1990 a large percentage of the Nepali population could read and write. Literacy, it could be maintained, was also the bedrock of political consciousness.

The contradiction about encouraging education while at the same time constraining political activity became evident to many Nepali intellectuals during the 1980s. A young Nepali engineer said, just a year before the revolution: 'If I were a Panchayat politician I would be worried about the expansion of education. If our leaders want to maintain the Panchayat system they should immediately shut down all institutions of education.'

Yet, the field of education was not the only area in which the Panchayat government was at fault. At a deeper level the government's repeated emphasis on economic development and growth also led to its undoing. The Ranas, who had ruled Nepal for over a century, perceived any economic development not related to their own interests as a political threat. The Panchayat government appeared unconcerned about such a link between politics and economics. In fact, King Mahendra's justification for the introduction of the Panchayat system, when he seized power in 1960, was that this system would better serve the further development of the country.

Foreign aid began to flow freely into the country which totally changed the lifestyles of Nepal's urban population. Nepalis began to long for western consumerism and Kathmandu began to take on the trappings of a modern, western city. Consumer products had flooded the markets. Though this materialism only affected a tiny percentage of the population, it was precisely this percentage which was close to the centre of Nepali political life. These were the people who had the dynamism and ability to translate their aspirations into action. These people found that their material lifestyle improved, but they still lacked the civil liberties and political freedom often associated with modern society. Increased material wealth, therefore, led only to increased political discontent. A professor at the university in Kathmandu said just before the revolution: 'This regime which has been in power for the last 25 years, what good has it done anyone really? It has not prevented the privileged few from leading a fully western consumer lifestyle in the name of modernisation, but it takes away the rights of people to say "No" to it.' Material change and social change thus fed on one another.

The caste system had been the strongest social institution in Nepal. The Panchayat constitution of 1962 had banned caste as a way of distinguishing people. Of course, as a deeply ingrained tradition sanctioned by religious values, the caste system could not be done away with overnight. From 1951 onwards, however, a slow erosion of values was evident in Nepal. By the end of the 1980s this process had amounted to nothing less than a social revolution. The old rigid caste rules of pollution and purification were now laughed at by many people. Inter-caste marriage was still unusual, but no longer unheard of. Similarly, the concept of love-marriage had gained noticeable acceptance—although a large majority of young Nepalis were still married off by their families. Now a small, but growing group of educated women were filling important jobs in the towns.

This social revolution, which had reached furthest in Kathmandu, also had its negative aspects. Ethical, moral and religious values which had previously held people in check now began to lose their grip. The Brahmins, who according to Hindu law were not allowed to touch alcohol, began to suffer from a growing alcohol problem. The growing social malaise was perhaps summed up by young Nepalis stealing idols from temples in the Kathmandu valley and selling them to tourists from the West.

What seemed to be happening was that the urban, modernized and educated élite were in search of new values and a new identity. Naturally, ideas had flowed into Nepal along with aid. The ideologies of India, China and the West caught the imagination of the newly-educated segment of the population. Nepal had never been a colony. In fact, Nepal had been closed to the outside world. Now that the country was open, Nepali intellectuals experienced an intoxicating freedom in trying to pick and choose an ideology which would fit their own way of thinking. What held most appeal, however, were Marxist and communist ideas in some form or other.

In order to understand the Nepali revolution of 1990 it is necessary to scrutinize the 1980s and what they brought by way of changes to Nepali society.

The 1980 referendum had been a watershed. Since the Panchayat government had defeated the multi-party camp by only a narrow margin, Nepal had become a different country in many respects. The 1980s saw yuppies ascendant in the West. Closer to home, Rajiv Gandhi's economic reforms in India aimed at creating a two hundred million strong middle class. It was during this decade that modernization in Nepal was felt most strongly. A liberal pancha pointed out that 300,000 people were given a proper education in Nepal during these ten years. From the point of view of numbers alone, this was a large enough group to upset the delicate political balance of 1979.

In the referendum of 1980 the majority of young people had backed the multi-party system. This new educated group was growing and their sympathy did not lie with the ruling regime.

This group was now so large that the government was no longer able to placate it. In the past, educated people were almost automatically given jobs in government service and that served as a means of neutralizing them politically. People now outstripped jobs in this, the largest growing bureaucracy in the world. Fears grew that there might be large-scale white-collar unemployment as in India. For the time being at any rate, largely due to foreign aid, most educated people did get jobs. Those who did not find government jobs did find employment in the slowly growing private and semi-private sector.

This professional middle class was a totally new feature of Nepali society and formed the backbone of the pro-Democracy movement in 1990. Ironically, it was this group who had largely enjoyed the limited measures of freedom brought about by the Third Amendment to the Constitution after the referendum in 1980.

The early 1980s also saw other kinds of freedom develop. An autonomous press was created in the country for the first time. Weekly newspapers such as *The Nepali Awaj* and *Saptahik Bimarsa* and several other Nepali language dailies were launched. These newspapers, as well as many of the older ones, criticized the Panchayat system openly. This criticism stopped short of the King, but the royal family did not escape reproval between the lines.

The Panchayat government tried every means it could think of to silence the press. The government banned newspapers, confiscated issues and arrested journalists and editors. These attempts were in vain, however, and at best half-hearted. Newspapers were generally left to write what they wanted, and when a newspaper was banned it would mysteriously resurrect itself just a few days later under a different name.

Another feature of the new freedom of the 1980s was the continued existence of the political parties. Though the political parties continued to be officially banned after the 1980 referendum, they were allowed to carry on with their activities within certain limits. As long as they did not organize demonstrations or public meetings it was, more or less, business as usual.

These small measures of freedom came nowhere near appeasing the new educated middle class of Nepal. Rather, the taste of freedom encouraged people to press for more. Gradually the lack of full political freedom and civil liberties became unbearable and these unbearable constraints were what finally galvanized the population into political action.

In addition, a new form of politics began to emerge towards the end of the 1980s. Previously, political opposition had been the monopoly of the banned political parties. Very quickly, however, a number of formal and informal organizations sprang up through which the new class of intellectuals expressed their dissatisfaction with their lot and the government. Most prominent amongst these were the human rights organizations. Though the government imposed some limits on these new organizations, they were largely left to fend for themselves.

More important to the final outcome of the 1990 revolution were the professional organizations and intellectual forums which appeared. The Medical, Engineering and University Associations were vital to the democratic struggle throughout the revolution. The intellectual forums, for their part, acted as a more subtle force in the period just before the revolution started.

These forums were composed largely of the same people and appeared and disappeared with bewildering rapidity. One central member of these groups explained: 'The same groups of people were active in the name of different forums. Sometimes organising meetings for religious unity, sometimes organising forums to propagate democratic norms and concepts of equity among the people and against exploitation and many other things. So we did not form specific formal groups. Just for some time, for example, we formed the forum for religious unity. If it continued many people would be arrested, so we just formed another forum and the whole thing was very fluid.' Because of this there were a large number of people already politically active even before the pro-Democracy movement officially began.

It was largely due to pressure from these groups and from the new intelligentsia that the Nepali Congress and communists joined the Movement for the Restoration of Democracy. Unity among the opposition parties, which had proved so elusive in the past, now came about as a direct result of the demands of Nepal's new middle class.

Former Home Minister, Nirenjan Thapa pointed to one of the main failings of the Panchayat system when he stated: 'We failed to forge links with the intellectuals and obtain their sympathy.' The reason why this new class could not be accommodated within the Panchayat system has its roots in the main principles and ideology of the whole Panchayat enterprise.

When King Mahendra staged his royal coup in 1960 he argued that Nepal was not yet mature enough for multi-party democracy. Instead, he claimed, he would introduce a new form of democracy more suited to the needs of Nepal. While King Mahendra's coup came as a shock to the politicized élite of the time, there was very little actual opposition. A small group of party leaders, either in prison or in exile, did protest, but the large bulk of educated people, many of whom had been party members, quickly accommodated themselves to the new regime. To understand why the transition from democracy to royal dictatorship went so smoothly, one has to understand Nepali society in 1960.

In 1960 Nepal's modern history was only a decade old. The educated segment of the population was still pitifully minuscule. The vast majority of the population lived in remote villages and did not even know that a change of government had taken place. When they did, they hardly grasped its importance. It is also true that while many intellectuals did not approve of King Mahendra's action, they did not really mind. There were several reasons for this. The 1950s had been an unstable period of successive governments racked by rifts and squabbles. Even after the Nepali Congress came to power in 1959, the problem of law and order in the country did not change. Educated Nepalis came to realize that democracy could not solve all their economic, social and political problems at once. Many lost faith in democracy and began to believe that it was not the political system best suited to Nepali society. As one ex-pancha, involved in the Panchayat system from the beginning stated: 'Democracy actually seemed to strengthen the traditional power structure. It did not transform and change the fundamental social structure. Most of the political parties were managed and headed by upper caste people and they were only interested in giving lip service to the political aspect of democracy: liberty, fraternity, and equality. There were very few and only half-hearted attempts to transform those idioms and concepts into economic change to make an effort to alleviate poverty.'

There was also the uncomfortable feeling that the whole of the Nepali democratic system had been imported from India and was being managed by India. All party leaders had connections with Nepal's southern neighbour and many Nepalis believed that political decisions affecting their country were made in New Delhi rather than in Kathmandu.

This was the mood in Nepal when King Mahendra introduced the Panchayat system. Thus the Panchayat emphasis on economic development, nationalism and gradual democratization based on village councils or Panchayats, appealed to many who had been discontent with the previous system.

Yet the Panchayat system was not unique. There seemed to be an international movement amongst the post-colonial Third World countries away from multi-party democracy. A former Panchayat Prime Minister, Surya Bahadur Thapa, explained: 'Throughout Asia and other Third World countries there was a wave. Two types of democracy were introduced. One, guided democracy: the second, basic democracy. The name was different, but it was the same thing. The Panchayat system was also such a system introduced as a result of this international movement.' The twin goals of these systems were, as he went on to say: first, build democracy slowly and gradually: secondly, promote economic development. These new systems were introduced by way of a solution to a general problem which Third World countries had to deal with. 'The problem was that these countries had to catch up with a process of democratisation and economic development which in the West had taken a hundred, two hundred, even up to a thousand years. There was the industrial revolution in Britain and the political revolution in France...and so many other revolutions. We had to catch up with all these dramatic changes in a very short time. The global, economic and political scenario was changing so fast that we felt we had no time left. Our question, then, was how to synchronise all these changes and make them happen simultaneously.'

When the shock of the royal coup had passed, some idealism and enthusiasm for the new Panchayat system actually emerged. Furthermore, it was conscious Panchayat policy to attract newly educated people into the system and give them government jobs. A symbol of the major Panchayat ideals was the National Education System Plan announced in 1971. This plan's aim was to implant patriotism, practicality and political consciousness into the new generation. In this way the school children of Nepal were to be trained for the slow and steady economic development of their country and for its gradual democratization. The plan, as has been stated, was never properly implemented. Even before the National Education System Plan's introduction, many had already lost faith in the Panchayat system. For by then the Panchayat system had begun to show its true totalitarian character. By then, too, some of the Panchayat leaders appeared to have understood that such an education system, if implemented, would in the long run, not benefit their hold on power.

The great appeal of the Panchayat vision was its programme of an evolutionary process leading towards democracy. The system's supporters agreed with King Mahendra that the people of Nepal in the 1960s had not reached a level where they were able to cope with multi-party democracy. They did believe, however, that with the growth of education and the passage of time, full democracy would be introduced in Nepal. Gradual political reforms, therefore, were seen as the main characteristic of the Panchayat system. A former pancha minister described how a kind of political evolution had taken place within the Panchayat system during its thirty year history. 'The initial panchayat was nothing. Members of the parliament, the Rashtriya Panchayat, were not elected, they were chosen—and they were only asked to raise their hands. When a representative was to be elected, a high administrative official would come to the local district panchayat and ask who they wanted to be their member in parliament. The first person who raised his hand would automatically become the representative. The Panchayat system started that way, but within its lifetime it changed a great deal. And when the Third Constitutional Amendment came, it was very clear that it was heading towards the multi-party system.'

There was, however, a growing frustration among liberal-minded panchas that the government had deliberately tried to check this process of reform. A former member of the Rashtriya Panchayat said: 'Everything went well until 1970. Then the vested interests started to come in and take over and since then the whole system has gone bad.'

The main difference between the Panchayat system and parliamentary democracy was the principle of 'partylessness'. Political parties were banned—supposedly to strengthen unity and national identity. In fact, 'partylessness' merely encouraged disunity as factions and groups developed and squabbled within the system. As no other political identity was legal, elections were fought on a communal basis and national identity, if anything, was ruptured further. The widening gap between liberal and conservative panchas did, in effect, give rise to two or more political parties within the non-party system. Finally, this political system, which had been created to accommodate diversity, began to suppress even its own dissenting members. In the late 1970s several prominent panchas demanded a widening of the electorate and open sessions in parliament. For this they were imprisoned.

This *de-facto* pluralism within the non-party system perfectly illustrates the wide gap between ideals and realities within the Panchayat regime. The longer the system continued, the more obvious it became that King Mahendra had merely introduced autocratic dictatorship under a thin democratic guise.

The Third Amendment to the Constitution in 1980 made the Panchayat system almost fully democratic on paper, but changed little in daily life. What was worse, after thirty years of Panchayat rule, general economic conditions in the country had only deteriorated. The poor became visibly poorer while the palace circle amassed more and more wealth. Corruption was widespread and reached the Palace itself. It was the blatant corruption, more than anything else, which made the population as a whole finally lose faith in the government and the Panchayat system.

It is natural to ask whether King Mahendra's Panchayat vision was ever genuinely intended. It was obviously in Mahendra's interest to do away with the Nepali Congress government in 1960 in order to maintain his own position. Thus the Panchayat system might be seen only as a tool to retain power for the King and his immediate circle. However, it is also true that during the first years of the system the large majority of the educated population obviously felt that they could work within it. It was only during the Panchayat's latter stages, especially the 1980s, that the educated classes began to agitate for alternative forms of government.

The rampant corruption within the Panchayat system and even within the palace itself caused the Nepali population to become deeply disillusioned with the political system.

Yet, more than this, the lack of political freedom made many turn their attention to other systems. Many knew that better forms of democracy existed elsewhere in the world. Unlike their parents and grandparents, the newly educated listened to radio and watched TV and even travelled. What the media disclosed were reports of how people in other parts of the world had revolted against the regimes oppressing them.

The 1986 revolution in the Philippines made a strong impression on many in Nepal. The uprising against Ferdinand Marcos gave many in Nepal heart that something similar might come about. The student protests in China and the Tiananmen Square massacre of 1989 also challenged Nepalis, even though these events were scarcely covered by the Nepali media owing to the country's delicate relations with China. What finally galvanized the Nepali people into action, however, were the democratic revolutions in Eastern Europe in 1989, particularly the revolution in Romania. All these revolutions appeared to be striving for the same goals: the introduction of multi-party democracy, political freedom, and a respect for human rights. These were the same stated objectives of the pro-Democracy movement in Nepal. The Nepali Congress and communist parties had already agreed to a minimum common programme which included these points before the planned revolution began. But what did these vague political goals actually mean in a society like Nepal where democracy had flourished for only sixteen months thirty years ago?

A teacher at the university in Kathmandu said a year before the revolution: 'It doesn't matter what you call it as long as there are basic freedoms and human rights.'

People wanted democracy because to them it spelled freedom, but they did not know what kind of democracy they wanted. A natural model would have been the Indian political system—but India was too close and Nepalis were only too well aware of India's political shortcomings. Moderates, especially within the Nepali Congress, favoured the British political system. The British combination of constitutional monarchy with parliamentary democracy firmly set in tradition seemed a suitable system for Nepal to adopt.

Democracy, most importantly, meant freedom. Liberalism and pluralism in the Western sense were alien concepts to Nepali society.

Moreover, they were hard ideas to translate into political slogans which would appeal to ordinary citizens. Therefore many Nepalis looked for more practical political ideas.

The only real alternatives to the ruling Panchayat ideology in Nepal seemed to be either communism or socialism. Both appealed to the demands in Nepali society for equality. Equality was an intoxicating, even an explosive, political idea for people living in a society governed by caste hierarchy and feudal structures. When asked to define the nature of Marxism, communists and socialists alike from the extreme left Mashal Party to the Nepali Congress Party all declared firmly that it was, 'the new idea of equality'.

Historically, Nepali communism and socialism began in India with the anti-imperialist movement against British rule. After India gained independence the struggle moved to the subsequent fight against the Rana regime in Nepal. The first politician to introduce socialism as an official ideology in Nepal was B.P. Koirala. He was more radical than later Congress leaders. His Congress government, the first democratically elected government in Nepal in 1959, followed a path of idealistic socialism which culminated in the announcement of the Land Reform Act and the abolition of the rent-free *Birtha*; however, Koirala's political philosophy, which he expressed through his literary essays, was criticized by many as being too theoretical and too impractical.

The communist movement did not exercise any real power in Nepal until the 1990 revolution. The communists were always critical of Congress. They lambasted the Nepali Congress continually for fine words, but little action. Action was a major topic as far as the communists were concerned. Their many splits, conflicts and realignments during their forty year history were mainly to do with what political action they should take. Differences in political doctrine often seemed to be secondary—the communists were more occupied with how to deal with the practical situation facing Nepal.

When the Panchayat system was introduced, the Nepali Congress had been defined as the main enemy of the regime. Over the years, the Panchayat government did try to woo communists into their ranks.

They were successful to a certain degree with men like Keshar Jung Rayemajhi and Shailendra Kumar Upadhyaya. These politicians had been central figures in the communist movement when it began and later became active panchas.

In the early years of the Panchayat system many communists did feel that the best way to realize their goals was to work within the system. Certain features of the Panchayat system even appealed to them. One was the formation of the 'Back to the Village National Campaign' in 1967 which had been inspired by the Cultural Revolution in China. Communist involvement came to an end when the Campaign became corrupt and was revealed as yet another tool for the political puppeteers in the Palace to control local elections. Many disillusioned activists turned to the Communist Party which operated underground from Mahendra's coup in 1960 until the referendum announcement in 1979.

By 1990 the communist movement in Nepal was stronger than ever before, but it desperately lacked unity. Mikhail Gorbachev's Glasnost and Perestroika, the Chinese massacre in Tiananmen Square and the revolutions in Eastern Europe had all left their mark. The communists desperately needed to defend an ideology which was manifestly dying elsewhere in the world and show that it was still politically viable for Nepal. There was also a realization that much could be achieved if only the communists could unite and overcome their differences. This was easier said than done. There were no fewer than fourteen communist parties and each contained a wide body of opinion.

On the far left there were still communists who advocated an armed struggle and the Dictatorship of the Proletariat. These communists continued to speak text-book Marxism and viewed Marxist ideology as a waterproof system of thought which could provide answers to any question. They explained away the events in Eastern Europe merely as popular uprisings against revisionism. A leader of the extreme left Communist Mashal Party commented: 'Communism has not failed. Some experiments have failed, but that does not mean that the whole science itself has failed. A machine based on scientific theories may sometimes fail, and even break down, but that does not mean the whole science has broken down. Similarly, Marxism is a social science tool to change society, to change the whole of history. That a few experiments in Eastern Europe and China failed does not mean that failure is forever.'

The overriding communist goal was democracy based on economic redistribution. The communists saw their support and participation in the pro-Democracy movement as necessary before launching their 'real' revolution at a later date. Parliamentary democracy was bourgeois in their eyes, but at least it was a stage further along the road to a true people's revolution: 'In a parliamentary democracy,' the Mashal member went on to say, 'you don't redistribute the property, you just advocate free competition. Free competition among unequals is naturally in the favour of the more powerful ones. When we perform this new democratic revolution we will immediately redistribute property. We will confiscate all landed property and redistribute the wealth among the poor. The political institutions may remain the same. We believe in political freedom. We will have election, but the elections so far have only been dominated by money.'

These radical communists were characterized by their well-organized underground party networks. A member of the Nepal Communist Party 4th Convention, the most radical party in the United Left Front, said: 'Our party is disciplined. We have our own rules. No member is entitled to work or conduct any activity without the prior central committee decision. All such decisions are binding to the party's workers. We also have mass support. All this cannot be seen in the revisionist parties.'

Yet ideas were changing even amongst the radical communist parties. During the 1980s the biggest Communist Party, the Marxist-Leninists, had transformed themselves from a group of Naxalite-inspired terrorists into a democratic party standing for pluralism and a multi-party system. One of the party members explained: 'Our extreme thinking and violent movement had to change.

The situation of the country was no longer favourable to an armed revolution, so we changed ourselves and reformed our thinking. Previously we emphasised armed revolt. We attacked landowners and police and snatched their guns. But now we left the idea of an armed revolution and started mass politics. We still agitated for the implementation of the Land Reform Act and the protection of tillers' rights. But we now also tuned our eyes to exploited workers in the cities as well as demanding increase of wages.'

He explained this extraordinarily radical change of policy as follows: 'The fundamental theory of Marxism is dialectic materialism. This is a moveable process. To every action there is a reaction. This makes society go ahead. There are many types of thinking in society and also in the party. If such a dialectic situation does not exist in the party, how should it survive and how should it at all be able to rule the country? The true and actual thinking of Marxism is therefore the same as democracy.'

'Political exercise should be encouraged. Every party should have inner party democracy. Only then can we give democracy to the people. And this will help us to finally reach a stage where we can find communism.'

The younger members among Marxist-Leninists were not the only ones to have changed their views. The old generation of communists, who had been founder members of the original Communist Party of Nepal seemed even more willing to revise their opinions. Their pragmatic attitude made the formation of the United Left Front possible. This front, which helped lead the pro-Democracy movement, consisted of seven communist parties working with the Nepali Congress. The United Left Front's goals seemed more social democratic than communist. The leader of the United Left Front and the Nepal Communist Party (Marxist), Sahana Pradhan, explained how this turnabout was possible: 'We all said "let's agree for the time being"—and we all agreed with constitutional monarchy. The world is changing and we shouldn't be dogmatic. In Russia there is glasnost, in China, modernisation. All these things are happening, so at this time we too, should think in different ways. We decided it was better to join hands with the Congress and say we believe in constitutional monarchy and the multi-party system. For these things to come about we believe that peaceful methods should be used. We no longer believe in violence.' Sahana Pradhan went on to comment: 'We believe in this now. It's tactical now. We said republicanism might come later. First let us bring democracy. Let us have some fundamental rights. Unless we have some political freedom how can we go any further and take the next step?'

So radical communists had reformed and embraced the ideals of multi-party democracy and constitutional monarchy. This was the situation amongst the large majority of communists in Nepal just before the pro-Democracy movement launched its campaign. But how could these people still call themselves communists?

Populist leader and independent left-wing politician Padma Ratna Tuladhar claimed that he still believed that communism was the only possible solution to Nepal's many problems. 'Marx said that society should give according to the individual's needs and demand according to his ability. This should be the guiding principle of our government.' He readily accepted that no country had yet reached this utopian position, though he believed stoutly that that was no reason to give up communist principles.

But what was the main principle of the Nepali communists' ideology? Radha Krishna Mainali, a leading member of the Marxist-Leninist Party, said: 'Communism works for the sake of the poor and lower class people. Gandhi said that the poor person should come first. This poor person is the basis of society. Poor people are discriminated against and Marxism is essential for their betterment. The real goal of Marxism is to help the poor and the labourers. Therefore we embrace Communist ideology.'

This expressed the core content of Nepali communist ideology: liberation for the poor, the downtrodden and exploited in society. Transforming the lot of the poor was these people's main motivation. Narayan Man Bijukche (Comrade Rohit), of Bhaktapur, founder and president of the Nepal Peasants' and Workers' Organization, said this of his first encounter with Marxism: 'Then I got to know about the new principle of Marxism to serve the poor.' Thus communism appealed to Nepali idealists who wished to do something good for society. At the same time the ancient Hindu and Buddhist principles of compassion, charity and equality appealed strongly to them. Veteran communist leader, Tulsi Lal Amatya explained what he thought communism actually was: 'What is Communism?' he asked, 'In our ancient days our Rishis (Hindu Sages) used to recite a "Shloka" (a Hindu saying) which was like this: "Let us live together, let us eat together, let us work together, let our intellect grow and let us not be envious of each other. Let us live together like friends, as a family." And this is what we mean by Communism. What we oppose in Capitalism is that in those countries, however rich they may be, a section of the people always suffers. Only the upper class of the people enjoy the whole fruit of civilisation. What we think: let nobody suffer under the system because they are all human beings—they must also have right to enjoy life, but this can only be done with the communists, through Communism.'

To Amatya and many other communists there was a strong link between communism and religion. 'Real Hinduism is Communism itself. In ancient times Hindu Rishis talked of equality for everybody. They thought that every human must be happy. I even think that Communist philosophy lagged behind the philosophy of Hinduism. Think of Krishna's philosophy, for instance, or that represented by the Upanishads. Krishna does not say that there is any god above the humans. God is the heart of all people and in the heart of the poor. What is the difference between us and the poor boy suffering on the road? We are all one. This philosophy teaches us that I must feel your problem as my own problem. Hinduism and Communism can go together completely with identical views. But today Hindu philosophy doesn't talk about these things. Instead the Hindu rulers are suppressing the poor and exploiting the workers.'

However, Hinduism in Nepal became too closely identified with the establishment which communism had sworn to fight against. Because of that it seemed easier to combine communist thought with

Buddhism, the second religion of Nepal. Buddhism did not have royal or government patronage. 'Buddha said that the principle of the ruler must be "Uttistha"—the definition of this is that there should be nobody in this kingdom who has tears in their eyes. And what the Buddha stands for is also what we Communists stand for. Communism is a way to make people's lives happy, to allow them to prosper and live a happy life.' For many, therefore, communism was accepted along the same lines as religion. Comrade Rohit said: 'The aim of religion has always been to reform society. Therefore religion went through various developments in the different ages or "yugas". Every time a new injustice became rampant in society a new religion would appear. In this way socialism came to Europe in the form of a religion when economic exploitation of the workers had reached its most extreme, just as Buddhism came to India in the age of slavery to give the oppressed liberation.'

These idealistic communists emphasized the importance of creating a Nepali form of communism. 'The same ideals were preached both by religion and Communism. It was because of this that we slowly became Communist and tried to develop a Nepali form of Communism.'

Another radical communist said: 'First we thought we could have a revolution along the lines of the Soviet revolution. Then we thought we wanted a Maoist peasant revolution, but now we have reached the conclusion that we need our own Nepali form of transition to Communism.'

An attempt to formulate a specifically Nepali form of communism granted the freedom to alter unwanted aspects of communism found in other countries.

'Communism contains quite a lot of impractical elements. That is why in Eastern Europe the people have tried to purify socialism through the recent revolutions. Subsequently, there must always be a multi-party system in socialist countries. The people must be allowed to encourage the progress of science and technology and there must be freedom.'

The dream of realizing an ideal communist society obviously held a strong appeal for many Nepalis. But could it ever be more than just a dream? After all, what the communists were striving for was as different from the realities of Nepali society as one could possibly imagine. Were their dreams merely theoretical—just an intellectual élite chattering about wishful impossibilities? Or did the communist movement really represent the first signs of a genuine revolt against age-old traditions and socio-economic and political constraints? However genuine this alternative ideology might have been, it must still be seen in the context of traditional Nepali society. What one must always remember is that the modern history of Nepal dates back only to 1951. Speaking about the development of his country, the distinguished geographer and ex-minister, H.B. Gurung, pointed out: 'Political change in Nepal will be slow because we are not talking about a long history. Changes have to be measured only after 1951 and the fall of the Ranas.'

Drastic changes had taken place in Nepali society in just forty years. These changes made the 1990 revolution possible. This was an event which would have been unthinkable in the still-feudal society of 1951. However, the changes since 1951 had been in number rather than depth. Although a large educated class had indisputably appeared, the basic Hindu-Brahmin attitude towards education had remained unchanged. Higher education conferred a certain social status and this was often more important than the training itself. Degrees served as entrance tickets to secure positions within the government bureaucracy and not as a preparation for any kind of useful work. While the caste system had been officially abolished, the old social values still remained. Nepal's élite were still composed of largely Brahmins and Chetris with a number of high-caste Newaris thrown in for good measure. One Newari, an important government official, shrugged and said: 'Whether they are Panchas, members of the Nepali Congress Party, or Communists, they are all Brahmins.'

While this remark needs some qualification it was nevertheless true that the old upper caste groups were slowly metamorphosing into the new economic and political upper class of Nepal. Even though life had changed in the cities, at least on the surface, old casteist ideas were still maintained in the rural areas. The two main features of the classical Hindu world-view, which had informed and sustained Nepal before 1951, were the caste system and the cyclical world-view. All ethnic groups and nationalities had belonged to a system of four 'varnas' or classes and thirty-six 'jats' or castes. This meant that every member of the population had a fixed status. Interaction between the different social groups of Nepal was regularized. Many ethnic groups accepted the caste system only superficially, but in practical terms they were integrated into the Hindu order sanctioned by the rulers. Hinduism stated that every individual was born into the caste which he or she deserved. An individual could only hope for better in the next life. Underlying this view was a cyclical or repetitive understanding of history. The person died only to be reborn, but this pattern was also traced in society which went through different cycles. First came 'satya yug' or the 'age of truth'. From this golden age life slowly deteriorated through four different ages until the last, 'kali yug' or the 'age of darkness'. After the age of darkness was completed the whole process began over again. Given this perspective, there was no room for a modern understanding of development based as it was on a linear or progressive view of history. Neither was there room for the individual to change history. Fate was all encompassing and human beings could do little to improve their lot.

As important as the Hindu world-view's continuing influence on modern Nepali politics, was the political legacy of the Rana government. Until 1951, the government of Nepal had been the personal rule of the Maharaja. The Maharaja sat at the centre of an intricate web of rituals and ploys in order to maintain his absolute rule. Government servants were transferred constantly from post to post so that they could not build up their own power base. Nepal's nobility had to show continual loyalty to the Maharaja or they would fall from grace. The institutional methods of showing loyalty which, in Nepali, are called 'shakari' survived the Rana regime, embedded in the new government bureaucracy. The old idea of personal rule remained alive and well in government departments where even minor decisions would be referred up the long hierarchy to ministerial level. Powerful politicians, such as the Prime Minister and members of the cabinet or Palace secretaries, would have crowds of individuals gathering outside their homes before office hours. These people turned up to ask personal favours or just show submission and loyalty.

Nepali conservatism encouraged stability and this meant that even after a period of upheaval order would be restored quickly and the streets of Kathmandu would look as though nothing had happened. At the same time the survival of these same traditions hampered economic and political development within the country. This was the environment in which the 1990 revolution in Nepal took place. Nepal was a society where rapid economic change and educational growth challenged the ingrained social structure and traditions. It was where promised political reforms had not been implemented. The pace of change had raised political hopes, but these hopes could not be accommodated within the ruling Panchayat regime. The early enthusiasm for the Panchayat system had long faded and by the late 1970s and 1980s it had been completely discredited in the eyes of Nepali intellectuals. The result of this was a widening rift within the Panchayat system itself. Liberal panchas openly criticized the government, while conservative hardliners accused these dissidents of disloyalty. More importantly, the educated classes were looking for an alternative. This new class was now ready to fight for political freedom. These people were attracted by the banned parties who offered a spectrum of options ranging from the moderate Nepali Congress Party to the extreme left Mashal Communist Party. Their message of social and economic equality gave the communists a mass appeal. This mass support was hard to measure, however, as Nepali conservatism was likely to encourage the Nepali people to opt for less radical solutions than what the communists proposed.

The crucial questions during the 1990 revolution were: to what extent were the masses mobilized? And what was the relationship between the political leaders and the educated élite on the one side, and the masses on the other? The answers to these two questions were decisive, both for the outcome of the revolution and for its long-term consequences. Even the question of whether there really was a mass movement elicited a wide range of responses from the different political leaders.

As Nepal is riven by colossal differences between urban and rural areas as well as between the mountain villages and the Terai, participation in a political movement such as the 1990 revolution would obviously take on a different colouring in different areas. It seems evident that, in Kathmandu and the towns of the Terai at least, the educated classes were the first to take to the streets. Does this mean that Nepal's 1990 revolution was only bourgeois, similar perhaps to the revolutions which rocked Europe in 1848? Was this revolution merely the forerunner of other revolutions and political shocks to come? The answer to this important question may become clear as one looks in more detail at the actual events which took place in Nepal between January and May 1990.

In Gorbachev's Shadow

When the Berlin Wall fell on 9 November 1989, the world was aware that something profound had taken place. The slow thaw which had begun with Mikhail Gorbachev's announcements of Glasnost and Perestroika in the Soviet Union just a few years earlier had now become an unstoppable torrent. As the entrenched communist regimes of Eastern Europe toppled one after the other, the people of Nepal grew jealous. They watched TV and listened to the radio and saw the possibility of achieving the same freedom that the East Europeans had suddenly won merely by pouring out on to the streets.

In an interview on 1 May 1990, Ganesh Man Singh, the Supreme Leader of the pro-Democracy movement testified to the importance of the current international situation in helping to bring about democracy in Nepal: 'You must understand that the international environment was favourable to our movement. With Gorbachev's announcement of perestroika and glasnost something like this became possible even in Nepal.'

So it was, that events in Europe had a dramatic impact even on the Himalayan kingdom of Nepal as waves of democracy spread out to places as scattered as Mongolia, Bangladesh and Madagascar.

Yet, the international situation was not the only factor that contributed to the timing of Nepal's 1990 revolution. Another important factor was the Indian Trade Embargo which had been imposed on 23 March 1989. A year of severe shortages had resulted in discontent. Many put the blame for the situation on the government. They claimed it was Panchayat stubbornness which had brought about the Embargo in the first place. Thus the 1990 revolution took place when the situation at home and abroad was most favourable for political change.

Favourable conditions, however, were not enough to spark off a revolution. There had to be leaders, a vision, a purpose and a plan. There had to be organization. What happened in Nepal between 18 February 1990 and 9 April 1990 has to be seen as the result of several forces at work at the same time. Conditions at home and abroad were favourable. The Congress and communists had finally united to plan the pro-Democracy movement, and the Panchayat regime was on the brink of collapse. In addition, the Nepali people had lost faith in the Panchayat government and desperately wanted a change.

When a whole regime collapses, as the Panchayat regime did, the situation begs the question: to what extent did the regime itself willingly give up power? The Panchayat system was in disarray, and obviously disintegrating. As was the case in Eastern Europe, the Panchayat regime collapsed as much through its own inertia as through the revolutionary activity which challenged it. In Nepal the main driving force throughout the revolution were the opposition leaders. Nevertheless, it was the King's settlement which caused the pro-Democracy movement to call off its campaign. King Birendra's capitulation was the necessary signal that the Panchayat system had irretrievably collapsed and the pro-Democracy movement had finally won.

The Panchayat government had been growing increasingly jittery in the months leading up to the launch of the pro-Democracy movement. The most obvious sign of the Panchayat government's waning self-confidence was the way it tried to bolster itself in the press. The government newspaper, *Gorkha Patra*, ran repeated headlines of 'The Panchayat System—True Democracy' and 'Nationalism—Democracy and Unity—the Pillars of the Panchayat Polity'. Similar sentiments were voiced by Nepal TV and Radio Nepal. The government's media propaganda was supplemented by officially organized Panchayat rallies which became more and more frequent as the opposition gained momentum.

The government at this stage was more eager to show some kind of consensus within its own Panchayat ranks than to attack the opposition parties. Yet even that failed. The calls for Marich Man Singh Shrestha's resignation grew louder with every day that passed. Liberal panchas took to organizing their own rallies and demanded that the Shrestha government be dismissed. They also demanded the implementation of the Third Amendment to the Constitution along with certain political reforms. These liberal panchas turned their tirade against the opposition parties while at the same time drawing more and more panchas into their camp.

Marich Man Singh Shrestha was left isolated. Everyone had turned against him. He survived because he was backed by the most important element of the whole Panchayat system—the Palace. The majority of politicians regarded him only as a puppet and even Shrestha himself admitted that he had a close relationship with the King. It was certainly true that he met him frequently for consultation. Yet in the end even the King abandoned him. Mathura Prasad Shrestha, later Health Minister in the interim government, spoke scathingly about him: 'He never acted as a prime minister. I saw him several times even before the movement, and once during the movement. But I always had the impression he did not belong to himself. He was completely subservient to another group of people. And he always looked foolish, rather than a respectable person.'

In early January 1990, the royal family left Kathmandu on their annual tour of one of the four development regions. On this occasion they headed for Pokhara in western Nepal. This meant that King Birendra was not in Kathmandu for the entire duration of the revolution. When he returned to open the new airport terminal building in Kathmandu on 18 February, the day the pro-Democracy movement started, the King flew straight back to Pokhara after making his speech. It could be that Shrestha's harsh measures during the pro-Democracy campaign were the acts of a desperate man who felt all support ebbing from him.

But what of the King, the one single person who really mattered in the Panchayat system? What of King Birendra? Did the decisions to suppress the pro-Democracy movement come from him or not? How much did he really know about the situation in his own country? How much was he misinformed? To what extent did he ignore the promptings of his immediate circle of advisers? The truth can only be found behind the locked doors of the Palace. A close aide of the King described the position of the King during the Panchayat regime: 'The King is like a computer. His understanding of any situation will reflect what information the people around him have fed in. During the recent movement he was mainly fed information by people who wanted to conceal the realities, though this does not mean that the King was not warned. He was told on several occasions that unless he did something the situation would become grave. But he didn't listen to these warnings.'

Whether the King knew the situation was serious or whether he simply did not want to believe it is hard to know. During the demonstration of 1979 the King only announced the National Referendum when he actually saw the masses marching up towards the Palace through Durbar Marg. It could have been the case that news was kept from the King and his isolation in Pokhara rendered him ignorant of what was happening in Kathmandu.

When the King finally did return to Kathmandu he acted swiftly by lifting the ban on the political parties and opening negotiations with the opposition—so perhaps there is something to be said for this version of events. It is important to remember that King Birendra was the inheritor, not the creator, of the Panchayat system. Many believed that Birendra had never been happy with his position as political autocrat. Some went as far as to say that the King's transfer of power to the interim government in May 1990 actually came to him as a relief.

So the Panchayat system collapsed and the King gave in. But there was more to the revolution than just the self-destruction of the old regime. The Panchayat system would undoubtedly have continued at least a few more years had it not been for the well-planned campaign by the banned parties and the mass support they received.

Though the political parties had been banned by King Mahendra after his royal coup in 1960, they had never totally disappeared. At first they worked underground or in exile. After the 1980 referendum their activities became more public. They had campaigned tirelessly against the Panchayat system from the very beginning, but their struggle went through various changes. These parties, dating back several decades and with a democratic tradition, were profoundly affected by the changes in Eastern Europe. At last, what they had struggled for seemed within their grasp.

It must always be remembered that the revolution in Nepal was planned. Furthermore the opposition had leaders of stature and experience able to step into the shoes of the old regime. The revolution was well-organized, but not totally controlled. Yet, in contrast to the East European countries where the opposition had to organize itself almost overnight to catch up with events taking place on the streets, the parties in Nepal were united and gave guidance and co-ordination throughout the campaign.

The most important opposition party was the Nepali Congress Party established in Varanasi, India, in 1947. Having led the short-lived democratic government in Nepal in 1959, Congress saw itself as the natural symbol of democracy in the fight against Panchayat totalitarianism. After the dismissal of the Koirala government in 1959, Congress found most of its leaders in prison and launched an armed campaign from India. The raids across the border had little effect, however, and were called off by the Indian government at the start of the Sino-Indian conflict in 1962. Congress's democratic struggle abated until B.P. Koirala, released by the King's amnesty in 1977, announced his new policy of National Reconciliation. Unfortunately, Koirala's hope of creating a working relationship with the more liberal-minded King Birendra was unable to bear any fruit. Student unrest and the King's announcement of a National Referendum in 1979 threw the Nepali Congress into an election campaign for which they were unprepared but over-confident. After the referendum defeat, Congress fell into disarray and it was not until 1985 that the party was sufficiently organized to launch 'satyagraha' against the government. This movement, however, was called off after the bomb blasts in Kathmandu. Five more years passed before Congress was able to stage a successful challenge to the Panchayat system. Congress's new confidence drew strength, of course, from its new alliance with the communists.

Nepal's Communist Party was established only two years after the Nepali Congress, in 1949 at Calcutta. Though they had played a part in all the major political events since 1951, it was not until the 1990 revolution that the communists really emerged as a potent political force. The Cold War fear of communism had played a part in this as well as the innumerable splits and conflicts within their own ranks over the years.

The communists had only four members in the 1959-60 democratic parliament. King Mahendra's coup made the party illegal along with all the others.

Soon after the coup the communists split into three factions. One group wanted to work within the system; another wished to fight against it. The majority, led by Pushpa Lal Shrestha, opted for an alliance with the Nepali Congress. The aim was to re-establish the old parliament. In the 1970s and 1980s the communists splintered further and by 1989, there were at least fourteen different communist parties in the country. Yet the communist movement as a whole was now a force to be reckoned with inside Nepal. Now Congress needed to unite with the communists in order to be sure of any political success.

The 1980s therefore brought a new understanding between the Congress Party and the communists. The two parties came to see that they needed to rely on one another. Even so, the formation of the United Left Front under the leadership of Sahana Pradhan on 10 January 1990, comprising as it did seven communist parties working with the Nepali Congress was a remarkable political feat. When the seven remaining communist parties voiced support for the Front without actually joining it, all opposition forces within Nepal were united for the first time since the revolution of 1951. This unity gave the opposition leaders the firm belief that this time their efforts would be successful. They believed they would finally witness the downfall of the Panchayat system. Before the pro-Democracy movement began, Krishna Prasad Bhattarai, the President of the Nepali Congress Party, said: 'This time we are going to win. We will force the King to be constitutional. If everything goes well, only a few weeks and we will be in power. If things go wrong, I and my colleagues might end up in jail, but that's not a threat—we know that if that happens it can only last a few months and then we will win.'

The United Left Front and the Congress Party had tabled their demands before the movement even started. These were, 'the establishment of a multi-party democracy and a constitutional monarchy.' Though the two parties never merged it seemed taken for granted that the communists were the junior partners in the movement.

The towering personalities of the pro-Democracy movement during the days of the revolution were the Nepali Congress veterans. They set the tone of the movement and seemed to decide the line of action. Their age, ascetic lifestyles, and history of persecution made them apt symbols of an alternative democratic order.

But what was their strategy? It appeared to be two-fold. They were uncompromising in their demands to the Panchayat government and the King, though they stopped short at calling for violence. At the same time they nourished the underlying hope that the King would announce reforms before the situation got out of hand. The opposition leaders gave the King repeated opportunities to state a more liberal position and even postponed the whole movement a month to give him more time. Most people in Kathmandu had believed that the movement would start on 18 January when the Nepali Congress Party held its convention at the house of Ganesh Man Singh.

That the opposition leaders hoped so deeply that the King would act showed, perhaps, a real fear that they would lose control of the movement. The opposition's demands were not extreme, however, and their fight was never directed against the King. Rather they saw the King as a necessary unifying force within the country. But they wanted political freedom and wanted it so badly that they would have paid the high price of sacrificing the King if that had proved necessary.

To observers the seven-week revolution in Nepal was astonishingly disciplined and well-organized—and this was despite the fact that most of the opposition leaders were under arrest by 18 February, the day the movement started.

For the first full month of the revolution there was blanket censorship in Nepal of a kind not seen since the days of the Ranas. Even *Newsweek* and *Time* were confiscated the moment they arrived at the airport and virtually all of the private newspapers had been banned. What newspapers remained, printed subversive news and attacked the government, but in such a manner that it was impossible for the government to strike back. Such writing was a renaissance of the indirect style of political writing which had become so developed under the Ranas. Nepalis passed information by word of mouth and circulated leaflets and illegal newspapers. This ensured that everyone knew where protests and demonstrations were to take place. Last, but not least, foreign news broadcasts in Nepali played an important role. A surprisingly large percentage of the population tuned into All-India Radio, the BBC and the Voice of America. These foreign radio stations used various means to make direct contacts with the opposition leaders. Consequently, they became the only platform available for the opposition leaders in their isolation—though they were able to smuggle out messages and directives to a limited extent. Thus Nepalis were able to take the news printed next morning in the government papers with a pinch of salt.

The party leaders were locked up and could not act publicly. Those who did act were the students who bore the brunt of the police violence. One student leader in Kathmandu said proudly: 'We have been the most important political force in Nepal. We are the people who have suffered the most in the fight for democracy, not the party leaders. The students have been imprisoned, beaten, tortured and some even killed.' When the campaign entered its most critical phase at the end of March, activity first started up on the various university campuses in Kathmandu which the government then promptly shut down.

Besides the students, the professional organizations also played a vital role in galvanizing people and bringing them out on to the streets.

In order to coordinate all the demonstrations and protests, it had been necessary to develop an elaborate underground network of communication. Kamala Pant, a young student leader in Kathmandu, described this network as follows: 'When many of the leaders were arrested and the rest went underground I also went underground on that day and remained there until the end of the movement. Almost all our planning and work was done over the phone, even recruiting people to take part in our demonstrations and protests. For example, when we organised the major women's demonstration, I phoned different key persons, women I knew, and asked them to take along whoever they knew, and we always knew each other's phone numbers even though almost all of us were constantly on the move. When too many people and police in uniform or civil dress arrived I would be hurried off to a new place. And it continued like this. At all political meetings and demonstrations and other protests I would be present, but the rest of the time I would stay underground. I would be transported back and forth in the back of a tempo, a motorised rickshaw, so that nobody could see me. I would arrive late and leave early and there would always be planned escape route for me through a back door which I used several times when the police arrived. I always had bodyguards, other students, around me.'

Apart from a few minor incidents, the demonstrations throughout the revolution appeared to adhere to a strict code of conduct. Many were afraid that the movement would turn violent. However, the

Gandhian position of non-violence proclaimed by the major leaders of the pro-Democracy movement held firm. Fears of bloodshed were largely unfounded.

Though the revolution was organized, it was not controlled. The whole movement would have failed without the mass support it did receive, but this very support introduced an unstable element into the proceedings. The opposition leaders had to rely on the crowds to bring about any political change at all. However, these same crowds were capable of turning the whole movement into something quite different from what the opposition leaders had initially planned. Though the end of the revolution brought about a result which the opposition leaders had been dreaming of for decades, the method by which this was achieved and the extent to which this was achieved came as a surprise. The Supreme Leader of the Nepali Congress Party, Ganesh Man Singh, said just after the movement had come to an end: 'We thought our movement would get support, but we had never expected that we would get the kind of mass support we did get.' Similarly, Padma Ratna Tuladhar, the independent leftist, said: 'There was suspicion, you see, among the leaders that the people of Kathmandu would not participate in the movement. But on 18 February the participation of the local people was so big that the leaders became extreme. Even myself, when I went into the street on that day saw so many local people, shopkeepers, businessmen and others. So this made us convinced that now the people would come.' It was clear that the extent of the mass support for the revolution came as a surprise to the opposition leaders as much as to the Panchayat government. So what had the leaders of the revolution initially hoped to achieve through the pro-Democracy movement?

Most of the leaders had been confident that this would be the strongest movement in Nepal's history. Even so, the number of protestors on the streets, at least in the urban areas of the Kathmandu valley, far exceeded their wildest expectations. At best, many of the opposition leaders had thought they might attract enough support to force through some sort of political compromise. They had not expected a full-scale revolution. Yet this is what took place in the

Kathmandu valley during the first days of April 1990. The uprising swiftly brought about a situation in which the opposition, backed by the people, were able to dictate totally the terms on which the government and the King surrendered to them.

Yet while there had been steady support for the movement from 18 February onwards, it was, at that stage, far from being a mass uprising. The popular revolt came at a much later stage and did so as a reaction to police suppression and violence. Padma Ratna Tuladhar explained: 'The people became very angry at this suppression. They saw that innocent people were arrested and tortured. The police opened fire unnecessarily. So the people actually retaliated against this kind of suppression. In this way the government played a positive role for the movement.'

This violence was totally beyond the control of the opposition leaders. The Panchayat government's initial response to the pro-Democracy movement seemed to be to try and turn Nepal into a police state overnight. Police presence was heavy on the streets and the government suddenly introduced new repressive measures. Just picking up a leaflet from the pavement or watching a demonstration was now enough to land a person in police custody. The government actively encouraged citizens to inform on one another. What angered the population more than anything was the haphazard way in which the government acted. People were arrested for no apparent reason and at night police could swoop down on a neighbourhood and arrest all the young men and boys.

Many lost their final respect for the Panchayat government when the Mandales, the government sponsored thugs, were let loose in the Kathmandu valley. This brought about the impossible. People who had held back because they believed King Birendra would step in now threw in their lot with the pro-Democracy movement. The long-suffering people of Nepal finally lost their patience. Even old women and young children, who normally would have taken no interest in politics, saw what was happening outside their own doorstep and took to the streets.

Government violence was further inflated by its own censorship. With most of the private press shut down and government papers dishing up obvious lies, people relied on rumours for information. These rumours blew the violence out of proportion and this brought more people out into the streets.

In Eastern Europe the revolutions appeared to happen as much on TV as on the streets. The media did not play this crucial role in Nepal. One Nepali investigative journalist claimed, however, that the Nepali media did help prepare the ground for the movement: 'Over a long period the shortcomings of the system were exposed to the people both through the programmes of independent reporters especially on TV and in government media, but mainly in the private press. In this way people slowly understood that the system no longer had anything to offer. In addition came the coverage by Nepal TV of the revolutions in Eastern Europe. You know, the Nepali government never practised any censorship on international news as in China or Burma.' He pointed out that TV did play an indirect role during the revolution, even during the first period of total censorship: 'Everybody who works in TV knows how fatal over-exposure is. The movement began just at the time the King and Queen made their annual tour of the Western region. As usual TV and radio covered their movements daily. This, however, did not work for their benefit. The people were daily confronted with how bad the political system was and then they had to watch the Queen every evening on TV, which made their resentment grow even further.'

While the media kow-towed to government censorship, on 1 April Nepal TV finally went its own way. In a programme covering the unrest in Kirtipur in the Kathmandu valley, the broadcast called for a dialogue between the government and the opposition. Leading opposition panchas were interviewed and B.P. Koirala's picture was shown for the first time ever on Nepal TV. Nepal TV had always enjoyed more freedom than other sections of the government media as its director, Nir Bikram Shah, was a relative of the King. Even so, this programme went too far and both the journalist involved and his boss were asked to resign. But by now it was too late. The revolution had gathered momentum. Nepal TV, having broken the government ban once, continued to report events as they happened, unabashed.

One feature of the revolution which also took the opposition leaders by surprise was the imagination displayed in some of the protests. On 3 March artists sat down outside Trichandra College in Kathmandu with black scarves tied around their mouths in silent protest against the Panchayat government. Such black scarves became the most common symbol of defiance throughout the revolution. On 31 March a large number of housewives gathered outside the gates of the Padma Kanya University Campus in Kathmandu and raised a din by banging pots and pans together. In the eastern city of Biratnagar, dogs, cows and donkeys decorated with black scarves and anti-government slogans were let loose into the streets. Most remarkable, however, were the voluntary blackouts which began in Narayanghat in the Terai. They spread quickly to Kathmandu and the other towns in Nepal. For half-an-hour every evening Nepal's towns were plunged into darkness. One of the leaders of the revolution said: 'It was during these evening hours we finally knew that a victory was imminent.'

Two events in two different places were vital to changing the whole course of the revolution. These were the incidents which took place in Bhaktapur and Patan, the former principalities in the Kathmandu valley. What happened there took the form of local revolts. On 19 February the people of Bhaktapur turned against the police making the protests of the previous day seem timid by comparison. A battle raged in the streets of Bhaktapur for two days and several people were killed. The revolt in Bhaktapur showed the government that the people meant business and that it would be no easy task to restore the status quo. Later what happened in Patan pushed the revolution into its most critical phase and showed that the defeat of the government was just a matter of time.

Kathmandu, Patan and Bhaktapur all lie within easy reach of one another. Patan and Bhaktapur, however, are quite different in some respects from Kathmandu. Bhaktapur consists of almost 100 per cent Newaris. Despite its distance of just 10 km from Kathmandu it is relatively undeveloped and unchanged. The longstanding grievances resulting from this state of affairs was probably one reason why the Panchayat system never took a stronghold there. This may explain why one organization, the Nepal Workers' and Peasants' Organization, led by Narayan Man Bijukche, amassed such overwhelming support from the community. Therefore, while the revolt in Bhaktapur was spontaneous, it did have a guiding hand.

Patan, being to all intents and purposes part of the capital, has a much more heterogeneous population. While the people of Patan were more educated and politicized than the people of Bhaktapur, they had no corresponding binding force such as a common political party. The uprising in Patan on 30 March started after a clash between police and demonstrators in Mangal Bazar, the centre of Patan, which left several dead. Once the people of Patan unleashed their protest there were many similarities with what had happened in Bhaktapur six weeks earlier. Almost everything that happened happened in the city centre which, like Bhaktapur, was inhabited almost entirely by Newaris. United action seemed to spring from close-knit communities who saw their neighbourhoods, families and friends threatened. Two young activists described what happened. 'During the night we went from tol to tol, block to block, telling the people that they should defend their brothers and sisters, daughters and sons, of whom some had already been killed and injured by the police. The people came out with knives and rods and whatever else they could find in their household, both women and men, old and young. The activities really started at Chyasal Tol where the people all belonging to the same caste which practised intermarriage were the most unified block in Patan. But from there it spread to all the other tols and areas.'

All revolutions find success or failure in the interplay between the revolutionary leaders and the masses. This was certainly the case in Nepal. The leaders planned the pro-Democracy movement and called for action. The masses responded, but their response made the movement theirs and took the initiative away from the opposition leaders. The opposition leaders were forced to adjust and then make a concerted effort to regain control of the movement.

While the opposition leaders were in prison or under house-arrest, the masses pushed the revolution to its climax on 6 April. That morning when King Birendra broke his long silence and announced the dismissal of the Shrestha government, the crowd flocked out into the streets in good spirits. But their mood suddenly changed. This happened after the open air meeting at the Parade Grounds, Tundikhel, in the centre of Kathmandu. Shouting slogans against the King and Queen, a thick phalanx of people began to move slowly from the Parade Grounds up towards the Palace. This was bound to end in disaster and did so when the military were called out to stop the crowd advancing any further. In the massacre which followed more people were killed than in the previous seven weeks put together and this was followed by the two-day curfew.

The events of 6 April remain something of a mystery. Why did the mood of the crowd change so suddenly and why did they move towards the Palace? Everybody must have known that any threat to the King would bring about severe reprisals. Did Mashal activists incite the crowd or, more sinisterly, were Mandale thugs at work? Or, as some people believed, were members of the crowd listening to the radio and learned that the police had been given orders not to attack? Did this encourage the crowd to go too far? What was evident was that the King's speech had worked against him. If the forty eight-hour curfew had not been imposed it is possible that the King, and perhaps even the moderate opposition leaders, would have been swept away.

Something similar happened on the night of 15 and 16 April when the masses again took over and dictated events. Though the King had lifted the ban on the political parties he delayed further reforms and the people once again lost their patience.

On the night of 15 April the opposition leaders had finally agreed to negotiations with members of Lokendra Bahadur Chand's government. 'Unfortunately,' as a minister in Chand's cabinet, Achut Raj Regmi, also a member of the interim cabinet, said, 'the venue for the negotiations had been officially announced.' Because of this, thousands of people gathered outside the Royal Academy Hall in the centre of Kathmandu where the politicians were meeting. And at 3 a.m. a defeated Prime Minister Chand walked past the remaining crowd into his car and drove directly to the Palace where he tendered his resignation. Thus, the course of events in both these incidents seemed to be totally in the hands of the masses.

Looking back on the revolution as a whole, it was clear that neither the opposition leaders nor the masses could wholly dictate the outcome of the movement. One moment the opposition leaders appeared to be in control, then the crowd appeared to have taken on a will of its own. The revolution was characterized by two distinct eatures: surprise and plan. Broadly speaking, the masses supplied the surprise while the opposition leaders supplied the plan.

Given the context of surprise and plan, the revolution appeared to develop through three distinct stages. The first stage might be called the 'build-up'. This consisted of the two parallel processes of a situation building up which was favourable to the pro-Democracy movement combined with the opposition leaders' well-laid plans. This period covers the events both before the launch of the movement on 18 February and the first part of the revolution up to 30 March.

The second stage of the revolution could be termed the 'climax'. This began when the crowds erupted into the streets. The sheer volume of the crowd rendered the opposition leaders temporarily impotent. They had to act quickly to regain the initiative. During this period it was the mood of the crowd, not the time-table of the opposition leaders, which dictated events.

The third and last stage of the revolution might be referred to as the 'step back'. In order to regain control the opposition leaders had to calm the crowd and ensure that they would be satisfied by the fulfilment of a specific set of demands. The opposition leaders began doing this on 9 April when they called off the movement in response to the King's decision to lift the ban on the political parties.

Regaining the reins of the revolution did not prove so easy. The very next day the Mashal Communist Party appealed to the masses to disobey the revolutionary leaders. They claimed that they had betrayed the movement. The masses did not heed the Mashal, but nevertheless some initiative remained with the crowd. The opposition leaders could not tolerate this and, as a further calming action, allied themselves with some of the elements from the old Panchayat regime. In other words, they sought to draw the King and the armed forces on to their side. As a result the moderate elements in the revolution, especially the Nepali Congress, succeeded in stabilizing the situation at last and found themselves once more at the helm. But at some cost. The communists did not agree with Congress's tactics and there almost was a split. Padma Ratna Tuladhar described what happened: 'At that time the Nepali Congress wanted to make a settlement with the Palace as soon as possible. They were afraid the movement was getting out of hand, and they wanted to stop it. In this way they were also ready to accept a negotiated settlement based on compromise. The communists still wanted the government and Palace to surrender totally. But they were in a dilemma. They couldn't afford a split with the Nepali Congress, as that would damage the whole base of the popular movement, the people's movement. They were forced to accept a compromise, but only after the Palace had given into their minimum demand, the dissolution of the Rashtriya Panchayat.'

What the opposition leaders tried to do during the third stage of the revolution was to maintain their own position. They also wished Nepal to return to the normalities of everyday life. The celebrations of late March and early April had infected people to such an extent that their usual concerns were quite forgotten. It was only weeks or months later that people seemed to shake their heads as though waking from a dream and ask 'What really happened?' In the aftermath of those seven momentous weeks that was not an easy question to answer. The most elementary facts proved elusive. The most glaring example was the actual death toll. Even the Prime Minister maintained for several months afterwards that between 500 and 1,000 people had died. Yet the commission of inquiry appointed by the government reporting a year later, could only establish sixty-two deaths.

Turning from what happened to how people had actually perceived the revolution also proved confusing and contradictory. The Nepali Congress and communists liked to give the impression that the pro-Democracy movement had enjoyed large-scale support from the first day and that the movement had affected all the districts and villages of the country. The conservative panchas, however, scorned the idea that there had been any movement at all. According to them the King had freely given away his powers to the people.

The consensus view, of course, was that there was a movement and that this movement had brought about radical political changes in the country. That established, the true story of the revolution was still hard to determine. One important question left unanswered was: what went on behind the scenes during those seven weeks, especially inside the Palace premises? As long as the royal family sheltered behind their immunity this crucial information would remain unrevealed. Most people felt, however, that the revolution had brought about the end of secret politicking and intrigue within the Palace. From now on Nepali politics would be conducted out in the open to an extent it never had been before.

It would be of interest historically to compare the 1990 revolution in Nepal with the earlier one of 1951 which had brought Rana rule to an end. There were obvious parallels. In 1951 and 1990 internal and external factors were at work to make change within Nepal possible. The 1951 revolution occurred during a period of rapid decolonization only three years after India had gained its independence. The 1990 revolution took place in the midst of a democratic wave which had already changed the face of Eastern Europe and was now moving beyond. The role of India, too, was crucial in both revolutions, though probably more directly so in the 1951 revolution. Many of the leaders who took up the struggle to open Nepal in 1951 were still leaders forty years later in 1990. In both cases the power vacuum caused by momentary political instability within Nepal led to similar forms of unrest.

It is true to say, however, that similarities between 1951 and 1990 were not just a matter of coincidence. The veteran opposition leaders seemed to exploit any similarities they could find between the two events. When the Nepali Congress leaders gathered for an emergency meeting on the morning of 23 April to discuss the worrying violence and unrest still simmering in Kathmandu the repeated comment was made: 'This is just like the Khukuri Dal and the Raksha Dal revolts in 1951 and 1952 and we will have to deal with this accordingly.'

One significant difference between the Nepali revolutions of 1951 and 1990 was that the 1990 revolution enjoyed a mass support which the 1951 revolution did not. The 1951 revolution was rightly called a Palace Revolution. What happened in 1990 was a popular uprising—at least in the Kathmandu valley. Even the opposition leaders had shown amazement at this—for the impossible had happened. Politics had at last taken a democratic course in Nepal which could no longer be easily reversed.

The Foreign Factor

The 1951 revolution ended a century of Rana isolation. By the 1970s and 1980s Nepal had become internationally famous, but only as a place of high, dazzling mountains, exotic temples, and a particular photogenic poverty. Nepal also became known as the sixth poorest country in the world and a large recipient of foreign aid. It took the 1990 revolution to push Nepal into the limelight as a country with its own particular political problems and conflicts. For the first time Nepal hit the headlines around the world. As reports of the violent suppression of the pro-Democracy movement reached newspapers, radio and TV in other countries, people were shocked into realizing that the myth of the peaceful, isolated Himalayan kingdom was no longer true. Reactions to the news came swiftly. Many Western countries condemned the violence at once.

Nepal's isolation, however, was a myth like any other and a myth which was finally shattered in 1990. There had actually been a long history of foreign involvement in Nepal and in 1990 foreign involvement played both a direct and indirect role in determining the outcome of the revolution.

As early as 1 February 1990, Krishna Prasad Bhattarai, President of the Nepali Congress Party, declared that the pro-Democracy movement had received promises of support from several other countries. This support, he stated, would make it morally impossible for the Panchayat government to suppress the movement once it had started. The United States and Britain both played an important role at this point. Although neither government took a direct stand for the pro-Democracy movement until much later, individual politicians pledged support for the democratic cause from an early stage. This gave the opposition politicians a degree of self-confidence.

In addition to declarations of moral support, the leaders of the pro-Democracy movement hoped that foreign governments would exert direct pressure on the Panchayat government. Everyone was aware that the Panchayat regime was totally dependent on the billions of rupees which were pumped into the country annually through foreign aid. A threat to this income could topple the Panchayat system overnight. Knowing this and knowing that Western governments were increasingly linking aid to human rights, the opposition leaders asked foreign governments to withhold aid until the political situation in Nepal had settled.

Foreign response to this request was cautious. Only West Germany stated publicly (and four weeks after the movement had started) that the country would consider freezing all aid unless the suppression of the pro-Democracy movement and the violation of human rights came to an end. Other countries considered a move, but no one acted until the revolution was over.

Though the Western governments did not act, the fact that they were obviously favourable towards the pro-Democracy movement was enough to frighten the Panchayat government. In an official answer on 22 February to the US Secretary of State's condemnation of the suppression of the pro-Democracy movement, the Panchayat government replied that the recent unrest had been led by a few extremists who did not respect the political system of the country—a system which had been backed by the majority of Nepali citizens in the referendum of 1980. Statements to this effect were issued almost daily by the Panchayat government in the weeks that followed. The

Slogans appearing in the days before the launch of the pro-Democracy movement (February 1990)

Democracy Day protest (18 February 1990)

Democracy Day official procession (18 February 1990)

Nurses and medical staff protest at Maharajganj Teaching Hospital, Kathmandu
(23 February 1990)

Writers' and artists' protest (16 March 1990)

Buddhist monks in Kathmandu demand equal rights for all religions (photo: Gopal Chitrakar)

Arrests at the beginning of the Patan uprising (end of March 1990)

Temple idols used to build barricades around the city centre during the uprising in Patan (end of March 1990)

Two young boys killed during the Patan uprising (end of March 1990)

People in Patan barricade the road with burning tyres during the mass agitation which brought multi-party government in Nepal (photo: Gopal Chitrakar)

Demonstrators coming closer to the Palace (6 April 1990)

Soldiers on the alert before the afternoon massacre (6 April 1990)

Protest procession in Kathmandu demanding the promulgation
of the 1990 Constitution (photo: Gopal Chitrakar)

Climax of the revolution:demonstrations in downtown Kathmandu (6 April 1990)

Mass meeting at open-air theatre at Tundikhel (9 April 1990)

Communists celebrating the victory of the pro-Democracy
movement in Patan (9 April 1990)

Demonstrators carrying the Nepali Congress Party flag, celebrating the victory of the pro-Democracy movement (9 April 1990)

Ganesh Man Singh, his face covered in vermillion powder, celebrating the victory (9 April 1990)

A suspected Mandale killed by civilians in Kathmandu during the re-emergence of violence just after the revolution (April 1990)

Panchayat Prime Minister, Marich Man Singh Shrestha (photo: Gopal Chitrakar)

Interim Prime Minister, Krishna Prasad Bhattarai

Election slogans (late April 1991)

The National Democratic Party campaigning in a village outside Kathmandu in 1991

The Nepali Congress Party campaigning during the 1991 elections

Madan Bhandari, leader of the UML Communist Party, speaking at an election rally

Comrade Rohit

Election rallies in Kathmandu last year (photo: Gopal Chitrakar)

Police in Kathmandu charge with lathis on the mob which tried to disrupt the counting of votes during the general elections held last in Nepal (photo: Gopal Chitrakar)

Sahana Pradhan

Member of Parliament, Padma Ratna Tuladhar, addressing
a mass meeting at Kathmandu recently (photo: Gopal Chitrakar)

Prime Minister Girija Prasad Koirala (photo: Gopal Chitrakar)

government media in Nepal even went as far as to accuse the BBC, All-India Radio and the Voice of America of lying and wilfully misrepresenting the situation.

This foreign pressure mainly from Western democracies achieved two ends. First, the opposition in Nepal was encouraged to continue its struggle. Secondly, foreign support for the pro-Democracy movement alarmed the Panchayat government which was already demoralized over a number of other issues.

The two countries which had the most direct influence over Nepal, however, were close at hand. They were India and China. China was suspicious. The Chinese government had traditionally supported the Panchayat system and was wary of any political change close to its borders. Chinese action in Tiananmen Square in 1989 had shown the world what China thought of democracy movements. Yet if China was negative, Chinese influence turned out to be insignificant when the revolution did take place. As in all previous political conflicts and changes in Nepal, the one neighbour who really counted was India.

Geographically, economically and culturally—at least as far as the Hindu State culture was concerned—Nepal was part of the Indian subcontinent. The border of this region followed the main peaks of the Himalayas.This same border formed India's argument for supremacy in the region. There was also a historical precedent for India's paternal, some might say bullying, regard for Nepal. When India became independent in 1947 the new government entered into the same kind of relationship with Nepal as the British had done. This development appeared to be what the British had wanted, judging by the correspondence between the Foreign Office in London and the British Resident in Kathmandu at the time. This may have been one reason why half the Gurkha regiments, Britain's closest link with Nepal, were handed over to the Indian army.

The government in New Delhi, led by Jawaharlal Nehru, soon became even more involved in Nepal than the British. India and Nepal signed a Treaty of Peace and Friendship in 1950. On paper this was fully reciprocal, but the colossal difference in size between the two countries gave India the upper hand. A complicating factor was that this treaty was signed with the Rana government which was swept out of power shortly afterwards. As a result, the 1950 treaty gradually came to be seen as a symbol of Indian domination.

More important than the 1950 treaty was India's role in the 1951 revolution. Though the revolution came about as a result of several forces, the final settlement between the Rana government and the Nepali Congress was engineered by the government in New Delhi. This opened a period of close co-operation between Kathmandu and New Delhi. Many Nepalis did not like Indian interference in their country to this extent and when Nehru visited Nepal in 1951 he was met by a mass of protesting black flags.

Indian influence over Nepal began to wane in the late 1950s. This was largely as a result of the single-minded resolve of Nepali Prime Ministers such as Tanka Prasad Acharya and the democratically elected B.P. Koirala. Furthermore King Mahendra proved far more political minded than his father, King Tribhuvan, and wished to steer his country on an independent course. Special relations between Nepal and India continued in principle, however, right up until the royal coup in 1960. King Mahendra's coup brought relations between India and Nepal to low ebb. India was a democracy and had to react negatively. Though the Indian government gave no official support to the now-outlawed democratic forces, it did allow the Nepali Congress to conduct armed raids across the border into Nepal. What complicated the political situation from India's point of view, however, and rendered the climate very different from that of 1951, was the growing conflict between India and China. India needed Nepal as a loyal buffer state and so needed the support of King Mahendra. Now Nepal—at least King Mahendra—had a lever of power to use against India. When war broke out between India and China in 1962, King Mahendra found himself free to act.

The Nepali Congress raids were swiftly brought to an end by the Indian government for fear of antagonizing Kathmandu and the Panchayat government led by King Mahendra began a policy of 'balanced dependence' between India and China. In effect, King

Mahendra played one country against the other and this remained the mainstay of Nepali foreign policy right up to the revolution in 1990. The last Panchayat Foreign Minister, Shailendra Kumar Upadhyaya, defended this policy: 'Any government in this country will always face one problem. India is a big country. There is no reason to pick a quarrel with India. It doesn't help Nepal to be an enemy of China either. Now there is a school of thought in India which wants Nepal to break with China. We say no. We are an independent country. We will not permit our soil to be used against India or against China. Generally India feels that Nepal should not side with China. I think we have to give India that type of assurance. Similarly, the Chinese have to feel comfortable as far as our borders are concerned. So this is not the pride of Panchayat. It is the pride of a nation, a nation that doesn't want to take sides.'

Despite such rhetoric, Nepal remained almost entirely economically dependent on India throughout the Panchayat period. Virtually all goods had to travel through India to reach Nepal and almost sixty per cent of Nepali trade was with India. Quarrels between India and Nepal over trade and transit were frequent and intensified every time the Trade and Transit Treaty between the two countries came up for renewal. India wanted to use Nepal's vulnerable economic position to pressurize the country into submission; Nepal wanted to retain as much independence as possible. Usually a compromise was reached, though the compromise tended to be in India's favour.

In 1989, however, no compromise was reached. Instead, India imposed a virtual trade embargo on Nepal. Negotiations had been taking place, but when the current treaty expired on 23 March 1989 India terminated all existing arrangements instead of prolonging the old treaty until a new one had been signed.

India's move came as a sharp shock to the Panchayat government in Kathmandu. More than half of the country's trade simply disappeared overnight along with essential supplies of fuel and medicine. These now had to be imported at a much higher cost from a third country. In Kathmandu traffic vanished from the streets and kerosene and sugar became difficult to obtain. The Panchayat government did its best to import goods from third countries, but price hikes were inevitable. As a result Nepal's weak economy was weakened even further.

In principle goods from third countries could still proceed through Indian territory, but India put obstacles in the way of transit. Calcutta was the only Indian harbour used for Nepali goods and the facilities used by Nepal were partly closed several times during the embargo period for 'construction work'. Nepali nationals working in India were not allowed to carry their salaries back over the border. Even Nepali planes were not allowed to refuel at Indian airports.

India's actions seemed extreme. But India was impatient and had been dissatisfied with the government in Nepal for a long time. India's main complaint was that Nepal did not respect India's security interests as agreed in the 1950 treaty. The Indian government was particularly annoyed that Nepal had imported Chinese arms. Another major point of irritation was that Nepal allowed luxury goods to be flown into the country which were then smuggled across the border to India. The Indian government also claimed that Indian nationals living in Nepal were not being treated fairly. The Indians especially disliked Nepal's new system of work permits which, the government in New Delhi claimed, breached another clause of the 1950 treaty. There was a general feeling, however, that India had exaggerated these complaints and was merely flexing its muscles as a regional superpower. India now possessed the world's third largest army and was already involved politically in several of its neighbouring countries.

Gradually, relations between India and China had been improving. This was manifest in Rajiv Gandhi's visit to Beijing in 1988 which signalled the end of almost three decades of Sino-Indian conflict. Nepal's successful policy of balanced dependence was now becoming obsolete. It seemed India would soon be free to impose its will on Nepal once again and return to the dominant position of the 1950s. Indian involvement in Sri Lanka and the Maldives suggested that this was exactly what Rajiv Gandhi's government wanted to do.

All the signs were present that India wanted to take some action against Nepal to bow the country into submission. Yet these signs were ignored or simply not taken into account by the Panchayat government. Unlikely as this may seem, it appears that there was simply a lack of communication and a series of misunderstandings both within the Nepali government and with the Indian government. Basically, bungling led to the Trade Embargo crisis. Shailendra Kumar Upadhyaya, who was the Foreign Minister, said: 'Well, I think at the political level there would have been no problems had this process been going honestly. But even the Foreign Minister of India used to say that there were things he understood, but then he could not move without the approval of the higher authority. In my country, of course, everything had to be cleared by the Palace. And Palace secretaries could play dirty games—and they did play dirty games. Had it just been for me to get clearance with His Majesty perhaps it would have been much easier. But, you know, whatever I felt, whatever went to His Majesty from me went through a distorted form and similarly His Majesty's views came to me in a distorted form. It was very difficult to negotiate on these terms.'

Shailendra Kumar Upadhyaya went on to blame the Nepali government for the resulting crisis: 'It was not handled in a proper way. We have to face the fact that India is a big country. We cannot afford to displease India. We have to think about what is helpful to India and not harmful to Nepal. This should be the basis of our foreign policy. But unfortunately it was not so at the time.'

The Panchayat government's initial austerity measures had met with a good deal of popular support, but people's patience wore thin as the situation worsened throughout the autumn and winter of 1989. Public opinion in Nepal swung further when the Panchayat government was unable to reach a settlement with the newly elected V.P. Singh government in India which had pledged to improve relations with Nepal.

Anti-Indian feeling was still strong, and the Indian Trade Embargo had caused unrest inside Nepal. What the panchas feared was that the Indian Trade Embargo was actually a camouflage and that what the Indian government really wanted was political instability within Nepal and the end of the Panchayat system.

Indian involvement in Nepal was, however, more complex than merely a large country wishing to dominate a smaller one. India had been a democracy since independence in 1947. As a democracy it was the main point of reference as well as support for the Nepali opposition. On the other hand, Indian dissatisfaction with Nepal was not only due to Nepal's lack of democratic rights, but dated back to King Mahendra's policy of balancing India and China. Later King Birendra also played his part in displeasing India. He proposed that Nepal be declared a 'Zone of Peace' around the time of his coronation in 1975. This proposal received immediate support from the Chinese and as a result the Indian reaction was sour. Many Nepalis, however, saw India's attitude towards Nepal as a thirst for power tainted with paranoia. Madan Mani Dikshit, editor of the Nepali newspaper, *Samiksha*, said: 'The Indian government is completely opposed to the Peace Zone proposal of our King, because in their perspective this goes against the provision of the 1950 treaty. Secondly, they do not want Nepal to maintain their relations with China on the same conditions as with India. Our government policy over the last thirty years some analysts have called that of equi-distance with China and India. I don't think it should be described that way, but India thinks this is a policy of equi-distance and they reject it. They want us to have the same relations to China as they have, ignoring the fact that we have a completely different history and have had completely different relations with China over the last thirty years.'

India's involvement in Nepal's 1990 revolution was certainly significant—if not consistent. At first it seemed that Indian support for the success of the pro-Democracy movement would be as crucial as in 1951. When Chandra Shekhar, leader of the Janata Dal in India and later Prime Minister, spoke at the Nepali Congress Convention in January 1990, he openly declared his support for the pro-Democracy movement, and stated that this was the view of all Indian political leaders. Furthermore, in an interview on 1 February 1990, the President of the Nepali Congress Party, Krishna Prasad Bhattarai, said that although the Indian government had not given any official support to the pro-Democracy movement, 'privately they have assured us that they will put on all sorts of pressure.' Bhattarai even claimed that the Indian leaders had gone as far as to promise that no new Trade and Transit Treaty would be signed, 'until there is an understanding about democracy in Nepal.'

Pressure from India did come. On 15 February, All India **Radio** announced that the Indian government would close all the remaining border crossings with Nepal on 18 February, the day the pro-Democracy movement was due to start. Then on 21 February the Indian government expressed concern that the Nepali government had used the military to quell the uprising at Bhaktapur.

On 23 February, the Indian Prime Minister, V.P. Singh, publicly stated that his government had no intention of interfering in Nepal's internal affairs. However, the Panchayat government had felt Indian pressure and Singh's statement was quite acceptable to the Nepali opposition as a compulsory diplomatic move. What worried people was that rumours had begun to circulate that the Indian government wanted to take advantage of the Panchayat government's weak position and push through all their demands in negotiating a new Trade and Transit Treaty. These rumours were confirmed by the Nepali newspaper, *Navaras*, on 28 February.

This newspaper revealed that liberal panchas had taken the government to task for being too lenient with India during the previous round of talks in New Delhi. The newspaper stated that the Nepali delegation had even agreed to a renewal of the 1950 Peace and Friendship Treaty which the same Nepali government had roundly condemned just a few months earlier. These rumours were given further substance by Rishikesh Shaha, the human rights activist, who was in New Delhi to monitor support for the pro-Democracy movement in Nepal. On 21 March 1990, he used his forceful personality to criticize the Indian government, for its recent dealings with Nepal. Any deal with the Panchayat government, he stated, would be a deal against the people of Nepal. Accordingly, he urged the Indian government not to negotiate with the Panchayat government and not to exploit its weak position to Indian advantage.

Meanwhile, resentment was mounting in Nepal against India. Nepalis felt let down by the Indian leaders, but most importantly they felt confused. No one seemed to know if India was playing a game or not. It was unclear if India was trying to rush through a new treaty or if the Panchayat government had simply become more lenient. In an interview on 3 March, Shree Bhadra Sharma, a liberal pancha and member of the Rashtriya Panchayat, explained the apparent change of heart in the Panchayat government's attitude towards India: 'Previously, during the whole of last year it was the strategy of the government in its dealings with India to bargain for two treaties of Trade and Transit rather than one and profess against the 1950 treaty. They said that this treaty was out of date and Nepal could not accept it without fundamental changes. That was the view of the government then. But later on the government found that it was fighting two fronts simultaneously: one internal against the multi-party system, the other international against the Indian government. It finally reached the conclusion that fighting on two fronts was not possible, so there were only two options—either to build the multi-party system inside the country and strengthen their position for bargaining with India, or to get India's sympathy by giving them some concessions and then crush the multi-party people within the country. Between these two options the government had preferred the second. They are now surrendering their sovereignty to India and at the same time crushing the multi-party movement inside the country. The government has already accepted the 1950 treaty and not only that, it has accepted India's conception of their own security perception. I have never had a clear idea of what this security perception entails, but whatever it means, the Nepali government has accepted it. This was the outcome of the Nepali delegation's recent visit on secretary level to New Delhi.' Commenting on India's strategy, Shree Bhadra Sharma said: 'I don't know what the opinion of the Indian government is, but as far as I understand India will first make the Nepali government sign the treaty and take all the concessions from the Nepali government. Then they will support the Democratic opposition to maintain their international image.'

Shailendra Kumar Upadhyaya, who was Nepal's Foreign Minister at the time, told a different story. He claimed that he knew nothing about any Indian attempt to exploit the weak position of the Panchayat government. On the contrary, after his visit to New Delhi in January 1990, Upadhyaya was of the opinion that India had begun to understand Nepal's position. 'I came with a great hope,' he said, 'so if there was any type of negotiation going on, it went on behind my back.' Upadhyaya had little faith in Marich Man Singh Shrestha, the then Prime Minister of Nepal. He could not totally rule out that such negotiations had taken place: 'Well, the Prime Minister is more of a conspirator than a politician,' Upadhyaya commented, 'and so were many of the people in establishment. So I cannot rule out that something like this happened. I have heard it from several sources. I was even told this from Indian sources. After I left the Ministry some people said that these things had taken place.'

Even taking Marich Man Singh Shrestha's possible leniency into account, there was little doubt that India was playing an ambiguous— some might say dubious—role in Nepal during the 1990 revolution. Indian leaders repeatedly supported the pro-Democracy movement and called for an end to the violence instigated by the Panchayat government. Yet the Indian government tried to pressurize the Panchayat government into accepting the provisions of the 1950 treaty—a treaty repugnant to most Nepalis who thought it only showed the Indian wish to dominate.

India itself was divided and its ambiguity towards Nepal may have been partly a result of this. Chandra Shekhar and V.P. Singh were both competing to lead the country and seemed also to use the issue of democracy in Nepal to bolster their own political positions.

On 1 March 1990 three members of the Indian cabinet—the Ministers of Finance, Railways and Textiles—all pledged their support to the pro-Democracy movement in Nepal. By 30 March the situation in Nepal had grown more serious and tempers rose in the Indian parliament when the matter was discussed. The Janata Dal leader, Chandra Shekhar, said that a treaty signed with the Nepali government now would be a treaty signed against the Nepali people. Shekhar was supported in his statements by the Nepali Congress leader, Bhasanta Sate. Countering this opinion, the Indian Foreign Minister, I.K. Gujral, who was responsible for negotiating the new treaty with Nepal said: 'Even though we support democracy in Nepal, we will not interfere in another nation's internal affairs.' Chandra Shekhar retorted that it was the duty of the Indian government to give Nepal's pro-Democracy movement all the support it asked for. The Indian parliament remained divided. Only on 9 April when King Birendra announced the multi-party system did the Indian government at last officially declare its support for democracy within Nepal.

If official Indian support was lacking, this was not true of unofficial Indian support. The close ties between the Nepali opposition, Congress and communist politicians alike with India, ensured that many Indian politicians were deeply involved in supporting the pro-Democracy movement. Chandra Shekhar was one of many. As the revolution continued, even Indian political parties began to pledge their collective support. This support came from all quarters—surprisingly even from the Bharatiya Janata Party. This growing Hindu party has strong links with the World Hindu Federation and had always supported the monarchy in Nepal and the Panchayat system. In a statement on 7 March 1990, the party's General Secretary expressed support for Nepal's pro-Democracy movement. This party went further than any of the other Indian political parties in stating that it supported the formation of a constituent assembly and a constitutional monarch in Nepal.

In addition to political support from New Delhi, there was a good deal of local support from the areas of India closer to Nepal. This was especially true of the Indian state of Bihar. Indian politicians in Bihar organized a series of demonstrations in support of the pro-Democracy movement. On 9 March Indian communists and Janata Dal workers blocked the main border station at Raxaul for more than six hours. Then on 14 March Indian politicians halted the railway to the Nepali town of Janakpur in the eastern Terai in order to show support for the general strike in Nepal on that day.

Indian involvement, therefore, was mixed. At best Indian politicians genuinely supported the cause of democracy inside Nepal; at worst the Indian government appeared to be calculating to infiltrate and gain influence in Nepal.

It was Panchayat policy throughout the revolution to accuse both liberal panchas and opposition leaders of being manipulated from the outside—especially by India. Shailendra Kumar Upadhyaya explained why: 'The assessment of the Prime Minister and his followers inside the cabinet was that this movement would not get widespread support from the people. They thought that the nationalist sentiment of the people would not go against the system which was being harassed by India because of the blockade.' Upadhyaya explained how Indian participation in the Nepali Congress Convention in January 1990 had given the Panchayat government more leeway to criticize the opposition: 'You might recall that following the statement by Chandra Shekhar at the Nepali Congress Convention, a demonstration was organised by many panchas to ask Chandra Shekhar to leave the country. And there was a day to oppose this foreign interference and there was a mass meeting in which many, including the Prime Minister, spoke.'

Yet, Panchayat accusations that the pro-Democracy movement was manipulated by India, may have held more than a grain of truth. Former Prime Minister, Marich Man Singh Shrestha said in November 1990 after the revolution was over: 'Of course the recent movement was totally engineered and manipulated by India. I can show you lots of proof. Just look at the records of the Nepal Rashtra Bank (the National Bank of Nepal). Until the third week of Magh there was a general deficit of more than 20,000,000 rupees. Then suddenly there was a surplus of 50-60,000,000 rupees. Where did this money come from? There is no doubt that it came from India, infused into Nepal to support various political forces in order to destabilise the political situation.' Describing India's attitude to Nepal during the last two years of his ministry, Marich Man Singh Shrestha said: 'Because of the relaxation in superpower tension, the Indian government saw that the time was right to take action in Nepal. They wanted to force us to accept the provisions of the 1950 treaty and their total domination. At first they imposed the embargo. Then they started the recent movement inside the country. The Indians destabilised the political situation inside Nepal in order to weaken the position of the King and government to accept their total demands. The Indians first tried to instigate student unrest at the same time as the embargo was imposed, but we managed to avert this. Then they launched the movement. Look, even B.P. Koirala's family and his main adviser warned the Nepali Congress leaders not to launch the movement because it was a trick from the Indian government to force the Nepali nation into submission. In the middle of the recent political crisis, when the Nepali government was in a weak position, the Indian government even tried to force us to reassert the 1950 treaty.'

Grishma Bahadur Devkota, Nepali historian and member of the Palace Assembly, the Raj Sabha, during the Panchayat period, was even less generous than Marich Man Singh Shrestha in describing the involvement of India during the period of the 1990 revolution: 'India had the following two interests or goals: the main interest was to bring Nepal into their own security sphere. In the same way as the Chinese controlled Tibet, the Indians wanted Nepal as part of their area of influence and they wanted to control Nepal in the same way. They wanted to create a state of unrest inside Nepal. Their first method to reach this point was to impose an economic embargo last year. They first created a situation of economic hardships for the Nepali people and they went on to step number two, the creation of political movement inside the country.'

Devkota admitted that the pro-Democracy movement had been initiated by the Nepali Congress, but he pointed to the close links between the Nepali Congress Party and Indian politicians: 'The movement really started last year when Nepali Congress leaders took part in a programme in Kathmandu to celebrate the birthday of the late Indian Prime Minister, Mr Nehru. On this occasion a Nepali Congress leader said that Nepal is not a fully sovereign nation, adding that sovereignty had been given to Nepal by India. If we look back at history, even before the Nepali Congress was established, the National Nepali Congress existed. In their first programme it was written that

Nepal was a branch of India. The argument was that every aspect of Nepali society, culture, religion and so on originated from India.'

Devkota pointed out that when the movement officially started with the Nepali Congress Convention in January 1990: 'The Congress Party invited a number of foreign political leaders for the meeting, but only Indian leaders arrived.' Clearly, Devkota was convinced that the whole pro-Democracy movement had been completely controlled by India.

There was, as has been stated, a great deal of intimacy between the Nepali Congress Party and Indian politicians. The Congress veterans had largely been educated in India and first became politically active there. Many had lived in exile in India and enjoyed the patronage of Indian politicians who supported their cause. It was natural enough that Nepali Congress politicians should have forged close friendships with Indian politicians such as Chandra Shekhar. Ideologically, too, the Nepali Congress Party drew much of their inspiration from India. B.P. Koirala's brand of socialism was allied to the socialist movement in India led by Jayaprakash Narayan. Still, even Marich Man Singh Shrestha admitted that these Nepali Congress politicians were genuine Nepali nationalists. Shrestha's opinion was that it was blindness and ignorance rather than anything else which made these politicians naïve about India's intentions in Nepal.

In contrast to the Nepali Congress politicians, the Nepali communists were ardent nationalists and deeply suspicious of India. In their eyes India was a regional superpower and a threat to Nepal's independence. The communists too, however, had close ties to India. Their communism was more Indian than Chinese and many of the factions and groups within Nepal were linked to sister parties in India. Like the Nepali Congress politicians, many Nepali communists had fled to India during the Panchayat period. These communists had also built up an organization inside India as well as an underground network inside Nepal. Even in 1990, some reports claimed that Nepali communists were training activists in camps inside India. On 1 March, the BBC's Nepali Service reported that communist leaders such as

C.P. Mainali were giving military training to activists in India. The communist government in West Bengal was allegedly giving covert support to these activities and supplying the communists with arms.

India was either a friend or a threat depending on which political camp you belonged to. This conflict of opinion surfaced again immediately after the revolution. After his appointment as Prime Minister of the interim government, Krishna Prasad Bhattarai said at a press conference on 16 April that one of the most important objectives of the new interim government would be to solve the trade dispute with India in a way which best served Nepal's interests. On 24 May Bhattarai announced that he would be leaving for New Delhi in two weeks. Bhattarai was known for having spent a long period in India and for being friendly with various Indian politicians. Many Nepalis expressed doubts before he left.

The Nepali delegation visited India from 7 to 11 June. The first report made by the Nepali delegation which included Minister of Industry and President of the United Left Front, Sahana Pradhan, and the Nepali Minister of Finance, Devendra Raj Pande, was fairly straight-forward. The Indian government had agreed to the restoration of status quo ante between the two countries. It was decided a new treaty would wait until there was a democratically elected government in Nepal.

Opinion in Nepal changed later when it was discovered that Bhattarai had held secret negotiations with Indian leaders of which not even Sahana Pradhan was aware. At these talks Bhattarai gave in to a wide range of Indian demands and this was reported by several Nepali newspapers. The two Prime Ministers issued a joint communiqué at the end of the visit. This communiqué stated that Nepal would fully respect India's security concerns and would not allow any activities on its soil prejudicial to Indian security. Furthermore, the two countries would consult with the aim of reaching a mutual agreement on defence-related matters. What caused an outcry in Kathmandu, however, was a speech made by Bhattarai in New Delhi where he mentioned that India and Nepal should work together on developing a policy to exploit the resources of their 'common rivers'.

The Nepali communists accused Bhattarai of selling out to India even though they themselves formed part of the interim government. The ex-panchas soon followed suit. The leaders of the new National Democratic Parties (which were largely composed of ex-panchas) roundly condemned Bhattarai's common rivers policy. These nationalist reactions were hardly alleviated when Indian Foreign Minister I.K. Gujral, visiting Nepal in early August 1990, mentioned the possibility of establishing a common currency for Nepal and India. When Chandra Shekhar visited Nepal again in 1991, this time as Prime Minister of India, he behaved in a much less provocative manner. Yet both the communists and the ex-panchas had now turned Nepal's relationship with India into one of the burning issues of the coming general election.

Shailendra Kumar Upadhyaya gave a balanced, if still nationalistic, account of Bhattarai's negotiations in New Delhi: 'No, I don't agree that it is a total sell-out,' he said, 'I would say that the Prime Minister, in order to appease India, had overlooked some of the phraseology and communiqués, or may be he has not been advised properly by his advisers, so there are some phrases which will create difficulty for any succeeding government for future negotiations with India. When it is said that both countries should engage in consultation to reach an agreement on security, one has overlooked the recent experience we have had of India flexing its muscles. Knowing this, it will be difficult for any future government to consult with India, unless it is a very strong government backed by the people, which can resist all items in an agreement going against Nepal's own interests. The so-called similar perception of security is so wide and encompassing that it could be a threat to Nepal. For India, China is an enemy still—for us, China is a friendly state. If we accept the Indian perception, the Chinese might not tolerate this attitude and this would be a dangerous game inviting China's anger. We know from experience that India's security interest views all territory south of the Himalayas as part of their territory of influence and this perception will naturally give problems to Nepal's government. Similarly, the Prime Minister's mentioning of common rivers will create big difficulties for a future government. The recent agreement with India was therefore not a total sell-out, but the Prime Minister did make several concessions which in the long run may not lead to a better understanding with India.'

With hindsight it is clear that foreign influence, overwhelmingly Indian influence, played an important role in determining the outcome of the 1990 revolution in Nepal. The long-term effects of this influence, especially in regard to Nepal's relationship with India, remained uncertain. Many Nepali intellectuals and politicians, especially ex-panchas, worried that democracy would actually strengthen India's hand in Nepal. Some even worried that Nepal's independence might be fatally undermined. Ex-Prime Minister Marich Man Singh Shrestha explained in an interview in 1990 the extent to which he believed India was involved in Nepali affairs: 'You must understand that the RAW of the Indian government, known as the research division and the equivalent of the KGB and the CIA, is active all over Nepal. Because of their strength and resources, India has a flexibility to do whatever they want to, to further their interests in Nepal. At the same time they support opposing political forces inside the country to ensure that there will never be a strong and stable government here. They want no party to obtain an absolute majority so that there will always be weak coalitions. Look, even the ML Communist Party is a total creation by India and this is an Indian move to weaken the Nepali monarchy.' Shrestha tried to emphasize the extent to which Indian forces had penetrated Nepal: 'You must have a long political experience as I have to understand how important and powerful these foreign political forces are in Nepal. It is not that the new political leaders do not have experience, not that they are not nationalists, but they lack the full understanding and will to assert Nepal's Independence.' It was not only hardline ex-panchas such as Marich Man Singh Shrestha who expressed such views. Liberal members of the old regime and some communists also worried publicly about India's involvement in Nepali affairs especially through the Indian intelligence service—the Research and Analysis Wing (RAW).

The major question concerning foreign affairs after the 1990 revolution therefore remained unanswered. Although opinion differed, it was too early to tell if the 1990 revolution would strengthen or weaken Nepal in relation to India. Some Nepalis worried that the revolution might mark the first step in a long process under which Nepal would succumb like Sikkim in the 1970s to becoming only another state in the Indian Union. Others repudiated this pessimism. They maintained that a strong, democratically-elected government in Kathmandu would be able to stand up to Indian demands. These people were saying that the old policy of balancing India against China to Nepal's benefit would reassert itself. Whether this was still possible or whether a capable democratic government would emerge in Nepal still remained to be seen.

THREE

The Day After

After the euphoria of the revolution had evaporated, the Nepali people and their new leaders were forced to wake up and assess their situation. Power had been transferred to the interim government in principle, but the government now had to build up a new political system. The spring promise of a society based on democracy and justice, however, seemed further away than ever. There had been a sharp increase in prices and the economy had sunk even further into depression. There was also a general sense of crisis in law and order which undermined people's personal security. Political freedom had come, of course, but this new freedom seemed intangible in a society which had been ruled by totalitarian diktats for so long.

The Nepali people and their democratic leaders were faced with two overriding questions which would determine whether the new order would survive. First of all, how should the new democratic system be built on the remains of the old Panchayat structure? Even more important, how should new democratic freedoms be handled? For democracy to prove viable it was vital that people should be able to exercise their rights within a framework of discipline and constraint.

What many of the new democratic leaders had not realized was how the Panchayat system had stifled a seething mass of conflicts and resentments. With the Panchayat regime gone, these conflicts were likely to rise to the surface and burst out into the open. In the days immediately following the revolution that is exactly what happened. New movements sprang up overnight. Demands were put forward and protests were launched. The ensuing upheaval touched parts of Nepali society which had never been affected by such unrest before. These conflicts were of a social, economic, cultural and even religious nature. Though challenging and difficult, this period of disruption was probably a necessary transitional stage between a closed society and an open one.

After he had dissolved the Rashtriya Panchayat, the King bowed to the demands of the interim government. He dissolved the village and town Panchayats and dismissed the Zonal Commissioners, the Anchaladhises, on 7 May 1990. As the last vestiges of the Panchayat system disappeared, the interim government hoped it would gain a tighter control over the country. In fact the opposite happened. The dissolution of the Panchayats and the disappearance of the once mighty Zonal Commissioners led to a loss of control in the districts. A long period of chaos followed and many months passed before law and order was restored satisfactorily. As has been mentioned earlier, the power vacuum immediately following the revolution led to a recurrence of violence in Kathmandu at the end of April 1990. The situation in the capital was soon brought under control. Yet in many places, unrest, almost anarchy, continued for the whole period the interim government sat in office. The government tried to restore some order through the Village Development Committees. These consisted mainly of local civil servants. Unfortunately, people were appointed to these committees in a rather arbitrary fashion and many degenerated into squabbling gangs of Congress members and communists with some ex-panchas. The new committees certainly did not function as the smooth-running organs of local government that the central government desperately needed.

The unrest during this period took two distinct forms. First of all there was a marked increase in crime. The root of this problem lay in the loss of morale suffered by the police force following the revolution. Ordinary police officers no longer knew whom to obey. Experience now told them that one ruling government could quickly be substituted by another—with an entirely different set of orders. They had been praised by panchas and blamed by democrats. Furthermore, the police had soiled their reputation during the revolution. Some had even taken part in burglaries, looting and violence. Many people felt they could no longer trust the police and neighbourhoods had set up their own security committees. Many complained that democracy had brought only disorder and crime.

As the days passed, the unrest in the country began to take on a more sinister form. Incidents of political violence broke out. Old grievances merged with fights between various political groups—and the 'Mandales', the former Panchayat thugs, reared their heads once again. The police were also involved more often than not. These incidents had one common factor and that was it was difficult to establish the truth of what had happened. On 15 May one person was killed and several severely injured at a public meeting at the District headquarters of Baglung in western Nepal. This was because police opened fire into a crowd. Reports stated that the police had first ordered the crowd to disperse, but people had begun throwing stones and the police had responded with gunfire. This, at least, was the official version.

Similar incidents occurred in many places during the following months. The most serious of these was a clash at Krishnanagar in the central Terai region in August, and another again at Baglung in November. This violence became more and more political as time passed. On 11 November a public meeting organized by the newly-established National Democratic Party (Chand) ended in a clash where several politicians were injured. These politicians included the former Prime Minister, Lokendra Bahadur Chand, and Rajeshwor Devkota. Several people were also injured the following day at another meeting in a neighbouring district. On 13 December, a former pancha, Surya Bahadur Thapa, organized a political meeting at Banepal, a town in the Kathmandu valley. Six people were injured, one of whom later succumbed to his injuries. Such incidents became more frequent as the election campaign gathered momentum during the initial months of 1991.

Most of the violence, however, was merely the settling of local disputes. It was a time when law and order was slack and old scores could be settled without fear of reprisals. A typical example of this occurred in the eastern hill district of Ramechap towards the end of September 1990. A large crowd of people used force to move their District Headquarters to another locality. The crowd moved everything including all the official papers and documents. This led to fighting between different groups in the area and the police had to call in reinforcements.

The unrest in the Terai region in the south of the country, which was bad enough, was made worse by the Hindu-Muslim conflict in India. In India, the city of Ayodhya had become a flashpoint of national conflict as Hindus wanted to build a temple on the site of a Muslim mosque. Some of this sectarian violence spread over the border into Nepal. On 8 August houses were set on fire in a village in the Sarlahi district of the eastern Terai region. Fighting broke out between Muslims and Hindus and several people were severely injured. On 16 September Hindu reactionaries placed a dead cow in a Muslim village to inflame the inter-religious conflict and two months later two Muslims were killed in clashes in the eastern Terai.

Former panchas used these incidents to point to the new government's failings. Law and order, they claimed, hardly existed and where it did there was rule by force, not rule by law. One former pancha minister complained: 'In the name of democracy, mob-ocracy has been established!' He described the current state of affairs by saying: 'If a group forms in a village and suddenly decides, "This is a bad man, so let's go and burn his house", they are left to do it. Nobody feels secure any longer, not even in the villages or the remote districts. These days a young woman cannot walk alone. People cannot wear their jewellery or other valuables. You are afraid to walk in the streets and people no longer let the traffic pass easily.'

Nevertheless, the unrest during this period was not only caused by mobs or reactionary elements from the old regime. Conflicts also resulted from genuine social conflicts which were now allowed to come out into the open. Such an incident took plac on 4 February 1991 at Naval Parasi in the Central Terai region. The Shukumbasis, landless people who squatted on government land, tried to block the main road between Butwal and Narayanghat. Their protest developed into a clash between police and demonstrators in which three people were killed and several wounded. This was the official story. However, Chandra Bahadur Gurung, President of the Landless People's Organizations of Nepal and organizer of the demonstration, gave another version: 'The whole thing started on 30 January when we spread our pamphlets in the districts stating our simple demands for citizenship and land rights. The next day we surrounded the Civil District Officer's office. When this had no effect, on the evening of 4 February we put up a road block across the main road between Butwal and Narayanghat, stopping all the traffic. The road block lasted until the next morning when the CDO told us that the Prime Minister would arrive before 6 o'clock in the afternoon to answer our demands. The afternoon passed and no Prime Minister turned up. Heading back to put up our road block we clashed with the police just as we entered the main road. About 200 policemen tried to chase us with batons, but they had to give up. We surrounded the police station and after three rounds of tear gas they opened fire. People were falling all around. As I tried to drag somebody with me another person was hit just behind me. In the end three people were killed—two on the spot and one at the hospital—and many were wounded. We also know that three others were killed, but the police would not give us their bodies.'

The problems of the Shukumbasis had a long history which was closely linked to the politics of the Panchayat regime. Chandra Bahadur Gurung explained: 'Though there have always been landless people in Nepal, the problems really started during the last years of the Panchayat system. In connection with elections and especially during the referendum campaign of 1980, the Panchayat politicians lured poor people from the hills to vote for them, promising them new land in the Terai. People left the hills in hundreds, sold what little they had of land and moved to the Terai. Arriving there, they settled down on government land and cleared bushes and forests. But the Panchayat politicians forgot what they had promised and the land was never officially given to the settlers. Instead, these new farming communities on government land were seen as illegal squatter settlements and the government did everything it could to evict us. The police arrived reading out statements saying that we must leave and they would set fire to our village. But we had nowhere to go. Our land in the hills no longer belonged to us and we had no money to buy new land. Instead, we rebuilt our houses as best we could and planted our rice and other crops on the lush, beautiful land surrounding us—and waited patiently for the next round-up.' Gurung further pointed out that the problems of the Shukumbasis were not only landlessness and poverty: 'We Shukumbasis are non-citizens in Nepal. It is almost impossible for us to get a passport. The government will ask for our landholder's certificate or the name and address of our employer and we have nothing to give them.' Gurung explained that the coming of democracy had spurred the Shukumbasis to rally for the first time and put forward their demands for land and citizenship.

The Shukumbasis, who numbered several hundred thousand, were only one of the many underprivileged groups in Nepal who emerged with demands in the months following the revolution. When direct action failed, these groups took their grievances personally to members of the interim cabinet. But follow-up action was not forthcoming. Chandra Bahadur Gurung related how he had spoken to the Prime Minister and Home Minister in Kathmandu after the incident at Naval Parasi. The Home Minister had been dismissive. Two people killed was not enough to make an impression, he said. As a last resort, Gurung and others went on a hunger strike, but their protest went largely unrecognized.

Hunger strikes, strikes and demonstrations occurred continually. A new feature of the revolution was the 'gheraos' which occurred frequently. 'Gherao' means to 'surround'. Buildings or employers were surrounded by a crowd as a form of protest. Nepal was further racked by serious labour unrest. The Panchayat government had set such strictures on the workplace that natural relations between bosses and workers were impossible. The time had now come to change this situation—but also to settle old accounts. Unfortunately, the workers wanted all their demands met at once. As a result, both the government and private sectors were stalled by strikes during the year of interim government. Whether the demands put forward were reasonable or unreasonable, it was generally impossible to meet them owing to the desperate economic situation. The Indian Trade Embargo and the revolution had crippled business to the extent that wage increases were out of the question. But the workers were not demanding just more money. Their demands had now become political. Both Congress and the communists competed for the support of the workers and they became politicized in the process. These two major political groups really wanted to exploit the volatile situation for their own ends and use the workers as a lever. Often the real goal appeared to be to create disturbances. What followed, as former pancha Keshar Bahadur Bista pointedly said, was a crisis in discipline: 'Nobody is working. You go to some offices and people come only once a week to sign that they have attended and get their pay. The lower staff isn't obeying the senior staff. The senior staff cannot handle the situation and find it impossible to give orders. Everywhere employees bang tables against their own chiefs. The workers are always on strike—even if the government has decided a minimum facility and wage. If a group of workers go on strike today, things will be settled today and they will go back to work today. But tomorrow again another group of Communists or rightists or leftists or extremists or whatever they are will get out and organise a strike again.'

All manner of professional groups—whether teachers, civil servants or journalists—organized protests outside government offices to put pressure on the interim government. Faced with such a battery of demands, how did the interim cabinet cope with the situation?

On 24 June 1990 the Education Minister, Keshar Jang Rayamajhi, brought a hunger strike organized by the Nepal Teachers' Association to an end by promising that all their demands would be met. He spoke at the open-air theatre in the centre of Kathmandu. On 13 August the Prime Minister visited a group of journalists who were staging a hunger-strike. He told them that their demands would be looked into within the next month. The government was criticized for being harsh or lenient by turns. One thing was clear—the interim government was not willing to use repressive methods to suppress the strikes and unrest. Yet many claimed that the interim government's shilly-shallying in half-encouraging, half-punishing the strikers, actually encouraged the unrest.

The most serious challenge to the interim government came from government employees. Just as the revolution had begun on the university campuses, so the university was the first institution to experience the new wave of unrest after the revolution was over. On 11 May professors and lecturers demanded the removal of their Vice-Chancellors because of their allegiance to the old Panchayat system. The government gave in to these demands on 26 May and a new so-called democratic leadership was appointed at Tribhuvan University and the Nepal Sanskrit University. On the same day, all the members of the Royal Nepal Academy, a palace-sponsored research institute, were forced to resign as a result of popular pressure. Within the university itself, the library was the first place to be hit by strikes and disaffection. The Chief Librarian, Shanti Mishra, gave her own account of events: 'A few days after the revolution had come to an end, I was told about the University Employees' Ad Hoc Committee. This body, which was engineered by the ML Communist Party, with the help of two or three infiltrators among my library staff, managed to turn members of staff against me. They who were themselves Mandales called me a Mandale and accused me of political activity—I who had always kept aloof from politics and had criticised anything which I thought was wrong even in the old system! They forced me into a situation where I eventually resigned saying that I could no longer work with my staff.' Shanti Mishra drew breath and continued: 'The rest of the university didn't do anything to stop this. The new rector and vice-chancellor had been put into office because they belonged to the Congress and communist parties—and they did not lift a finger! They came privately and expressed their support for me and their opposition to what was happening. But all of them said they couldn't oppose it publicly.'

Shanti Mishra's experience was common at this time and reflected what happened to many people. The most serious threat to the government actually came from the civil servants. One member of the interim cabinet said: 'Unfortunately the civil servants became directly involved in the movement for democracy. Thus those who should be neutral government servants became politicised—and this is why we had problems, problems with the civil servants' agitation after the revolution.'

Soon after the revolution the lower level civil servants formed their own illegal organization. They pressed for a rise in salary and for the firing of corrupt bosses. They staged various protests and organized direct action in government offices. The government negotiated a compromise, but this settlement lasted only a few months. The civil servants went on strike again at the beginning of December 1990. This time their campaign attracted much more support—even from out in the districts. The government again succeeded in bringing the civil servants' agitation to an end by setting up a commission to look into their demands. Once again, however, all the government achieved was to postpone facing the real issues. As a result, the third and most serious civil servants' dispute became the main challenge to the new Congress government after the general election in May 1991.

In practice the civil servants' disputes meant that all government offices came to a standstill during the interim government period. Decisions were simply not taken and while corruption may have been wiped out at the highest political level, it increased at the lower levels.

The corruption, more than anything else, was what disillusioned the Nepali people during the autumn months of 1990. Government corruption, after all, was one of the main reasons why the previous regime had been swept away. Now people saw corruption continuing and even increasing.

Doing away with corruption was one of the main goals of the new democratic leaders. Several of them had admitted that this would take a long time and would be no easy task. Communist leader Tulsi Lal Amatya said: 'We are the leaders. We have to show the people how to behave and slowly our incorruptibility will trickle down.' This method would obviously take years to bear fruit. The Nepali people did not seem willing to wait for a slow change to be brought to bear. What caused the most resentment among ordinary citizens was that government officers retained their jobs—unpunished—even if they had acquired very bad reputations during the Panchayat period. In September 1990, a former Prime Minister expressed what by then had become popular opinion: 'These new rulers talk about corruption. Let them do whatever they want to do. When they are talking about property, family property, and this or that, they must start searching for this property among people. Why don't they? They can easily come and check how much a house, a car, or some furniture would have cost and where the money came from. But instead they just make speeches.'

The disillusionment which had spread amongst the citizens of Kathmandu was markedly different from the enthusiasm they had shown six months earlier. People were bitterly disappointed that the interim government had not fulfilled its promises. One highly-educated Kathmandu citizen said: 'The main failure with the interim government is their style of thinking. They promised so many things, even impossible things, during the time of the movement. So the hopes and aspirations of the people were raised too high. Now they are in power they have to face the backfire from those things—what they promised the people. You see, people are expecting so many unlimited things from a government like ours in a poor country—how can they fulfil the people's aspirations overnight? Even in remote places people think that they will get a private car and a house. Poor people thought they would get a lot of land after the revolution.'

The most immediate cause of popular resentment was the steep rise in prices. The new democratic leaders had promised a cut of as much as thirty-five per cent once they came into power. Instead inflation increased steeply. The Indian Trade Embargo and the revolution were the main reasons for this—but these reasons were not appreciated by ordinary Nepali citizens. The communists used the price rise to criticize the Nepali Congress and public protests against rising prices became more and more frequent as autumn passed.

Yet what had people expected? What did ordinary Nepalis really believe that democracy, a multi-party system and human rights would actually bring?

First and foremost, people associated democracy with freedom. Freedom spelled freedom of speech and freedom of action. A Kathmandu taxi-driver hailed by police as he drove the wrong way down a one-way street retorted: 'Don't you know that we have human rights now?' Generally people were more restrained. There was, however, a widespread feeling that more was possible and permissible than before.

Outside Kathmandu and the other major Nepali towns, there was not much understanding of the multi-party system. Many villagers believed the new political system to be the harbinger of disorder and crime. Even so, there was an underlying optimism that the general situation would improve. People did genuinely believe that democracy would improve their lot and bring about the end of poverty and exploitation. One influential member of the old regime had this to say about the Nepali people and their attitude towards democracy: 'People's understanding of democracy is like the blind person describing an elephant—one said it's a pillar, another said it's a wall and a third person said it's a tail. Nepal does not seem ready for democracy. The best illustration is to be found in the streets. The streets are always a good sign of how a people can govern themselves. Now the streets are dirtier than ever.'

Was the chaos following the revolution merely a sign that the Nepali people were not, in fact, ready for democracy? Was the interim government to blame for the confusion in the country? Everyone agreed that the interim government had a tough job on its hands—but everyone also seemed to agree that its performance was not quite up to the mark. One senior civil servant said: 'This is the most powerful government since Jang Bahadur Rana. They have all the powers. Nothing can stop them. Why have they not done anything? Why have they not been able to manage and control their civil servants? The whole university is in a mess. Everybody is on strike. The same might soon happen in Singha Durbar (the main government offices). The government are the ones who have established internal "ad hoc committees" in the ministries to handle internal administrative problems and these have again turned themselves against the ministers who have lost control over them.'

Four months after the revolution, one former pancha minister said of the interim government: 'The basic minimum achievement of the interim government turned out a complete failure. Even then I don't oppose this in public because the situation has been exceptional and these people are very inexperienced. They do have thirty years experience in organising an underground movement. They know how to oppose and how to criticise, but they don't know how to run a system or a government.'

As most of the new democratic leaders took office straight from jail or house-arrest it was undoubtedly true that they did lack experience in running a government. Some of the veteran Congress members had held office in B.P. Koirala's government thirty years earlier, but thirty years had passed and Nepal had changed dramatically during that period. What added to the interim government's difficulties was that they had to take up the reins where the Panchayat regime had left off. In other words they had to take over the running of a system whose practices they had opposed and which they wanted to change. The Home Minister in the interim government, Yog Prasad Upadhyaya, said: 'I could not be satisfied without achievement. Of course, much could have been done had there been ordinary circumstances and had we inherited a machinery undisturbed by political turmoil. Because we had to inherit the administrative set-up—the law enforcing agencies, for example, which were geared for a different purpose than we intended—we had to change things gradually and this meant we lost a lot of time.'

Yet the interim government not only had to change Nepal's political system, it also had to change many of the basic attitudes of the Nepali people. Yog Prasad Upadhyaya observed: 'It's a question of psychological adjustment!' The long period of dictatorship had come to an end—now working conditions for democracy and pluralism had to be created. The interim government had assumed office to act only by the tenets of democracy, but many people grew impatient with what they saw as stalling tactics. Yog Prasad Upadhyaya said: 'The people want us to do this or that, but they do not understand that in democracy the political leaders do not have unlimited power.' Many Nepalis seemed trapped in the contradiction of having high expectations of democracy while at the same time urging the interim government to use non- democratic means to be effective.

The interim government's task was made even harder by the fact that the cabinet was hardly a homogeneous body. It consisted of three very different political groups whose views and interests rarely coincided—the Nepali Congress, the communist members of the United Left Front, and the two royal nominees. Even so, Yog Prasad Upadhyaya expressed satisfaction about the way the cabinet worked: 'I am happy that most of the ministers have very strong common sense and that has compensated for their inexperience, if any at all. Our Finance Minister is an experienced administrator himself and, for example, the Prime Minister is a great organiser who knows human weaknesses and strengths. He has guided us more than anything else to stabilise and maintain a certain continuity in the administration, and it is because of his views that we have been able to work as a team. With all these different elements in the government it is a miracle that it has worked!'

Krishna Prasad Bhattarai, the Prime Minister of the interim government, was undoubtedly a key figure during this period. He seemed personally responsible for changing and restructuring the government. No one doubted that he had a difficult job to do. He was beleaguered constantly by crowds of people. Each morning at Baluwatar, the Prime Minister's residence in north Kathmandu, several hundred people gathered outside the front doors. All of them wanted to meet the Prime Minister personally. All of them wanted something— either political or personal. How did the Prime Minister deal with such an impossible situation? How could he cope with the daily barrage of requests? Bhattarai smiled and replied: 'Postponement is the best medicine here. You say, "Come again—come after the festival. Come after Dasain, come after Tihar". No one can solve all the problems in a developing country at once. Party members who are not ministers keep coming to me and ask when it will be their turn to be a minister. So even they are suffering from too high expectations.'

Somehow Bhattarai was able to cope with the situation. He dealt with the pressure and the seemingly impossible conflicts and proved himself to be adept at handling human relations. Yet these very qualities were what was perhaps wrong with the interim government.

Bhattarai's continual patching up of conflicts led to the interim government being criticized for the lack of a clear-cut policy. The interim government's publicly stated aims were to build a new democratic order in Nepal and hold elections. Yet how did they go about this?

There were two options open to the interim government. Either they could do away with the old system and build democracy from scratch—or they could somehow transform the old Panchayat structures into a new democratic form. What seemed to be the case was that the communists wanted a complete break with tradition while the Nepali Congress wanted some continuity. During the period of interim government, however, this choice never seemed to be made. If it was made, it was never publicly stated and a certain confusion and dissatisfaction resulted.

The King's decree did away with all the old Panchayat institutions. The Rashtriya Panchayat, village and town panchayats, and Class Organizations became suddenly obsolete. What this meant was that officially non-political institutions such as the university and government offices became the focus of fervent political activity. These were the only outlets the political parties had to agitate, persuade and recruit.

Yet the official political bodies of the Panchayat regime had never actually been the channels through which political activity had been organized. Power had been exercised primarily through the Palace and the interim government did not pay due attention to this. In doing away with the Rashtriya Panchayat the interim government did not do away with the real power structure of the old regime. Furthermore the interim government had to take over an administration including the civil service, police and army, which had been built up and run by the old system. Even the formerly powerful Palace secretariat was still in place.

If this situation did bring about problems for the interim government it was, at least, a matter of conscious choice. The moderates in the cabinet were certainly in favour of some continuity with the old system. Moreover, the whole cabinet agreed that they needed the civil service to enact new democratic policies, despite its long-standing reputation for inefficiency and corruption. The interim government hoped to win the loyalty of the civil service by slow degrees and so win control of the whole government administration. The interim government was also bound to respect the legal system set up by the Panchayat regime—at least until new laws could be passed and a new constitution brought into being. Yog Prasad Upadhyaya, Home Minister at that time, explained his dilemma: 'Ours is a government by law. It has got to run by law. We are challenged in the law courts. Never before have government actions been so seriously challenged in this country. And we are functioning with the same old laws. Even when the new constitution comes, the old laws will have to be amended and we have got to stick to some law. We cannot function arbitrarily. The people want us to function as generals, but we are against this despite the powers that we have.' According to him the problem was that many Nepalis did not seem to understand this.

The police and army certainly posed a visible challenge to the interim government. A former close aide of the King said: 'The army is totally loyal only to the King personally. But the army is mainly inactive. The police is 100 per cent under the interim government, but the police force is utterly demoralised. They do not dare to do anything. They remember what happened just after the revolution when several police were injured and police were even refused medical care. They are constantly worried that the power balance might tip once again, and that once again they might find themselves on the wrong side.'

It was clear to all that the police force needed some kind of thorough purge. Corrupt officers needed to be retired or brought to court. Yog Prasad Upadhyaya claimed that this was not a task for the interim government, however: 'Restructuring the police? We can't do that, you know, unless we pass a law. We are engaged in framing a constitution and in maintaining law and order within the existing framework. So we have no time. We were planning to have a police commission to look into the matter and the government is still considering that. May be this government or the next will form a police commission which will review the position and advise the government

on what sort of fair police force one should have and what powers
should be give to them....But we have not been able to correct the
situation. It would entail a very big burden on our government. As you
know this is the only sphere, the Ministry of Home Affairs, which is not
under any foreign aid or any foreign group. We have to do everything
on our own.'

The interim government's dealings with the police and army were
not only a matter of reorganization. According to Mathura Prasad
Shrestha, Minister of Health in the interim government speaking on
15 October 1990, it was also a matter of loyalty and control: 'We have
power—but the law enforcing forces, the police and the military, are
not entirely under our control. For this reason, you see, despite our
commitment to human rights, the police still commit atrocities and
human rights violations.' There was also an uneasy feeling in the air
that the police, army and Palace might combine to mount a coup—at
least, there was the feeling that it was possible. This threat made the
interim government cautious. Consequently, it may have been that a
certain wariness on the part of the interim government in dealing with
the old regime was publicly perceived as a lack of resolve.

Krishna Prasad Bhattarai and his cabinet were committed to
changing Nepali government and Nepali society. Strong democracy
meant both rule of law and accountability. Now even the government
had to be responsible for its own actions and, if necessary, cabinet
members could face trial and imprisonment. In order to bring about this
new situation, the government had to deal with the past. Most of the
interim government agreed that members of the old regime should be
investigated and tried where necessary. The interim government,
however, did not appear willing to do this. Certain half-hearted
measures were taken, but nothing actually happened. This apparent lack
of resolve led to a great deal of criticism. Bashu Dev Dhungana,
Chairman of the Bar Association of Nepal, said in April 1991, almost a
year after the interim government had taken office: 'The government
could have done one thing. It could have removed the people who had
tried to suppress the movement. These people even continued in the
administration. This way the masses were not satisfied. After all, many
people were killed and then these people just continued in their jobs.'

The government stalled partly because of internal dissent. The radical communists had posted hit lists on walls and buildings in Kathmandu during the final days of the revolution. These lists mentioned so-called culprits by name. In contrast some of the more moderate communists and the Congress members, including the Prime Minister, Krishna Prasad Bhattarai, openly preferred reconciliation to recrimination. The two royal nominees in the cabinet were not clear about their preferred course of action.

What the interim government did about this pressing matter was quite simple—it did nothing. The first commission formed to investigate what happened during the movement was actually set up by Lokendra Bahadur Chand during his brief fourteen-day ministry before the interim government came to power. This commission was headed by the Supreme Court Judge, Justice Prachanda Raj Anil. The interim government appointed two new members to this commission, but they soon resigned in protest saying that the members of the commission had been too involved personally in the old regime. As a result, the commission was dissolved. The Mallik Commission was put in its place. This consisted of three judges led by the Supreme Judge from the Eastern Regional Court whose name was Mallik. The commission's brief was to investigate what had happened during the revolution and find out who had been responsible for violence, loss of life and damage to property. At the same time another commission was set up to look into the question of missing persons during the Panchayat period from 1960-90.

Both commissions faced an uphill task. One member of the commission investigating missing persons, Prakash Kaphley, explained: 'Our commission was formed for three months. We conducted our work for six months, however, because we needed more time to get information out of the police. The police were not co-operative. We asked the government many times to do something because when the police did not give any information, how were we to get hold of material and conduct our investigation? When we asked, Bhattarai said that the police were not even co-operating with the government, so how could we expect them to co-operate with the commission?' Even so, Kaphley said: 'The commission managed to trace the cases of more than 100 people who had gone missing. Many of those responsible for the disappearances held high positions in the police force and government. For fear of antagonising the police, Bhattarai and his government did not take any further action.' The Mallik Commission found itself in a similar position. The police did not co-operate and the interim government shied away from giving the commission too much direct assistance. Despite its difficulties, the Mallik Commission did present its report on 31 December 1990. The commission was very clear. It stated the names of those it believed legally responsible for the atrocities committed during the period of the pro-Democracy movement. These included people in the administration and the police force. It also included politicians such as Marich Man Singh Shrestha, the former Prime Minister, ex-Home Minister Nirenjan Thapa, and the Chairman of the Panchayat Policy and Evaluation Committee, Navaraj Subedhi. The commission recommended that the rank and file government workers and police officers be dealt with in terms of the framework of the administration. As regards the politicians, the Mallik Commission recommended strongly that criminal charges be filed against them and that they be brought on trial. Despite advising the interim government on such a direct course of action, the Mallik Commission brought no legal proof against those it accused, nor did it refer to the actual laws which these people were supposed to have breached. Instead, the commission argued that evidence should be presented in a trial.

On 1 February 1991 the government did finally act. Five high-level government officers, including the Chief Cabinet Secretary, were dismissed. Furthermore, the passports of all the ministers in the Shrestha and Chand governments were confiscated, pending investigation. Lokendra Bahadur Chand appealed in court and the passports were returned.

That same day the government announced that no action would be taken against individual police officers or civil servants until after the elections. This was quite different from what Krishna Prasad Bhattarai had announced at a public meeting in Janakpur just a month earlier. Then he had assured his listeners that strong action would be taken against the culprits with no mercy. In an interview nine months later, Bhattarai defended his decision not to prosecute. 'I did not want to take action because the election was the target. I did not want to antagonise the police and therefore to disturb its fabric by punishing them on fictitious or—in certain cases—real grounds. I also did not want to antagonise the civil service because they were the people who would hold the elections.'

There seemed however, a real fear on the part of the interim government, especially the Congress members, of acting against members of the old regime—and this went further than purely practical considerations. The Mallik Commission's report was kept secret. It was then sent to another judge, Motikaji Sthapit, for study and for further recommendations to be made to the government. Sthapit replied that the report lacked the legal proof and legal references necessary to accuse the so-called culprits. He added that the government's decision not to prosecute police officers and civil servants rendered further investigation impossible.

Naturally, the interim government's inaction on this issue led to vocal opposition. Demands for further investigation and trials grew daily. These came mainly from the communist parties.

There was, however, a major problem. How could government officers or even cabinet members be held responsible in a political system where the real power lay in the Palace? Every person interviewed by the Mallik Commission replied almost in unison that they had only obeyed orders from above. The word for this, 'mathi', was repeated over and over again. Even Achut Kharel, the man believed to be responsible for the fate of many missing persons—persons last heard of within the premises of the Police Training Centre in North Kathmandu—shrugged and answered that he had only, 'followed the order of the "mathi".' Needless to say, none of these orders had ever found their way into print. It would be fair to say, therefore, that the greatest hindrance to people being brought to trial was probably the Palace. One human rights activist complained: 'No political force is interested in confronting the Palace.' Because of that, he insisted, it was impossible to find out the truth and who the true culprits were.

This situation begged the question: why were politicians unwilling to confront the Palace after the King had given up all his power? What was there to fear? One political activist stated: 'It is a question of balance among the three political forces left over by the revolution—the Nepali Congress, the Communists and the Palace. The Congress is now trying to bring the Palace nearer to them.'

During the summer and autumn of 1990, two distinct trends became obvious as the interim government's term of office continued: the Nepali Congress's quest for normalization and communist dissatisfaction. Ex-panchas had begun to flock into the ranks of the Nepali Congress from the very first day after the revolution. Six months later the ex-panchas actually outnumbered the original number of Congress members. At the same time, Krishna Prasad Bhattarai continued to steer a course of tolerance and reconciliation. Many people objected to this—especially the communists. They wanted action taken against the old centres of power such as the Palace and certain sections of government administration. The communists had a dual complaint. They complained that they had been allotted a minor role in the interim government and they complained that the Prime Minister was not being tough enough. Several communist parties began organizing public protests—even though these same parties were still involved in the interim government. It was clear by now that a split between the Congress and the communists would come sooner or later.

As already mentioned, Padma Ratna Tuladhar pointed out that this split was inevitable. It was already apparent in the settlement which brought about the end of the revolution. 'The Communists wanted the Panchayat government and the Palace to surrender totally, but they were in a dilemma. They couldn't afford a split with the Nepali Congress which would damage the base of the popular movement.

They were therefore forced to accept compromise and, as a result of this unhappy settlement, we still have many problems.'

Unfortunately this split when it came meant the end of consensus and the beginning of open political rivalry. One student leader expressed her frustration: 'Before the Congress Student Association worked openly and the Communist Student Group worked underground—but we always took part in each other's activities. This is not the situation any longer. Instead the Communists boycott every initiative coming from the Nepali Congress and vice versa. But who can blame us students? Even in the cabinet the Nepali Congress and Communists are fighting each other. The present government has not been able to do anything, because there is virtual stalemate in the cabinet between the Congress, the Communists and the Panchayat ministers.'

This political stalemate was probably what made the political vacuum after the revolution so apparent. What happened was that all kinds of social, political, economic and cultural groups suddenly came out into the open to fight for their own cause. The government, with its hands tied, left these groups undisturbed to fight. This ongoing tussle remained a disruptive element in the normal functioning of Nepali society.

Freedom: A Call For Further Revolution

The political change which swept through Nepal during the spring of 1990 did not only lead to a partial breakdown in law and order and to social unrest. The pro-Democracy movement actually released another, potentially stronger movement which threatened the very fabric of Nepali society. This second movement took the form of a religious and ethnic revolt.

The six-month period between the end of the revolution in May 1990 and the promulgation of the new constitution on 11 November brought the issues of language, religion and ethnic conflict to public attention.

Warnings about this had been given even before the revolution had begun. Speaking on 16 February 1990, two days before the movement was launched, Madan Mani Dikshit, editor of the weekly newspaper, *Samiksha*, said: 'Restoration of the multi-party system in this country naturally will weaken the authority of the monarch. The cultural and social backwardness of Nepal is such that it might lead to internal disintegration. See, we have more than 30-35 ethnic groups spread around the Himalayan mountains and even in the plains. We have several languages—at least three or four major languages and more than 50 dialects. Take the Magar community, for instance. That community is asserting its rights to organise on a community basis. They want a recognition of their language. They want a recognition of their script— recognition of their worklife and economy. Other groups are demanding the same thing. The argument from the partyless side has been that the people are united because the King is there. Otherwise, under the multi-party system the elections will demand that they exploit these ethnic divisions and linguistic differences as has taken place in India.'

It certainly became clear that Nepal with its thirty ethnic different groups and almost a hundred different languages might not remain satisfied with one national language, Nepali, and one national religion, Hinduism. Many Nepalis began to worry that the strife caused by communalism in India might one day spread to Nepal. There was some cause for worry. Nearly every week during this unstable period a new ethnic or regional party appeared, sworn to fight the political and economic domination by the high-caste Hindus.

At the same time, the position of the Hindu religion in the new constitution came to be questioned. The communists naturally wanted a secular state. Minority religious groups such as Christians and Muslims suddenly became visible in public life. More importantly, Buddhists made themselves felt as a political force for the first time. This emergence of a new Buddhist consciousness was quite unexpected. Previously, Buddhists in Nepal had been reckoned a kind of sect within Hinduism and their interests were seen as no different from the Hindu majority. The appearance of religious conflict worried orthodox Hindus who were influenced by the spread of Hindu fundamentalism in India.

What brought this new religious conflict out into the open was, strangely enough, caused neither by the communists, the Hindus nor the Buddhists. What happened was that the Nepal Christian Fellowship held the first ever public meeting in Nepal on 7 May 1990. The Christians were a small group, dating back only forty years. They were also a harassed group. It was illegal to change religion under the old Panchayat constitution and there were still several Christians serving prison sentences because of their religious convictions.

Christians speaking at this public meeting called for minority rights in the light of new democratic freedom. They also called for the release of all religious prisoners and for a secular state.

Besides Christians, human rights activists were present at the meeting. Also present was the Congress leader, Mashal Julum Shakya, Minister for Transportation and Physical Construction in the interim government, and the Supreme Leader of the Nepali Congress, Ganesh Man Singh. All of them expressed sympathy with the Christian community. They too had been persecuted under the Panchayat regime and they, too, supported the Christian demands for religious freedom.

A few days later, the remaining religious prisoners were released. In the weeks that followed, communist leaders and members of the interim cabinet publicly declared their belief that Nepal should become a secular state.

Many Hindus took fright at this. Reaction was strong to the proposal, especially in the press. Commenting on the release of religious prisoners, the weekly newspaper, *Bimarsa*, wrote on 15 June that, 'the state has thus become secular even before the framing of the new constitution. Followers of the Hindu religion are now feeling frightened lest the influence of Christians should increase.' The World Hindu Federation, which had received royal patronage and enjoyed strong support from the Panchayat regime, was scathing. In an article in the *Gorkha Patra*, the Federation complained that the release of religious prisoners, 'had undermined the rule of law and hurt the feelings of ninety-five per cent of the Nepali people as well as millions throughout the world.'

Thus the debate on secularism grew—though attention soon shifted away from the Christian community. More and more groups demanded a secular state and correspondingly the reactions from conservative Hindus became even stronger. One of the royal nominees to the interim cabinet, Achut Raj Regmi, declared that if the new constitution did not include provisions to retain Nepal's status as a Hindu state then he personally would stage a hunger strike at the gates of Pashupatinath, the main Hindu shrine in Kathmandu. The moderately conservative newspaper, *Motherland*, criticized the interim government's inability to handle the confict and wrote in an editorial on 26 June: 'Quite obviously very strong emotions have been aroused with the government itself taking up the question of secularism when practice was that the Hindu State tolerated the observances of any religion with remarkable co-existence and a fault-free history of mutual respect.' The newspaper went on to comment about the conflict between the Buddhists and Hindus: 'It is unfortunate thus that for the first time since Shankaracharya's epochal journey to the Valley nearly a millennium ago, Buddhism is being made distinct from Nepali Hinduism, something that only politics can explain and not logic in Nepal.'

Such attempts to smooth over the situation were in vain. The conflict had now spread too far. On 29 June, a protest of 5-6,000 people emerged form the gates of Pashupatinath and walked silently through the streets of Kathmandu. They held up an image of Lord Krishna in front of their procession and flourished banners with slogans such as 'Unity and Diversity—the Basic Characteristic of Hinduism' and 'We want a Hindu nation'. The following day, the largest demonstration since the revolution took place, organized by the Nepal Buddhist Association—25-30,000 people—walked through the centre of Kathmandu urging, 'Give us a Secular State. Buddhism is not just a branch of Hinduism.' This march, too, ended up at the open-air theatre at Tundikhel in the middle of Kathmandu. Several Buddhist scholars addressed the crowd including Bhikshu Amritananda. In his address he deplored the notion that Hinduism and Buddhism were the same and called strongly for a secular state. The speeches emphasized how Buddhism in Nepal had been suppressed. Speakers pointed out the differences between Hinduism and Buddhism—differences such as Hindu violence and Buddhist non-violence.

The Buddhist demonstration came as a total shock. Most Nepali politicians were Hindus and not at all vocal about their religion. To them Buddhism had just appeared as another kind of Hinduism. The Buddhist demonstration spurred even the moderate and rather traditional Nepali Congress to discuss secularism seriously.

On 6 July, Congress stated publicly that the party had no official position on whether Nepal should remain a Hindu state or become secular. Their only demand was that the King should remain a Hindu. The compromise did nothing to quell the mounting fervour of the conservative Hindus. On 11 August the leader of the Indian Bharatiya Janata Party, even travelled to Nepal to pressurize the interim government into retaining the country as a Hindu state. That same day, Achut Raj Regmi, a member of the interim government, said: 'Any person who ignores the feelings of the Hindus, who comprise ninety-five per cent of the people in Nepal, and says that Nepal should not be a Hindu state is not only an enemy of democracy, but a despot.' At a public meeting in connection with the Hindu festival, Krishna Janamashtami, the birthday of Lord Krishna, Regmi urged the Nepali Hindus to take to the streets and fight for a Hindu kingdom. 'We must fight for the continuation of a Hindu state!' he declared.

While Regmi may seem extremist, his background was actually liberal. He had been a member of the Nepali Congress Party, but later became part of the Panchayat system where he, in his own words, 'propagated parliamentary democracy'. The 1990 revolution brought him into the public eye. First he was part of Lokendra Bahadur Chand's short-lived ministry and then the King nominated him to the interim cabinet. Regmi was a founder member of the Hindu World Federation. He was also active in the Pashupati Development Trust. This was an organization which served as a focus for conservative Hindus. As the Queen was an active member, the Pashupati Development Trust was closely linked to the centre of power in Kathmandu. Religion, however, was more important to Regmi than politics. The walls of his house were covered with pictures of Hindu saints and his morning puja took more than an hour. He tried in every way to live as a strict, orthodox Brahmin.

Regmi argued that his strong desire to see Nepal remain a Hindu kingdom had more to do with culture than with politics or religion. He argued that Nepali culture was Hinduism. 'Hinduism and religion are different' he stressed. 'Hinduism is a culture, a nationality. There are so many religions inside Hinduism, Jain, Sikhism and also Buddhism are all part of Hindu culture. There are so many systems of worshipping God. Even within orthodox traditional Hinduism there are so many sects—some worship Vishnu, some worship the goddess Durga, Ganesh and so many others. To declare a Hindu state does not therefore mean a religious state—it means declaring a Hindu culture. Ninety-five per cent of the people believe in some way or another in Hindu culture and Hindu spirituality. That's why we need a Hindu state. There was no constitution at the time of the Rana regime and Nepal was called a Hindu state. That is why if you delete the word "Hindu" from the constitution ninety-five per cent of the people of Nepal will feel cheated.'

When asked about the Buddhist opposition, Regmi answered: 'They do not understand that if Nepal succumbs to secularism even their Buddhism will be punished.' Regmi saw secularism as something sinister coming from abroad—especially from India. He believed it was espoused by politicians who were bent on destroying Nepali culture. Regarding the communist call for a secular state Regmi laughed: 'Not even their wives support them in this.'

Though Regmi was a religious man and genuinely believed in religious freedom his views were, to some extent, connected with political power. As a high-caste Brahmin, Regmi himself was part of the élite who had occupied a privileged position precisely because

Nepal was a Hindu state. If the new constitution were to make Nepal a secular country this might directly challenge the high-caste Hindus' traditional hold on power.

Yet where did opposition to the Hindus come from? According to the official census the Buddhist population of Nepal was less than twenty per cent of the entire country. Moreover, the Buddhists had a reputation for living peaceably—almost invisibly—alongside the Hindus. It appeared to be the case that Hinduism and Buddhism in Nepal were simply indistinguishable. It was a fact, however, that the official census was misleading. Dubious measures had been used to try and show that the Hindus were by far the majority in Nepal. Dr Asha Ram Sakya, a Buddhist scholar and leader of the Nepal Buddhist Association, explained: 'In the 1981 census the Buddhist population was shown as 5.3 million. This is totally wrong. Tamangs were never Hindus—the Gurungs were never Hindus, nor the Sherpas, nor the Chepangs, nor the Rais, nor the Limbus of Eastern Nepal. In addition there are minor nationalities who are all Buddhists. In reality the Buddhists of Nepal are a majority. We are more than seventy per cent of the population. The problem was that most of the Buddhists of Nepal are not educated. When the census officers arrive they would not ask about their religion—they would ask "Do you worship Ganesh?" They would answer "Yes" and because Ganesh is a Hindu God they would be written down as Hindus. But in Nepal Hindus worship Buddha and Buddhists worship Ganesh. That does not mean that all are Hindus. It is a result of the long cultural intermingling and interaction between Hindus and Buddhists. And it does not mean that Buddhism is just a branch of Hinduism, which the previous government claimed.'

If it was the case that the vast majority of Nepal's Buddhists were not even conscious of their own religion, a small, but growing group of intellectuals like Asha Ram Sakya were attempting to reclaim their cultural and religious identity as Buddhists. These people saw Buddhism as providing an alternative ideology to the Brahminical Hinduism supported by the Panchayat government.

Sakya related how he had been born and brought up in a Buddhist *Vihara* in Patan. This was a Buddhist monastery which, throughout the centuries of Hindu domination, had become a sanctuary for a separate caste of Buddhist priests. Sakya explained that the Buddhist rituals had survived in this community—only there was no one to explain them. On inheriting his duties as a Buddhist priest from his father, Sakya decided that he wanted to study Buddhism. When he did so he found that he discovered something very different from Hinduism. 'It looked like a revolt against Hinduism—because Buddha never appreciated Brahmins and the division of people into four major groups.' Suddenly, Sakya claimed, he found that Buddhism was 'a modern religion for modern man.' According to Sakya, in a way Buddha 'supported a multi-party system' and said: 'Don't blindly follow—listen and analyse.' Sakya's position as a political activist and lecturer at the university in Kathmandu had also led him to believe that Buddhism was more important for Nepal's national identity than Hinduism. 'If Buddhism is taken away there is nothing. Nepal may just as well beome a part of India.'

Sakya's comment on the position of Buddists under the Ranas was: 'Under Rana rule they were repressed and subjugated. They have always been suppressed, but the Buddhists, tolerant as they are, meekly accepted what they were given. But they never accepted that Buddhism was a part of Hinduism.' Sakya totally rejected the popular view that Buddhists lived in harmony under their Hindu rulers: 'If Hindu suppression is what you call harmony,' he said distastefully, 'I would rather not have it!'

Naturally enough, Sakya became involved in fighting for Buddhist rights after the revolution of 1990. He was firm in demanding that Nepal become a secular state. 'All we wanted was the state to be secular,' he said. 'The state should have no religion—this is a universal law. Theocratic states have seen thousands of people being massacred every day. Look at Saddam Hussein—and you remember what Khomeini did, killing his own people in millions. And you see what has happened in Sri Lanka! It is all because of religion! Now if they don't say the constitution is secular we don't mind. But let the constitution be silent on religion. Let there be full freedom of religion.'

The communists were, of course, completely committed to Nepal becoming a secular state. Yet it was not only the communists, the Buddhists or the minority religious groups who believed in the benefits of secularism. In the weeks that followed the revolution, all the new democratic politicians and the intellectuals in Kathmandu seemed strongly in favour of a secular state. At that stage it seemed fairly certain that the new constitution would not make any reference to Hinduism continuing as the state religion of Nepal. The succeedng months, however, brought a wind of change.

There were many strong forces at work which aimed to keep Nepal as a Hindu kingdom. While some figures, such as Achut Raj Regmi, were public in their efforts—many of these forces worked stealthily and steadily underground. A large number of people believed that elements of the old regime were at work and that even the Palace was involved. By early September 1990, the mood in Nepal had changed to the extent that no one now believed the new constitution would be wholly secular. Many still hoped, however, that it would not prove as rigid on the question of religion as the previous Panchayat constitution had been.

Why then were the conservative Hindus able to gain the upper hand? How was it that events turned out in their favour?

One reason was that Hinduism was still a potent force in Nepali society, even in 1990. Ever since King Prithvi Narayan Shah had united the country in 1768, Hinduism had been the state religion. With the caste laws, the *Muluki Ain*, introduced by Jang Bahadur Rana in the middle of the nineteenth century, the Hindu social order had been the main means of governing the country. Put bluntly, Hinduism was in people's blood. Even so, Rana Hinduism was never state-sanctioned fundamentalism. Furthermore, Hinduism was only brought into the constitution of Nepal in the Panchayat constitution of 1962. Then its inclusion had seemed purely political to benefit the interests of a small élite in Nepali society. Rishikesh Shaha, one of the main advisers on the Panchayat constitution, described the debate at the time: 'Then came the question of calling Nepal a Hindu kingdom. I said, look, we've already said the King is going to be a Hindu. There is no point in rubbing it in. There are Muslims, Buddhists, Shaivites—all kinds of people. We have to be modern. We have to follow this secular state policy. King Mahendra made me discuss this proposition for the whole night and I convinced him. But unfortunately his sycophants in the cabinet were saying "Oh, we must have that" and then it was put in again.' Rishikesh Shaha then related how he had discussed exactly the same issue with King Birendra after the 1990 revolution: 'I told the King,' he said, 'look, do you want religious fundamentalism? I told your father King Mahendra the same thing and persuaded him not to put this thing in even at that time. Was not Nepal a Hindu country before 1962, although there were no references to that in the previous constitutions? So why should you have this? It will only have the effect of rubbing people up the wrong way. Now you see what the Buddhists are doing and the tribals and other groups. So I told the King to keep religion separate from the state, not to mix religion with politics.' Rishikesh Shaha's insistence was of no avail. The forces at work to maintain Nepal as a Hindu state were too strong.

This religious dispute was also linked to ethnic and communal questions. The six month period between the end of the revolution and the announcement of the new constitution saw the beginnings of some resistance to traditional high-caste Hindu domination in Nepal. Ever since King Prithvi Narayan Shah's reign in the eighteenth century the Nepali speaking Hindu high-castes had dominated the remainder of the population. In order to maintain their social position the high caste groups had used two powerful tools—the Nepali language and the Hindu religion. The ruling élite successfully incorporated all the ethnic groups in Nepal into the caste system and these groups came to accept a subordinate position as a direct result of this policy. It was not surprising, therefore, that these same ethnic groups were the last in Nepal to enjoy the benefits of modernization.

The months after the revolution, however, gave birth to new ethnically and communally based political parties and signalled that at last these Tibeto-Burmese peoples were ready to protest against the centuries-long rule of the Brahmins and the Chetris. The President of one of these new parties, the Nepal Rashtriya Jana Mukti Morcha (the Nepal National People's Liberation Front), said in an interview to the *Nepali Patra* on 7 September 1990: 'In Nepal Hinduism or Brahminism has been maintaining religious, political and social domination. Hindus have maintained a respectable status as the ruling class in every situation, such as Rana rule, Panchayat rule and the democratic period—whereas the other ethnic groups have always remained exploited and repressed. The Brahmins want to restrict us within their own narrow limits. It is therefore the goal of our party to organize the ethnic groups who have been left backward in the political, social and religious field. The Front does not oppose any prosperous ethnic groups, although it opposes their repression.'

This new ethnic movement focused on the questions of religion and language. It started among the Newari people of the Kathmandu valley. The Newaris were a Tibeto-Burmese people with a language of their own and possessed the oldest literary tradition in Nepal. With their complex mixture of Hindu, Buddhist and Tantric rituals and beliefs, the Newaris have maintained cultural and religious traditions which have disappeared from other parts of Asia. The Nwaris were, in fact, more of a nation than an ethnic group. It was true that a certain stratum of Newari society had held positions of privilege in Nepal, ranking only behind the Brahmins and the Chetris. It was also true, however, that Newari culture and language had been suppressed. A movement for the recognition of the Newari language had actually started after the 1951 revolution. During the 1950s Newari, together with Hindi, had enjoyed the status of semi-official languages in Nepal. This was recognized in the daily news broadcasts in both Newari and Hindi during that period. In 1957 there was even a brief debate as to whether Newari should be made the national language of Nepal.

King Mahendra's royal coup and the introduction of the Panchayat system put an end to all this. From then on Nepali was made the sole official language and the only medium of education in the country. Newari was not banned, as during the Rana period, but it was reduced to being only an optional subject at university level.

Thirty years later the Newaris resurged in the 1990 revolution. The uprisings in Patan, Bhaktapur and Kirtipur in the Kathmandu valley were crucial in determining the success of the pro-Democracy movement. Padma Ratna Tuladhar pointed out that these uprisings were not communal. They were aimed at bringing about freedom and democracy at a national level. Many of the Newari political leaders, however, were active in trying to push forward the cause of the Newari language. This was not done to the exclusion of all other languages in Nepal, but rather to try and force the central government to recognize the linguistic diversity within the country. Comrade Rohit from Bhaktapur, a writer as well as a politician, said: 'Nepal is just like a garden with a rich variety of flowers. Every ethnic group and caste has its own unique culture and art. The product of this is a rich and diverse natural culture. Therefore one should encourage the development of each one of these cultures and languages as they are there to improve the quality of life for the people.'

When Radio Nepal resumed news broadcasts in Newari and Hindi on 29 June 1990, therefore, political leaders like Rohit were not satisfied. Padma Ratna Tuladhar who was Chairman of the Newari language organization, the Nepal Basha Manka Khala, had become outspoken about the need for using mother tongues in Nepal's schools. He pointed out that most of the ethnic groups in Nepal were deprived of their basic right to develop their own mother tongue, in contrast to the relatively privileged Newari community: 'So far as the Newars are concerned,' he said, 'because they are the dwellers of the capital, Kathmandu, and they have been a very cultured race, they have such facilities as education, training and so on, and they can enjoy facilities in administration. Now, you see, we have so many ethnic groups besides these three—the Brahmins, Chetris and Newars, and almost all of these have been neglected. They have been deprived of such opportunities. So first of all now we must recognize that Nepal has so many ethnic groups, so many languages and accept that all these people are equal. And then the government should offer equal opportunities in education. We have no education system where the mother tongue is the medium. Nepali is the medium in education, even in primary education—and we have a huge population who do not know the Nepali language from the very beginning. Only when the different ethnic groups get education in their own mother tongue will they get access to other facilities—and only then can they say that all the ethnic groups have equal rights in our country—in jobs, administration posts and so on.' Padma Ratna Tuladhar continued: 'The first priority of the new government should be to solve this problem democratically. I'm requesting the political parties to raise the question, because only through political and democratic means can we have an amicable solution to this problem.' He warned that: 'If this is not solved democratically and politically, the people may go communal. Once such a problem turns into communalism we may have a very bad situation in the country. We have so many instances in India where they fought each other for language, religion and so on.... But in Nepal, even though almost all the languages have been deprived of democratic rights, we have had no communal riots.' Tuladhar was critical of both the communists and the Nepali Congress: 'They must understand that in a democracy the people have a right to come openly and demand their rights for languages, ethnic equality and so on. Meeting these demands must be made an integral part of our political movement.' Tuladhar did not believe that the new ethnic parties in Nepal were reactionary: 'This is only the natural and healthy result of democracy.'

Despite the importance of religion and language, much of this movement was actually concerned with economic and political power. The first political party to be established after the revolution was the Nepal National People's Liberation Front. The party was established by representatives from the Tibeto-Burmese hill population of Nepal. Its programme was to fight for equality for all the racial and ethnic groups in the country. On 25 June the Party's general secretary handed over a memorandum to the Constitution Recommendation Commission demanding equal rights for these communities.

A more extreme party was the Jana Jati Party established on 19 August 1990 and led by Khagendra Jang Gurung, a seasoned politician. In addition, several other organizations sprang up all putting forward demands on behalf of the Tibeto-Burmese peoples. Among these, was the Nepal Tamang Bhada Ghendung, established in Kathmandu on 7 June. This group demanded a special constitutional recognition of the Tamang community who lived in the hills around the Kathmandu valley. Although the Tamangs were numerous, they were amongst the least privileged of all the ethnic groups in Nepal. Later another group, the Mongol National Organization, at a mass meeting in the Ilam District in Eastern Nepal on 6 November declared provocatively that: 'We are not Hindus. We are determined to establish a Mongol state in Nepal.'

These various organizations represented a spectrum of opinion ranging from the extreme to the moderate. Yet they all shared certain basic common concerns. The Tibeto-Burmese people were linguistically and racially different from the Hindu high-castes. These groups made up a large section of Nepal's population—possibly even the majority. Even so, the Hindu élite had suppressed and controlled them for several hundred years. The caste label for them was 'Matwali', meaning 'the alcohol-drinking castes'. They were given a position below twice-born Hindus (those entitled to read the Vedic scripts and wear the sacred thread), but still well above the untouchables. Most of them did not practice Hinduism, but rather a mixture of Buddhism and Shaivism. They also possessed a fairly egalitarian social structure amongst themselves.

Their integration into Hindu society varied greatly from group to group. The Magars, for example, reckoned themselves as proper Hindus, while the Tamangs claimed that they were Buddhists. The Limbus in eastern Nepal had managed to preserve large parts of their native religion and culture. They even possessed their own written alphabet. Economically speaking, these groups were also very different. The Gurungs, Magars, Limbus and Rais had prospered through serving in the Gurkha regiments. Recruitment to the Gurkhas was actually restricted to these four large ethnic groups. The Tamangs were not eligible to join the Gurkhas and so had remained cut off from a major source of income. In addition to these were the Thakalis, who were a small group. These people had made a good living on the main trade

route to Tibet. In recent years they had gone into the tourist trade with
marked success.

Though they were varied, these different groups united when it
came to political grievances. Ghore Bahadur Khapangi, General
Secretary of the Nepal National People's Liberation Front, summed up
Tibeto-Burmese feeling by saying: 'I have been deprived of all my
political rights in this country just because I am a Magar. That is what I
rebel against.' This ethnic issue was what forced Khapangi to break
with the other political organizations he had previously been involved
with—the Teachers' Association and the United National Democratic
Forum. He explained: 'My main conflict with the forum and the Nepali
Congress and the Communists had to do with the position of all the
castes and tribes in the country. I said that all organisations, institutions
and political parties should have proportional representation reflecting
the size of various ethnic and caste groups in the population as a whole.
The leadership of the political parties, however, should be elected
irrespective of nationality or caste. I started raising these opinions, but
nobody accepted my position. As a consequence I had to leave.' The
National People's Liberation Front was founded to do something about
this issue. 'Our main goal,' Khapangi went on to say, 'is to bring the
exploited groups of Nepal into positions of power, the so-called
"Matwalis". We want to change the relationship between the
high-castes, whom we call the Taghadaris ("those who wear the sacred
thread") and the other groups, the Atagadharis. We want the two
groups to work together and share power. We have no wish to throw
the high-castes out and dominate them instead. The only way for us to
come to power is through proportional representation and a federal type
of government.' Khapangi complained that what needed to be changed
was the situation of inequality upheld even by the new democratic
government. 'The present government is not only a class government,
but a caste government. In other words, the Brahmins dominate
everything: universities, governments and so on—and they form the
majority everywhere.' Khapangi noted how the pro-Democracy
movement had actually been led by Brahmins and Chetris. He claimed
that once in power these leaders had forgotten all about the
Tibeto-Burmese peoples and had even made life worse for them by,

'stopping those going to Hong Kong and Singapore on business.' The government, it has to be said, called this business 'smuggling'.

The suppression of these groups, however, also occurred at a deeper level and was closely linked to religion. Khapangi stated: 'In the name of Hinduism we have lost our whole identity, language, culture—everything is theirs. Therefore all castes and communities should not be forced to call themselves Hindus. Up till 1964 our country was governed by caste laws. Those who opposed Hinduism were thrown into jail. These caste laws have destroyed our identity.'

An obvious question was why these Tibeto-Burmese peoples, with a worldwide reputation for strength and bravery, had not rebelled earlier. 'The main answer to this has to do with our knowledge,' said Khapangi. 'Our people have no sense of our own history. We even lack self-respect.' Within Nepal, he said: '...we are still not accepted as proper citizens. Wherever we travel abroad we are the Gurkhas. As such we are respected and revered, and we are even awarded the Victoria Cross and the Queen of England shakes our hands. But once we come back to Nepal we are only the Mathwalis, the "fools". We have absolutely no "ijjat"—respect. Even peons will abuse us.' There were aspects of this problem which Khapangi felt would take a long time to disappear: 'They call us the Magar Jati—this means that we cannot wear the sacred thread, nor touch the food and water of the high castes. We are slowly trying to do away with this "jati" term, but it will take a long time.' Khapangi also mentioned that there were certain subtleties in the relations between high-caste Hindus and these groups which were difficult for outsiders to appreciate: 'To understand us you have to understand that our thoughts, our culture, our behaviour is totally different from the Brahmins and the Chetris. If we don't agree with what you say we will just sit quiet and listen and eventually go away. We don't have the education or the vocabulary to disagree or discuss.' Khapangi finished by saying: 'My main personal political goal is to prove that even a Magar can become Prime Minister of Nepal.'

Some members of the Tibeto-Burmese groups, however, had enjoyed positions of privilege and status within Nepali society. One was Khagendra Jang Gurung, President of the more extreme ethnic party, the Jana Jati Party. He was an important leader from the Gurung community in Manang close to the Tibetan border. Both before and after the introduction of the Panchayat system he had served as a cabinet minister. His career had been stormy, moving from government to jail to exile and back again.

Khagendra Jang Gurung had formed an especially close relationship with King Mahendra who had used him to make the first contacts with China. The Mongol groups, of which Khagendra Jang Gurung was a member, were geographically and culturally closer to China than India. King Mahendra had promised them special rights and internal autonomy as a way of forging friendship with the Chinese government. Khagendra Jang Gurung said, however: 'Promises given by the Brahmins and Chetris to our communities were not met.' He resigned in protest as a minister in the Panchayat government and was imprisoned shortly afterwards for seven years.

Khagendra Jang Gurung had always been single-minded about his political goals. 'Autonomous states for the different ethnic groups' was what he demanded. But he did not trust the government in Kathmandu: 'They promise us one thing, but they give us the opposite,' he stated. 'There is a saying in Nepali: "The tiger always kills the deer, even if it is yellow and white". This means that their behaviour is always the same, whether they are Communist, Congress or for the King. They are never genuinely interested in helping us. They only want to preserve power for themselves—for the Brahmins and the Chetris.'

The government's indifference had made Khagendra Jang Gurung confrontationist. His party, the Jana Jati Party, went much further than the Nepal National People's Liberation Front in its demands. According to Gurung, the latter party was only interested in, 'expanding the job opportunities for the Tibeto-Burmese people.' Khagendra Jang Gurung spread out a map of Nepal showing the country split into a dozen ethnic regions or states. 'We want separate administration in our own areas,' he said. 'We want our own parliament, our cabinet, and we only want contact with the central government in connection with foreign policy and security. We want full freedom!' He further stated that: 'Unless our demands are met peacefully we will take up arms and start a more bloody revolution.'

Khagendra Jang Gurung's remarks made little impression on the political élite in Kathmandu. Most of them did not take him seriously; some thought he was in alliance with reactionary elements of the old regime who only wanted to create problems for the new interim government. All agreed that Khagendra Jang Gurung was not the man to start an armed revolt or a civil war. But by ignoring him, the politicians in Kathmandu closed their eyes to important political developments outside the Kathmandu valley, especially in the eastern part of the country. The Rais and Limbus had a reputation for being restless. They were the least Sanskritized of the major Tibeto-Burmese groups—that is, they had been least affected by the imposition of Hindu culture and the Nepali language. The Limbus especially had never accepted being governed by the Hindu high castes in Kathmandu. The years following the 1951 revolution had been marked by political unrest and violence in this region. Many ex-Gurkha servicemen were involved in the incidents which took place. The period following the 1990 revolution was also disturbed—but the events which took place were more political and less violent than previously.

On 21 June 1990 Gopal Gurung, chairman of the National Mongol Organization, demanded that power be restored to the Limbus in accordance with the treaty signed by King Prithvi Narayan Shah and the Limbu King. Gurung wanted the restoration of Limbuwan which had been a semi-independent principality until 1909. This demand was followed by several demonstrations and protests in eastern Nepal.

In effect, Kathmandu ignored the Limbus. While the Limbus and Rais had made a strong impression in 1952-53, their demands now merged into the welter of protests from all the other ethnic groups, castes and communities in Nepal.

It seemed that nearly every caste, linguistic group or ethnic community raised its voice in one way or another in the six months between the end of the revolution and the announcement of the new constitution. Even groups such as the Tharus in the Terai, the Tamangs and the Hindu low castes—underprivileged groups who had never been politically active before—organized themselves.

It remained to be seen whether these new organizations would go on to enjoy mass support or whether they would just wither and disappear after a short time. No one seemed certain if they had arisen as a result of a genuine popular movement, or whether they were being manipulated by a small group of individuals who wished to exploit the new democratic freedom to build up their own power base.

Meanwhile a potentially more serious regional conflict appeared to be emerging between the Terai and the hills. There were several reasons why this particular division was more worrying than that between the Tibeto-Burmese peoples and the Hindu high-castes.

In contrast to the Tibeto-Burmese peoples who were spread across the whole hill region, the population of the Terai was concentrated in one well-defined geographical area: the flat land to the south which formed part of the Gangetic plain. The élite in Kathmandu still viewed the Terai as something of a hinterland, though they were well aware that the main part of Nepal's agricultural and industrial wealth was to be found there. Despite steady immigration from the hill regions in the 1970s and 1980s the majority of the Terai people retained strong cultural and linguistic links with India. In effect, the Terai dwellers were identical to the inhabitants of the two neighbouring Indian states, Bihar and Uttar Pradesh. The languages and dialects used in the Terai were the same—Bhojpuri, Avadi, Rajbansi and Maithili—and the different groups used Hindi as a common link language. There was an open border between the two countries because of political agreements between Nepal and India. This meant that there was a continual free flow of people back and forth and inter-marriage between Nepalis and Indians was common. The closeness of the Terai region to India gave many in Kathmandu cause for concern. Several people warned that if a conflict were to develop in the region then Nepal could turn into another Sri Lanka. The fear of a regional uprising, however, did not cause the politicians in Kathmandu undue concern. After a brief period in the 1950s when Hindi enjoyed the status of a semi-official language in Nepal and the people of the Terai were encouraged to participate in public affairs, there was a clamp-down. The Panchayat government recognized only Nepali as the national language and the hill Brahmins' culture was actively promoted as the dominant one within Nepal. People from the Terai were discriminated against when they applied for government jobs. Moreover, the electoral constituencies were drawn to ensure that the hill people were the majority in as many places as possible. The 1990 revolution did not change this situation. Accordingly, when Gajendra Narayan Singh, President of the Nepal Sadbhavana Party, the Nepal Goodwill Party, which represented the interests of the Terai people, said in the autumn of 1990 that he would fight discrimination against the Terai people—there was a general feeling that the government's policy as regards the Terai had backfired. Singh said: 'The Terai people were neglected. They have neither been treated as Hindus nor as Nepalis. We have always been called Madeshis (the inhabitants of the plains) and treated as second-rate citizens. All the Terai people, whether they are Muslims or Hindus are treated as Madeshis. The ruling people in Kathmandu have always discriminated against us. We will now fight against this and remove this social and political, economical, cultural and linguistic suppression.'

Unlike the Tibeto-Burmese peoples there was a tradition of a political party which represented the interests of the Terai. The Terai Congress Party had several representatives in the short-lived democratic government of 1959. The new movement led by Gajendra Narayan Singh was less gentle and more regional. Singh demanded regional autonomy and linguistic equality: 'Our party has two main political goals,' he said. 'One is that Hindi should be recognized as an official language in the same way as Nepali, Hindi being the link language between all the groups of the Terai just as Nepali is among the Hill people, and that Nepal should be divided into five provinces and federal government encouraged.' More specifically, Gajendra Narayan Singh wanted the hills divided into three provinces—the Eastern Hills, the Central Hills and the Western Hills. Similarly, he believed that the Terai should be divided into eastern and western Terai.

This movement among the Terai people actually started at the time of the referendum in 1980. What sparked it off was the question of citizenship rights. According to Gajendra Narayan Singh, when the Panchayat government began a campaign to distribute citizenship certificates in the Terai in 1976 conditions were such that two-thirds of the Terai population were deemed ineligible. The resulting dispute forced Gajendra Narayan Singh to leave the Congress Party, which he had been active in for many years, and led him to devote all his energy to fighting for the Terai people. The Nepal Sadbhavana Parishad began as a non-political organization set up to campaign for citizenship rights for the Terai people. In 1985 Gajendra Narayan Singh was elected to the Rashtriya Panchayat. His main concern was the citizenship issue and he said: 'I managed to convince the government that they should show more concern to this problem and teams were sent to every village in the Terai in the late eighties to distribute new citizenship certificates.'

This question remained a burning one as far as the Terai people were concerned, so much so that the Sadbhavana Parishad was turned into a political party. Gajendra Narayan Singh became its first President and 2,000 people attended a general conference at the Terai town of Janakpur dham on 29 June 1990. Gajendra Narayan Singh declared: 'At least twenty per cent of the Terai population have still not been given citizenship although they've always lived in the country. They are looked upon as Indians although they have always lived within the borders of Nepal.'

Many Nepalis still worried about the loyalty of Gajendra Narayan Singh and the Nepal Sadbhavana Party. How patriotic were they? There were rumours that the Nepal Sadbhavana Party was financed and steered by India. Gajendra Narayan Singh, now in his sixties and clad in a dhoti kurta, was something of a mystery. Singh himself rejected the many allegations against him. 'I'm trying my best for the uplifting of the socio-economic condition of the Terai people and their ethnic languages. All these endeavours are not digestible to the hill Gorkhali communities, so they are spinning out such untrue propaganda. Nepal is my country. I was born in Nepal. My ancestors were born in Nepal and they all died here. I've spent my whole life fighting for the development of this country. Politically I've been active since I was seventeen years of age, so I love this country a lot.'

Gajendra Narayan Singh's passion dissipated and he became rather vague when asked to define his Nepali identity in practical terms. He referred to the Nepal Sadbhavana Party and stressed that: 'We are not separatists. We do not on any account want to divide the country— rather we want to protect it. The only way this country can survive is by giving the Terai people their rightful demands through the governmental structure of a federal state.' These sentiments did little to relieve the fears of the Kathmandu intellectuals and politicians. Most of them hoped fervently that the Nepal Sadbhavana Party would turn out to be an extremist fringe party and would not enjoy any mass support.

The new regional, ethnic and religious movements which emerged after the 1990 revolution did come as a surprise to the political and intellectual élite in Kathmandu. Worry was mingled with genuine fear—even dread. One influential member of the old regime said: 'Everything can now happen. Nepal can become another Kampuchea, Afghanistan or Sri Lanka.' To most people, however, the demands put forward by these movements seemed quite reasonable. Many felt that these minority groups had honest grievances and were justified in organizing themselves politically. There was a general opinion that the new democratic government had an obligation to act and include all these groups fairly within the new political order. It seemed only sensible that Nepal's linguistic, ethnic and religious diversity should be reflected in the new democratic system. Arun Raj Joshi, a writer and journalist, summed up much of this opinion when he wrote in the English language newspaper, *Motherland*, on 11 July: 'Democracy will not be democracy if it will only continue to satisfy the demands of one segment of the population, even if that segment comprises the majority. Democracy, ideally at least, is a meta-system in which all systems, cultural and religious included, are given breathing space to explore and express their potential. In the new democratic set-up therefore, the state cannot patronise one religious system. This will not only have a negative impact on the growth and development of the favoured religion itself, but will also create a situation in which the state, which favours a particular religious segment, would not be trusted by many other segments who are not practising the same religion.'

Though the intellectuals in Kathmandu voiced liberal opinions and the religious and ethnic groups along with the communists pressed for a secular state, this position became a lost cause. When the new constitution was officially announced on 11 November 1990, it looked as if some compromise on this issue had been reached—but in practice the Hindu high-castes, the Brahmin élite and the Chetris had not budged at all. One reason why conservative Hindus had been so agitated may have been a deep-seated fear they had of conversion. A flood of Nepalis to another religion, probably Christianity, would have undermined the whole base and structure of Hindu society. Padma Ratna Tuladhar pointed out, however, that the main reason for the Hindu victory was the simple fact that Brahmins were in the majority in all the relevant political institutions. Either consciously or unconsciously they had put their own vested interests first. Tuladhar explained what had actually happened: 'The Constitution Recommendation Commission raised this question many times, as to whether there should be a secular state. There was serious discussion, although there was no agreement, but at one stage there was a compromise agreed. So it was written that Nepal is a multi-lingual, multi-racial, Hindu monarchical kingdom. That means that the King is Hindu, but not the kingdom. Then the draft constitution was discussed in the cabinet and the problem arose again. There was a division once again, but there was a domination of Hindus. We cannot say that they were all fundamentalists. We cannot charge them like that, but they held the majority. The majority were Brahmins and the cabinet could not support the draft constitution on this issue. There was also another problem. In the draft constitution there was a provision that there could be no amendment to the constitution regarding the multi-party system and the monarchy. The Communists were totally opposed to this, stating that when the constitution had accepted that sovereignty was with the people and not with the monarchy the people had every right to change any provision or clause of the constitution. So to reach a compromise on both these matters the cabinet accepted that a comma should be added in connection with the Hindu monarchy. In the previous draft there was no comma: it said that Nepal was a "Hindu monarchical kingdom" meaning that the monarchy is Hindu but not the kingdom. But because of this political compromise they added the comma after "Hindu" and the whole meaning was changed.'

In the new constitution therefore, Nepal remained a Hindu kingdom. Yet in contrast to the previous Panchayat constitution, the new constitution did recognize the existence of ethnic minorities. The new constitution still had a clause concerning conversion. Previously it had been illegal to change religion in Nepal—but now it was no longer an offence to convert, only to cause someone else to convert. This clause distinguished between the two Nepali words for the verb 'to do': 'garnu' and 'garaunu'.

There were negative reactions. Yet the instability surrounding the announcement of the new constitution probably rendered these milder than might otherwise have been the case just a couple of months earlier. On 17 November, just a few days after the announcement of the new constitution, the so-called Jana Jati groups, representing the interests of the Tibeto-Burmese peoples, staged a mass meeting at Tundikhel, the parade grounds in the centre of Kathmandu. This meeting condemned the new constitution. A week later the Nepal Sadbhavana Party also held a mass meeting at Tundikhel which degenerated into a clash and police had to intervene.

The real test for the new ethnic and regional parties came with the general election in May 1991. Apart from the Nepal Sadbhavana Party which won six seats, none of the other parties gained entry into parliament. This, naturally enough, produced a noticeable measure of relief in Kathmandu.

The 1990 revolution in Nepal had therefore paved the way for another revolution of a religious and ethnic nature but the interim period proved that this second revolution was still only potential. Nevertheless, warning bells had been sounded. Though the conflict had not come fully out into the open, there was a certain measure of fear for the future. As one Newari intellectual in Kathmandu put it—the Brahmins were in for an unpleasant surprise one of these days: 'The Brahmin clutch on our society is extremely strong,' he said, 'whether they are Communists, Congress or Panchas—they are all Brahmins. But they must be aware that the recent ethnic awakening is only the beginning. In the future ethnic rivalry will become prominent.'

The King And The People

The central pivot of Nepali politics during the modern period has been the King. All major political events in the country since the revolution of 1951 have been to some degree, centred on the role of the monarchy. This was also true of the 1990 revolution. Veteran politician Bashu Dev Dhungana, pointed out that the leaders of the pro-Democracy movement and the masses who took to the streets during the revolution had one main aim in mind—the end of 'Palace rule'. 'In every field the Palace was the centre,' he said, 'and the people wanted to get rid of that.' Dhungana stated that the real starting-point of the pro-Democracy movement was the speech Ganesh Man Singh made on 14 November 1990 at a function at the Indian Embassy to celebrate Nehru's birth anniversary. In it he compared King Birendra to the Roman Emperor Nero who watched Rome burn.

Ganesh Man Singh's speech gave people courage. Many began to criticize the Palace openly and the pro-Democracy movement gained strength. The pro-Democracy movement, Dhungana claimed, was profoundly a movement against the Palace. An acceptable settlement could only be reached if and when the monarch changed his role.

The King, therefore, was crucial. His role was a determining factor in the old Panchayat system and his role had to change if democracy was going to be introduced into Nepal. Sushil Pyakurel, a human rights activist, had this to say: 'Though the role of the King changed in

Nepal's modern history, he was always there. If you try to write anything on Nepal, you have to try and write something on the Palace and what happened in the Palace. What happened in the 1951 revolution? King Tribhuvan exposed himself as pro-people, but he tried to manipulate everything. He said he was even ready to declare this country as a republic—but he never did. And what did King Mahendra do—he just played with various politicians. What happened when he imposed the Panchayat system? Did he sincerely want to overthrow the Nepali government to defend democracy? And again, what did King Birendra do in 1979? He said he would recognise the so-called minority in the referendum, but did he ever do this? In the same way, we need to find out what the King actually did in this 1990 movement and what his attitudes were.'

The monarchy in Nepal was conditioned largely by Hindu philosophy and tradition even in 1990. King Birendra, the current monarch, was the direct descendant of King Prithvi Narayan Shah. The Shah dynasty had ruled Nepal, at least in principle, since the unification of the nation in 1768. This did not mean that the Shah kings had exercised political power during this whole period. Power had actually begun slipping out of the hands of the Shah kings in the early nineteenth century and into those of the ambitious courtiers who were ready to seize any opportunity to advance themselves. By the mid-nineteenth century, the Rana family were effectively the rulers of Nepal and the King had become no more than a figurehead. Even so, the idea that the monarch in a Hindu kingdom was an incarnation of Lord Vishnu, a Hindu God, remained and was even cultivated by the Ranas.

This may seem strange. The idea of the God-King, after all, has a place in many cultures, and is usually associated with one individual wielding absolute power in both religious and temporal spheres. The concept of Hindu Kingship, however, is much more intangible than this. It was not the case that the King's politically subordinate role under the Ranas conflicted with the basic ideals of Hindu Kingship. If anything, the Ranas used the ideal of Hindu Kingship for their own ends.

The Nepali King's position in relation to his subjects is an elaborate and complicated one. In the religious sphere, the King is subordinate to any Brahmin even though he is the incarnation of a God. A Hindu scholar in Kathmandu said: 'The King as a member of the second caste, the Kshatriyas, must bow down in front of a Brahmin.' This apparent inequality is balanced by the fact that the Brahmin's superiority is limited only to the religious sphere. The Brahmin is dependent on the King, who is a member of the warrior caste, to exercise worldly power. Furthermore, the King's godliness is open to several interpretations. This godliness dates back to the Hindu epic, the Ramayana. In the Ramayana, Ram, the incarnation of Vishnu, comes to earth to build a kingdom of justice and prosperity, known as Ram Rajya. In some interpretations the King can only be accounted a true incarnation of Vishnu if his deeds show him worthy enough. There are also scholars who believe that the King, because he comes from the right caste, sub-caste and lineage, is an incarnation of Vishnu in respect only of his inherited title and not of his person. Traditionally in Nepal therefore, the idea of Hindu Kingship had little to do with wielding political power.

A more enduring mark on Nepali society has been made by the strong sense of personal loyalty which was expressed to the ruler—whether that ruler was a Rana or a Shah king. Power was purely personal and exercised from above, from ruler to ruled. This principle enabled the Rana Maharajas to rule Nepal and its inhabitants as their personal property. This same principle enabled King Tribhuvan, and later King Mahendra, to consolidate and build up their own personal power after the 1951 revolution, despite repeated promises of democracy.

During the 1950s, King Tribhuvan did function, at least in principle, as a constitutional monarch. The 1960s brought King Mahendra into an active role in Nepali politics. His Panchayat system ushered in a new royal ideology which defined and buttressed the position of the King. The two main pillars of this Panchayat ideology were national development and patriotism. The King was proclaimed as a unifying figure and all-important symbol of nationhood. He was the

Father of Development, guiding his people and country without respect to any political party or group. The Panchayat system after all, was introduced to bring 'partylessness' to Nepal.

The principal private secretary to King Birendra, Chiran Shumshere Thapa, gave his own view of the Nepalese monarchy and the role of the King: 'The contribution of the monarchy is important, and I think people expect this contribution to continue. The King is a unifying force and acceptable to the vast majority of the Nepalese people. One cannot be specific about unity, national values and nationalism. It is as much emotional as intellectual. But I think these are important facts and it is important to have a single focus and this is what the monarch should be.'

Towards the end of the Panchayat period the monarchy had lost a good deal of its credibility. In a bid to legitimize its power, the Palace turned strongly once again to religion. The Queen's involvement in the World Hindu Federation and the Pashupatinath Development Trust was widely publicized—and in connection with repeated references to Hindu Kingship. Yet a problem was that Hinduism lacked doctrine—at least, it lacked a prescribed mode of conduct and institutions which could bestow or bolster power. Hinduism was consequently inadequate as a ruling ideology in a modern society.

Furthermore, to many in recent years the Hindu Kingdom had simply become synonymous with corruption and oppression. No ideology could paint over the intrigue and abuse of power inside the Palace. There was a long history of court intrigue, but the disclosure of scandal after scandal was quite shocking and was a powerful factor in bringing the crowds out into the streets during the revolution.

Much of the corruption within the Palace was not blamed on the King personally, but on other members of the royal family. Even during the last days of the Panchayat regime the King was still seen by many as a victim of the system and not a manipulator.

The King himself was something of an elusive figure, quite unlike his father King Mahendra. According to the Prime Minister of the interim government, Krishna Prasad Bhattarai, King Birendra showed two distinct sides. On the one hand he was a shrewd power broker. After the United Left Front split while the interim government was still in office, the King gave Bhattarai this advice:'Why don't you kick them out on their backs, since four parties out of seven have come out of the alliance? Why not kick them all out?' Bhattarai went on to say: 'The King, as an old Etonian, said this to me in English. I said, "You are a clever fellow. I know you also want to kick me out." ' Despite their sparring, Bhattarai was warm in his praise of the King. Bhattarai called him a, 'thorough gentleman—He was very kind to me and very respectful and I had no cause for showing him disrespect.'

Even so, after the movement started, the King bided his time and only agreed to negotiations with the pro-Democracy movement leaders after the Panchayat system had collapsed completely. The King's principal private secretary, Chiran Shumshere Thapa pointed out that the reason for this was that events had moved at a much more rapid pace than anyone could have foreseen: 'Hindsight is not always a good guide. I think many people expected the movement to last much longer, may be fifty weeks, but in fact it was over in fifty days.' At best this could only be a partial explanation. What most people came to feel during the period of the pro-Democracy movement was that the King simply would not listen. This impression could not be confirmed as the workings of the Palace remained cloaked in mystery. Sushil Pyakural, felt that the Palace's very inaccessibility was a screen which hid the truth and the Palace remained a possible threat which even the revolution had not been able to remove: 'It is a matter of saving the Palace. The Palace is involved in everything. If you try to isolate the Palace it is impossible. If you talk about democracy the King must admit his mistakes and say what the Palace has done and then say "From this day on I will do nothing." You cannot just create an illusion and tell the people a fairy story.' In the event, the King offered no explanation of his behaviour. Moreover, many people came to believe after the revolution was finally over that the King had not yet come to terms with the political situation.

By the beginning of May 1990, the interim government had been established and the entire Panchayat structure had been dissolved.

Furthermore, the King had expressed his support for constitutional monarchy in Nepal. Yet, as long as the old Panchayat constitution still existed, the King was still free, in principle, to act as he wished. Obviously a new constitution had to be drawn up in line with the new political situation in Nepal. There was also the question of the army whose loyalty was still firmly to the King. As late as October 1990, Rishi Kumar Pandey, military adviser to the King, stated: 'Like in all other monarchies the Nepali army is totally loyal to the King.' He toned down this remark by going on to say: 'But the orders don't come directly from the King. Everybody in the army accepts that the King delegates his power. Who actually controls the army will always vary. Politics are continually changing. Political leaders come and go, but the army always remains the same, being totally disciplined and loyal to whoever is in power.'

The anomaly of the King's position after the revolution remained a cause for some concern. Rishikesh Shaha commented: 'He had not given anything. He controlled the army. He had discretionary powers—and he had the right to gibe assent to cabinet decisions. As a political scientist and analyst, I also knew that there was royal command. There might be understanding, but the King could dismiss the government at any time he wanted.'

The immediate onrush of freedom after the revolution temporarily blinded people to the fact that the King's position remained legally unchanged. Opinion shifted slowly after several incidents occurred—incidents which made Nepalis question if the King had truly understood that he had lost absolute power. These incidents also led people to question if actual power still remained in the Palace more than with the government.

On 11 May 1990 the King announced the formation of a Constitutional Reform Recommendation Commission over Radio Nepal. The King had not thought of consulting the interim government in advance. Everyone was taken aback. Even though the King had included liberals on the commission, including Daman Dhungana, a member of the Congress Party, and Bharat Mohan Adhikari, a communist, the fact remained that the King had turned round and done something he was no longer supposed to do. This caused consternation. What added to the democratic leaders' irritation was that the King had set up a commission only to reform the old constitution and not to draft a new one.

Rishikesh Shaha maintained that the King really had not yet appreciated the profound change which had taken place in the country. He related how he had been phoned by the Palace to comment on the establishment of the King's commission and how King Birendra wished him to help draft a new constitution, just as King Mahendra had done thirty years ago. 'The King sent for me and asked me to help with the constitution,' said Rishikesh Shaha, 'but I said, "Look, this is no longer your job. It is for the Prime Minister and the interim cabinet to decide." ' Rishikesh Shaha shook his head. 'Seventeen years ago I warned him, but he never listened to me. Instead, he gave up meeting me. And in 1985 when the bombs exploded I told the King, "You are sitting on top of a volcano". And still now, after the revolution, he behaved the same way. He was just like a robot and kept saying, "Do help me to make this constitution. Do advise me." '

Reactions came swiftly to the King's announcement. That same day both the Nepali Congress and the communists issued an official condemnation. The following day they asked their own members who had been appointed to the King's commission to resign. They did so promptly and were followed three days later by the President of the Commission, Supreme Judge, Vishwa Nath Upadhyaya. The Prime Minister and the interim cabinet were more careful in condemning the King. They were still worried about a possible Palace conspiracy and thought the King still had a great deal of support. The Prime Minister, Krishna Prasad Bhattarai, became bold, however, when he saw the public backlash against the King:'Meeting the King on 13 May I had to resort to threats and say I'd resign from the cabinet if the King didn't remove certain persons whom he had included in the constitution-making.'

By now the King had resolved to act in a more realistic manner. He officially disbanded the Commission on 15 May. At the same time he announced that he had given the Prime Minister the power to repeal any laws which would interfere in the speedy establishment of a multi-party democracy in Nepal. Finally, on 20 May the King at last began to adopt procedures suitable for constitutional monarchy when he appointed a new leadership to the university on the advice of the cabinet. Two days later he also announced that the legislative powers which had been given to the Rashtriya Panchayat under the old regime were now in the hands of the interim government.

On 31 May the King proclaimed the formation of a new Constitution Recommendation Commission—only this time on the recommendation of the cabinet, and this time the word 'reform' had been left out. The new commission consisted mainly of Congress and communist members in addition to the Chairman of the previous Commission, Supreme Judge, Vishwa Nath Upadhyaya. The new commission was given ninety days in which to draft a new constitution.

The King had obviously learned a lesson, but his loyalty to the new democratic regime was still ambiguous. This became clear when two months after this affair, the King made another blunder in appointing the new Attorney General and two new commissioners of the Electoral Commission on the recommendation of the old Raj Sabha, the Palace Assembly, and not the interim cabinet. These appointments were met with strong reactions and criticism. The most severe criticism came from the Marxist-Leninists who accused the King of trying to regain power by actively working against the principles of constitutional monarchy. These communists also maintained that the King had appointed former panchas to government posts without consulting the cabinet.

Even though the interim government had been invested with power formally, it seemed unsure of its position at this stage. Because of this the leader of the Marxist Communist Party, Man Mohan Adikhari, warned the communists to play down their extremist attitudes and try and co-operate with the King. Even the Prime Minister, Krishna Prasad Bhattarai, said in an interview with the BBC: 'The King cannot be tied with a scrap of paper, for he had a 35,000 man army and the police behind him. Blood will be shed if we try to do so in the present situation. We can tie the King only by framing a constitution and holding elections immediately after. We should also try to change the King's heart by reminding him of the factors that have now compelled him to hand over power to the people.'

The democratic leaders were further shaken by several other incidents involving the royal family. These incidents seemed to raise the possibility that a Palace conspiracy might be in the offing. On 11 May the Queen resigned from her post as Chairperson of the Social Service National Co-ordination Council which was responsible for all the private aid money coming into the country. The following day at a meeting of the committee she broke down, maintaining that she had no association whatsoever with the Mandale group. Her public penitence seemed to indicate that she had relinquished everything and made a complete break with the past. Three months later, however, the Queen came in to public view once again. She was visiting the Pashupatinath temple, just outside Kathmandu, on 23 August. This was in connection with the Teej festival. For some reason the Queen and other members of the royal family were attacked. The official version was that extremists hiding just outside the temple entrance lobbed stones at them. The situation was brought under control only after police had fired shots into the air—and only after several police vehicles were damaged. Twenty-one people were arrested in connection with this incident. The Home Minister, Yog Prasad Upadhyaya, immediately expressed his concern and grief over the incident and for several days after all political parties came forward to condemn what had happened to the Queen. At a public meeting on 25 August both Comrade Rohit and Rishikesh Shaha condemned the attack. At the same time they warned of the possibility of a royal plot. After all, if the Queen was involved in an incident which somehow demonstrated that the interim government had lost control then the King might be persuaded to act.

The so-called attack against the Queen highlighted the vulnerability of the interim government and the growing fears that some kind of Palace conspiracy was brewing. Mathura Prasad Shrestha,

Health Minister in the interim government, had this to say about those who had been arrested: 'We didn't support the arrests. I personally didn't and neither did the Prime Minister Bhattarai, but even so the people were arrested.' Shrestha explained how the 'attack' against the Queen was not as straightforward as had first been supposed: 'There were lots of flaws when the incident happened. First of all the Queen should have gone to the Pashupati temple rather than the Guheshwori. She went to the Guheshwori temple and she took her adult son with her. No woman is supposed to take an adult son with them on this occasion. This in itself was funny. And nobody knew that she would take that road. Nobody could know this. It would be impossible. When she arrived, the song programme and meeting was already over. In the main area where the people used to concentrate—from that area to where the incident occurred—takes about ten to fifteen minutes to walk. How could the demonstrators know that she was going that way? Another funny thing is that her car stopped in the middle of the road. The car was in perfect condition—why should it stop like this? Another strange thing was that they hijacked a police car and that the car's windows were broken from the inside rather than from the outside. And after all this the Queen rather than going to the Palace went to Prince Gyanendra's house. Why should she go there? Everybody knows or suspects that Gyanendra is leading the mafia gang which is trying to turn the situation backward.' Asked if he thought the Queen had actually staged the incident, Mathura Prasad Shrestha replied: 'You cannot assume that, but you can neither totally reject it. Until these questions are answered people should not have taken action. Moreover, they issued a warrant against someone who at that exact time was at a political meeting at a very different location. I myself am a witness. They even issued warrants against a person who at that time was in Shyanja in western Nepal.' Mathura Prasad Shrestha was speaking on 15 October 1990. He went as far as to admit that neither the police nor the army were, 'totally under our control' and so the situation was potentially serious.

It was in this uncertain situation that the interim government had to oversee the framing of the new constitution. What that constitution had to do was embody the new democratic ideals of the country after the revolution and also restrict the power of the King.

It was true that the interim government had been given more or less unlimited powers in principle and that they enjoyed a public support that no previous government in Nepal had ever done. Yet the members of the interim cabinet were far from certain that their positions were secure.

What brought these fears to the surface was the wrangling surrounding the new constitution. This wrangling triggered off a situation of uncertainty and confusion which was comparable to the revolution period six months earlier. The stakes were high—for the new constitution would largely shape the political future of Nepal. In the troubled weeks that followed any outcome seemed possible—from another mass uprising to a royal coup.

The struggle over the new constitution was not only between the new democratic regime pitted against the old. There were three main power groups involved: the Nepali Congress, the communists and the Palace. All three groups were represented on the Constitution Recommendation Commission and all three were in conflict. The Nepali Congress wanted to limit the powers of the King and secure multi-party democracy in Nepal. The Congress was driven by a desire for stability and wanted to ensure some continuity with the old regime. Because of this, Congress wanted a mutually acceptable agreement with the King. They wanted the King to remain a powerful symbolic figurehead in Nepal, but without any political power.

The communists, however, wanted a clean break with the past. Some of them saw the new constitution as only a temporary measure, just as they had seen the 1990 revolution as the first of a series of revolutions leading towards the Dictatorship of the Proletariat. The communists as a whole were uncomfortable with the monarchy. At the very least they wanted to ensure that the Palace would never play an active role in politics again. They also wanted it made possible in the constitution that the Nepali people, if they so wished, should be able to abolish the monarchy.

The Palace, naturally enough, wanted to retain as much of its former power as possible. A close aide to the King said, just a few weeks before the new constitution was announced: 'The King wants to retain, say, ten per cent of his power and is trying to bargain.'

There was also the question of what the old panchas wanted, though they were now a weak political voice. The panchas complained that they had not been included in drafting the new constitution. Rajeshwor Devkota, leader of the National Democratic Party (Chand) which had been formed by previous panchas, said: 'Only the parties who have been represented in the Commission will respect the new constitution—nobody else. Neither I, personally, nor my party will respect the new constitution.' Their official complaint was that the new constitution was being drawn up improperly—either the King or a constituent assembly should forge the new constitution, not a Commission.

There had been demands for a constituent assembly to be formed as soon as the revolution was over. These calls came mainly from communists and Kathmandu intellectuals. There were fears that there might be a repeat of the 1950s, when the elections to a constituent assembly had been repeatedly postponed until finally the King himself relented.

The Nepali Congress argued, however, that there was no time to set up such an assembly. Instead democracy must be enshrined in a new constitution as soon as possible in order to offset any possible counter-coup. Congress wanted the gains of the revolution consolidated in the constitution. The communists, who had compromised at the end of the revolution, wanted a looser constitution in order to leave some room for manoeuvre later on. Congress disliked this, not just because they were suspicious of the communists but because they wanted the King's position firmly decided. The Nepali Congress was worried that the Palace might try to find an opportunity to regain power at a later date. In the light of these possible threats, the Nepali Congress urged all political groups to give their full support to the Constitution Recommendation Commission. They did want it made possible, however, for the new constitution to be amended at a later date by an elected parliament.

Though the proceedings of the Constitution Recommendation Commission were secret, it soon became apparent that the commission's internal conflicts and disagreements were serious. Some of these conflicts came out into the open in a fairly dramatic way. On 10 August, the people of Kathmandu woke up to find posters all over the city. These posters revealed some of the most controversial points that the Commission was dealing with—as well as some of its secret proceedings. The source of this rather public and spectacular leak was soon discovered to be Nirmal Lama, the most radical member of the Constitution Commission. He defended his actions by saying: 'I was a representative of my party on the Commission, so it was my duty to report what happened to the Party High Command. In this context I said some secret matters to the high command, but unfortunately, without my knowledge, it was leaked to the lower level party activists and they published it.' Many, however, believed that the appearance of the posters was a simple strategy for the communists to obtain public backing for the points they wanted to push in the new constitution. Only two weeks earlier other information had been leaked from the Commission making it public that the three communist members had boycotted a session. There was wide speculation as to why this had happened and the general consensus was that the disagreement had something to do with the position of the monarchy. Eventually, on 29 August, the Marxist-Leninist newspaper, *Drishti*, revealed that the real reason for the communist boycott was, in fact, their failure to have a motion tabled to put constitutional checks on the monarchy. The problem was finally resolved through a compromise between the United Left Front and the Nepali Congress and this enabled the Commission to proceed.

These disputes diminished in importance as the weeks passed. People became more and more worried instead by the long delays in the promulgation of the new constitution. This worry came to overshadow public opinion. Rumours of a planned conspiracy once again circulated in Kathmandu.

The Constitution Recommendation Commission was due to finish its work on 31 August and many hoped that the new constitution would be announced on this day. Many also claimed that the announcement of the new constitution would be accompanied by fresh violence and curfews. A large number of police on the streets on that day showed that even the government was nervous. But nothing happened. Two days later the Chairman of the Constitution Recommendation Commission, Vishwa Nath Upadhyaya, asked the Palace to allow the Commission another three days to complete its work. On the evening of 6 September, Radio Nepal broadcast that the draft of the new constitution had been informally handed over to the King. The following day the Palace issued a statement saying that the draft constitution would be officially handed to the King by the Chairman of the Constitution Recommendation Commission on the approval of the Prime Minister. Two days later on September 9 still nothing more had happened. The communists began to lose their patience. The Marxist-Leninist Party headed by Radha Krishna Mainali and Mohan Chandra Adikhari staged a demonstration of about 10,000 people. They marched through Kathmandu brandishing slogans like: 'Stop the Conspiracy of the Palace!'

Finally, on 10 September the draft constitution was finally handed over to the King by Vishwa Nath Upadhyaya. This news was broadcast by both Nepal TV and Radio Nepal. The King then gave the draft constitution back to the Prime Minister. For the first time in public the King proceeded to give a speech which had not been prepared by a speechwriter in advance. Talking to the people he used the honorific term 'tapai' instead of the lower form 'timi'. This calculated liberal gesture did little to assure the public of the King's good faith, however, as he added that he personally would receive suggestions for the new constitution. King Birendra's speech implied that he imagined he would play an active role in editing the draft constitution. After this very public display, the term of the Constitution Recommendation Commission was extended again on 11 September. Again the communist leaders pressed for the new constitution to be announced as soon as possible.

This rather muddled and unsatisfactory situation continued throughout September and much of October 1990. The delays in the announcement of the new constitution led to an upsurge in demonstrations and protests. Meanwhile the draft of the new constitution led to an upsurge in demonstrations and protests, and was shuffled back and forth between the Palace and the interim cabinet with minor points being adjusted each time.

In his yearly speech to mark the Hindu festival of Dasain, which began on 29 September, the King did state that the interim government would bring in a strong multi-party system under a constitutional monarchy. He used the Nepali word 'antargat' for 'under' which implied that the multi-party system would be subordinate to the monarchy. This, naturally enough, was a cause for some concern. He also promised that the new constitution would be announced before the end of the Nepali month, which meant before the beginning of the next Hindu festival, Tihar. Even so, yet another announcement came a few days later saying that the new constitution would now not be announced until after Tihar.

The worry and frustration of most of the political leaders in Kathmandu was expressed by the two moderate communists, Man Mohan Adhikari and Krishna Raj Varma. On 27 October they asked that an Election Act be passed so that elections could be held even if there was no constitution. Again, they were anxious to offset any move that the King might make. Many were of the opinion that the King might make a move but no one was sure. Most people were confident that a counter-coup would not succeed, but they did worry that the King and the army might act against the new democratic regime.

The conflicts between the Nepali Congress and the communists continued throughout this period. At first the communists did not want any changes made to the draft constitution, but they eventually relented and began negotiating. A series of compromises was reached. The Nepali Congress wanted certain features of the new constitution to remain unchangeable. These were constitutional monarchy, a multi-party democratic system and basic human rights. In order to achieve this they had to give in to the communist demands that all major foreign treaties should be passed with only a two-thirds majority in parliament. The Nepali Congress also had their own way on the number of seats in the new parliament. Krishna Prasad Bhattarai, pointed out: 'The Commission had given 175 seats and the Communists wanted to keep this number. We changed the number to 205 and said that smaller constituencies were better for the contest. We managed to convince the Communists that this also was in their interests.'

These issues were minor, however, compared to the difference of opinion between the Nepali Congress and the communists over the position of the King. Prime Minister Bhattarai handed over the final draft of the new constitution to the King on 11 October. The Palace then issued a statement on Radio Nepal saying that the King would study this draft. This statement also declared that the King believed the new draft contained many good points and that he would do his best to promulgate the new constitution as soon as possible. A furore resulted. This was the first time that the media had broadcast that the King wanted to play an active and independent role in framing the new constitution. Fears of a royal conspiracy grew even further.

A year later, Krishna Prasad Bhattarai, related how pressure from the Palace and other conservative elements such as the army had been present during the whole period. 'One day,' he said, 'the Commander-in-Chief rang at eight o' clock and said he was coming at nine. He walked in in uniform and gave me a file. It said that the King's prerogatives and powers and sovereignty should all remain with him. So I said that this is not my business, it is the business of the Constitution Commission. I put it before the Commission and they rejected it. Then I duly informed the Commander-in-Chief. Then one day I had a telephone call in the office. Some generals and the Commander-in-Chief wanted to see personally. All of them came—22 generals in uniform led by the Commander-in-Chief. They saluted and sat down. I gave them a cup of tea—each. They gave me a file which was the same thing again. Prerogatives and private purse and all that should remain not with the people, but with the King. I replied that the political changes were the result of a very big movement. "How do you suppose that I can do these things or get these things accepted by the people?" I asked.... Then the King called me one day suddenly. I said I'd come there after office hours and went there at 5 pm. He called in his Private Secretary and the King said he didn't agree what the Commission was doing. I said it was beyond my power to change anything. I could not get it accepted by the Commission or by the Cabinet. There were all kinds of people involved in this, I said, Communists and others—and they would become very angry.'

By 20 October when Tihar began, the situation had reached serious proportions. The leader of the United Left Front, Sahana Pradhan, declared that unless the new constitution was announced by 24 October, the interim cabinet would resign and the mass movement would resume. Ganesh Man Singh added his voice, saying there would be another revolt if the new constitution did not appear soon.

No one, however, was prepared for what happened on 22 October. The headline news on both Nepal TV and the government-owned *Gorkha Patra* was that an entirely new constitution, completely different from that drawn up by the Constitution Recommendation Commission, had been handed over to the Prime Minister by the Palace on 20 October. According to the *Gorkha Patra*, the three communist members of the Constitution Recommendation Commission, led by Bharat Mohan Adhikari, had approached Prime Minister Bhattarai on 21 October to ask about this new Palace constitution. Bhattarai confirmed that he had received this document from the Palace. He explained that he had immediately rung the King's Chief Secretary, Revati Raman Khanal, and said that this Palace constitution was utterly unacceptable to the interim cabinet, to the Nepali Congress Party, to the Nepali people and to himself personally. According to the *Gorkha Patra,* he had added that he would resign at once if the Palace announced their own document as the new constitution.

This Palace constitution wanted to retain much wider powers for the King. Practically speaking, it had much in common with the old Panchayat constitution. The main points of the Palace document were that sovereignty should remain with the King and the people, and not just the people, and that all the powers and rights in the constitution should be vested in the King. The King personally should be the source of all executive, legislative and judiciary powers and he would appoint an Advisory State Council to help him with domestic and foreign political matters.

The news on Nepal TV and in the *Gorkha Patra* of this new Palace constitution came as a complete surprise. Most people wondered what was happening inside the Palace and were of the opinion that just about anything could happen. There were even rumours of an imminent military crackdown. The prevailing feeling, however, was one of disbelief. It seemed impossible that the King could turn round and announce his own constitution after his repeated support for the new regime. Former Foreign Minister, Shailendra Kumar Upadhyaya had expressed his own opinion of possible Palace conspiracy in an interview only a month earlier: 'If the King wants, nobody can hold him,' he said. 'The Palace doesn't have the power to harm the King. I don't think the King can accept the new situation very well, but he had no choice. So I think it will be in his interests—it will look good—it will restore his prestige which is very low at the moment, if the King willingly accepts democracy.'

Many people suspected that this Palace constitution emanated not so much from the King, but from those around him who wished to hold on to as much power as possible. Many people were also worried that the Palace constitution was merely the tip of an iceberg. Behind it perhaps lay a larger plot to do away with the interim government and democracy itself. This view was held by some of the political leaders. Bhattarai himself said later that there was probably, 'a lobby inside the Palace which generally doesn't like the King playing a liberal role. So they wanted him to retain most of his powers. Among these were probably members of his Secretariat.'

The situation was further confused when the Palace issued a statement that same afternoon of 22 October stating that what Nepal TV and the *Gorkha Patra* had announced was totally unknown to them.

This statement condemned, 'these attempts to sow discord between the Palace and the people'. The Palace tried to maintain this position. When asked about it a year later, Chiran Shumshere Thapa gave a dismissive shrug and said: 'You have to sift fact from fiction.'

But the Palace could not dismiss this incident as fiction so easily. The Palace constitution had obviously come from somewhere and been leaked to Nepal TV and the *Gorkha Patra*. What seemed clear at least was that the Palace had circulated copies of their own constitution to influential politicians, intellectuals and journalists a couple of days before its existence was revealed publicly on 22 October. The Palace's defence may have been that what was being circulated was merely a suggestion and not an alternative constitution, but it was not received as such. Prakash Kaphley, summed up the mood surrounding this incident by saying: 'First the King said something, then the people demanded more and so on. Therefore the King was trying to know the people's response, what their reaction would be. In fact, there was a strong reaction both from the people and the political parties. In this way the King was trying to learn the nerves of the people—how united they were.' The Prime Minister, Krishna Prasad Bhattarai, believed that the King had more than just personal motives for releasing this Palace constitution: 'He wanted to tell that group of people inside the Palace, those strong people who wanted to retain all the powers in the name of the King, he wanted to show them that he had done his best.'

Bhattarai's own role was crucial during this period. He was diplomatic publicly and used all his charm and pragmatism behind the scenes in a concerted effort to reach a settlement with the King. Eventually he succeeded. On 24 October the three veteran leaders of the Congress Party, Krishna Prasad Bhattarai, Girija Prasad Koirala and Ganesh Man Singh met the King. They gave him their opinion about what the constitution should entail and how serious they thought the whole matter had become. The following evening the Palace announced that the new constitution would be announced on 9 November 1990. The newspaper headlines on the morning of 26 October read: 'The Palace Conspiracy has Failed.' This was, in fact, the end of the matter.

From then on the Palace did not try to act independently of the interim government.

Bhattarai later spoke about his negotiations with the King during this time: He thought that he could pressurise me, but I didn't give in. I referred to my cabinet and the Communists, saying that it was not for me to decide.' In fact, the end of this matter seemed to bring about a resolution in their relationship. 'After that,' said Bhattarai, 'we had a very smooth sailing.'

In the new constitution a few symbolic concessions were given to the King. The preamble to the constitution began with the full Sanskrit title of the King which covered about half a page. More practically speaking, the royal family was declared exempt from tax, though they were banned from any involvement in business or politics.

The interim cabinet amended the constitution for the last time on 1 November. Even so, fearing another postponement, or a conspiracy, Comrade Rohit and the Nepal Peasants' and Workers' Organization staged a dramatic protest. On 6 November nearly all the inhabitants of Bhaktapur walked the 10 kilometres into Kathmandu. The ensuing rush blocked all the main roads of the capital. The demonstrators denounced the Palace conspiracy and demanded the announcement of the new constitution.

Constitution Day was declared a public holiday, but many people were still sceptical. There had been so many delays and so much confusion that people half-expected another postponement. The day before the new constitution was due to be announced was actually the Queen's birthday. The birthday celebrations were muted and that evening there were several blackouts across Kathmandu to protest against the festivities.

Finally, at noon on 9 November 1990, King Birendra announced the new constitution. This announcement marked the end of a long power struggle. In the final rounds between Prime Minister Bhattarai and the King, the Prime Minister had won. Popular power had at last triumphed over traditional power in Nepal.

Bhattarai said in an interview on the day the new constitution was announced: 'This constitution is as democratic as the situation possibly permitted.' There was a general agreement that this was the case.

The new constitution was certainly democratic in a way the previous Panchayat constitution had never been. Sovereignty now rested with the people and the King had become a constitutional monarch. After so many years as an absolute ruler, King Birendra was now a national figurehead. He remained Head of State, but with a democratically-elected parliament behind him, and with human rights listed in the constitution. Considering the uncertainty of the previous few months this new constitution was a major victory for the new regime.

It was also the case that minor, symbolic concessions had been made to the King. If the King had lost his power, he had retained his position and he was still a person to be reckoned with. Furthermore, there were still some similarities between the old constitution and the new. The thorny problems of religion and language had not been solved to everyone's satisfaction and the clauses concerning these did not differ significantly from the previous Panchayat constitution.

Apart from the extreme and the new regional and ethnic parties, most groups welcomed the new constitution. The chairman of the Bar Association, Bashu Dev Dhungana, said: 'I'm happy in one sense. The King should be on the throne and the power should be with the people. But there are also bad things. Sovereignty in Article two, for example. Parliament has the right to amend the constitution and the King has to assent, but when you say that the people are sovereign, you cannot restrict the people from amending certain parts of the constitution. But more important, there is a lot that has to be put into practice.'

Here Bashu Dev Dhungana had touched on the overriding question. Would the new constitution be respected and implemented? The experience of the 1980s had been disappointing. Many people were also sceptical that the King would reconcile himself to his new position as a constitutional monarch. He was used to being political, not only ceremonial. They were not sure how he would react. Most people were sure, however, that the King would respect the new constitution in the beginning.

In fact, the Palace quickly adopted a new tone which implied that it believed democracy had come to stay. In his Dasain speech the King had tried to portray the year's political change as gradual. The Palace obviously wanted to create the impression that the King had given away his power willingly and had not been forced to do so because of a mass uprising. Chiran Shumshere Thapa, tried to make out that King Birendra was merely acting in the tradition of his illustrious ancestors: 'It was an ancestor of His Majesty who forged Nepal into a state in 1768. It was His Majesty's grandfather who first introduced democracy into Nepal, and now His Majesty has embraced the multi-party system and constitutional monarchy in the interests of his people. He is very conscious that his family is there to serve the interests of the Nepalese people. He is of the feeling that Nepal cannot be left behind and what changes are necessary should be made quickly. This has led to the present situation with an interim government and a new constitution.'

The Palace, then, wanted to show that the King was interested in stability and had no intention of trying to win back his power. Yet everyone knew that the situation could change. It had done so before in 1960. If the new government failed to re-establish law and order and if the Nepali people started to lose faith in their democratic leaders then a situation might very well arise where King Birendra would repeat the actions of his father King Mahendra and seize power back again. Some people felt the King had actually lost too much power under the new constitution and that this was bad for the country. Narayan Prasad Shrestha, an influential member of the old regime, said: "Nepal is a multi-ethnic, multi-lingual, multi-religious and now a multi-party country. Without a strong monarchy capable of bringing about cohesion and harmony, it may relapse into becoming a Lebanon or Afghanistan. It was monarchy that created the modern Nepali nation and monarchy that led the Democratic revolution of 1951. Monarchy saved Nepal from becoming a Korea or Kampuchea in recent history. We must not forget that Nepal is like a building made of many bricks where the monarchy is the mortar holding the bricks together. Sadly, the mortar is being turned into sand and there is a danger that without the monarchy Nepal will fall apart. As long as the present constitution keeps the monarchy above controversy, so well and good—but the way the monarchy is being dragged into the media, especially in the speeches of the radicals, it is difficult to say if the institution has been left intact. Such tendencies are as deplorably undemocratic as they are unconstitutional.'

The new constitution needed more than the King's blessing in order to be assured of a future. It needed the backing of the Nepali people and all the political leaders. Even after 9 November when the new constitution was announced, some people doubted if there was enough of a political consensus in the country for the new constitution to be anything more than a well-meaning scrap of paper. Many worried that the tension of the previous months might develop into open anarchy. Whether the new constitution was stronger than the paper it was written on could only be decided by a general election. That would be the test. If a general election could be held successfully in Nepal then and only then would the new constitution be guaranteed any chance of survival.

Elections

The long-awaited announcement of the new constitution on 9 November 1990, brought a final end to the uncertainty which had surrounded the revolution. The King had now accepted his new position as a constitutional monarch and there was no longer any fear of a coup or 'counter-revolution' headed by the royal family or forces from within the Palace. Though the old élite still existed (and still wished to restore the old Panchayat order), it had to accept defeat—at least for the time being. The new democratic system was now an established fact. Political activity henceforth had to take place within the framework of the new constitution.

The change in the political climate also meant a change of emphasis for the interim government. Having fought off the prospect of a Palace coup, the cabinet was now able to turn its attention to the day-to-day running of government and the strengthening of democracy. The immediate task was to organize the general election. Only when this election had taken place could the interim government claim that they had properly established democracy in Nepal.

In the first months of 1991 there were signs that the interim government had begun to act, but cautiously. It was impossible, however, to satisfy their many critics and the problems facing them were so overwhelming that it was difficult to know where to begin. The civil service was in a shambles and the economy in ruins. It seemed that only radical measures could make any difference, but the interim government was afraid of appearing to act too rashly or harshly.

Life returned to normal very quickly. The daily struggles became once again those against poverty and bureaucracy and the festive spirit predominant at the end of the revolution was forgotten. The interim government, steered by the Nepali Congress in the forefront, seemed even to adopt hints of the old Panchayat government and was praised in the same glowing terms in newspapers and on radio and TV. One main difference was that now the royal family were firmly out of the limelight. Rather, the Nepali Congress tried to build up their own democratic myths based on the person of B.P. Koirala.

The media reports did distort the situation somewhat as the interim government did not have total control. Law and order was far from restored. Violence and unrest continued and in several incidents the social upheaval which had come in the wake of the revolution was clearly evident. Fights broke out at public meetings and local members of different parties tried to settle their differences with fisticuffs. This new unrest was no longer blamed directly on the Mandales, the Panchayat thugs, who wished to re-establish the old political system.

The Mandales, as a group, had melted away and infiltrated the political parties. Now in a new disguise, they set about trying to disrupt normal life. Whether it was a strike in a private factory or a government office, whether an outbreak of violence at a political meeting—such as that which occurred at a meeting of the National Democratic Party at

Banepa—or even political murder as happened in Piuthan—there always seemed to be one or two of these former Mandales pulling strings behind the scenes. As the Mandales had become even more shady than before, an official investigation was almost impossible.

One the other side of the political spectrum, the left-wing changed tactics. On 20 March the radical communist party, the Mashal, split for the fourth time. Young members of the party had decided that they wanted to contest the elections. This left the remaining rump of the Mashal with the sole principle that it would boycott them. These young communists did not support the parliamentary system, however—far from it. Their aim was to gain power, expose parliament from the inside and replace it with their own structures.

The ideological clashes did not hide the truth of the situation: politicians of all shades had begun to scramble after power. The prospect of power, not the commitment to a political ideology, was what appeared to motivate many. Before the deadline expired, three of the most wanted of the Panchayat old guard, Marich Man Singh Shrestha, Nirenjan Thapa, and Nava Raj Subedhi, emerged like ghosts from the sidelines and filed their nominations for the election as independent candidates.

The general election was announced for 12 May 1991. As soon as this was known the new political leaders of Nepal began to behave like politicians in any democracy. Those who had suffered years of harassment and imprisonment to bring about a democratic system now concentrated on winning as many seats as possible for their party in the election—and securing a post for themselves in the new government. Overnight, politicians turned from declaring their similarities with the other democratic parties to emphasizing their differences. The inevitable result was a split between the Nepali Congress and the United Left Front. Though this only became official during the Nepali Congress Party convention in January 1991, the general trend had pointed in that direction for the previous six months.

Radical members of the United Left Front had attacked the Nepali Congress continually throughout the autumn. More than anything else they criticized the admittance of former panchas into the party and the Congress attitude towards the new constitution. At the same time, moderate communists in the United Left Front urged unity and the need for the two democratic blocs to fight the election together. Inside the Nepali Congress, the conservative wing of the party, led by Girija Prasad Koirala, stated that an alliance with the communists was utterly unthinkable. He declared that the natural alliance should be with the former liberal panchas.

Krishna Prasad Bhattarai, the Prime Minister, tried to keep the coalition of the pro-Democracy movement together for a long while. Then he changed his mind. During the Nepali Congress convention he suddenly changed track and criticized the communists. He declared that the Nepali Congress would fight the election alone—and win a two-third majority in parliament. The Nepali Congress convention was held in the main football stadium in Kathmandu. It drew 20,000 supporters and the sight of such a crowd no doubt gave the Congress politicians a great deal of confidence that they would sweep the coming general election.

The United Left Front also split at this time. In December, three members of the Front, the Nepal Peasants' and Workers' Organization led by Comrade Rohit, the Tulsi Lal Amatya faction, and the most extreme of the factions within the United Left Front, the Nepal Communist Party (Fourth Convention), complained that they had been overlooked and were unrepresented in the interim government. Now they declared their support for the broad coalition of leftist forces to fight the election. Such a coalition, they demanded, should include all leftist parties, including those which had not joined the United Left Front. They wanted all these parties treated on equal terms.

In practical terms this split brought all hopes of leftist unity to an end. This became even more apparent a few weeks later when 8 January 1991, the two remaining members of the United Adhikari, the Nepal Communist Party (Marxist) and the Nep party (Marxist-Leninist) merged. This surpri moderate Marxists, led by Sahana and the radical Marxist-Leninists led by Madan Bhandari and Radha Krishna Mainali, seemed to many to be no more than a marriage of convenience. As the two most important communist parties in the country, this merger seemed to be a tactical move towards creating a communist party strong enough to form a government without the help of the other, small communist parties.

In contrast to the communists, the strength of the Nepali Congress Party was its unity. Even here, however, a united party could not be taken for granted. The selection of the candidates to represent Congress in the election severely strained party unity. The Communist Party maintained a strong whip and chose candidates from above. The parties established by former panchas simply rounded up candidates who had previously represented different geographical districts in the now dissolved Rashtriya Panchayat. The Nepali Congress Party, however, was plagued by bitter infighting that threatened to tear the party apart.

On 25 March more than 5,000 members of the Nepali Congress Party gathered outside the main party office in Dilli Bazar in Kathmandu to await the decision as to who should stand in the 205 constituencies across the country. The crowd blocked one of the main roads in Kathmandu. Those waiting represented many shades of opinion. The large majority were new members of the party, with their background in Panchayat politics. There were a few, though, who had never given up their Congress membership during all the years that the party had been banned.

Most of those who sought nominations pointed to their previous political experience and hoped that this would be enough to ensure their continuance in government. Some resorted to more eye-catching methods: one man from western Nepal started a hunger-strike in the hope of influencing the nomination decision in his favour.

When the election board, consisting mainly of the old guard of the Nepali Congress such as Girija Prasad Koirala, Ganesh Man Singh and ⁓ Prasad Bhattarai, finally read out the roll of names chosen, the ⁓ as a shock. To many outside the party headquarters ⁓le it seemed that the old guard had staged

nothing less than an internal coup. What caused the harshest reactions
to the board's decisions was that Ganesh Man Singh's wife and son had
both been chosen to represent two prime Kathmandu constituencies.
The party was in uproar. Party members who had not been nominated
threatened to stand as independents. There was even talk of launching a
second Congress Party. Protests were staged outside the homes of
Ganesh Man Singh and Krishna Prasad Bhattarai. Bhattarai defended
himself by saying that the three main criteria for choosing candidates
were as follows: one, that they should have suffered for the cause of
democracy, two that they should stand a good chance of winning and
three, that they should be capable of taking on a political role. The fact
that competence was relegated to number three on the Congress's list
left many party hopefuls grinding their teeth in disappointment.
However, this tricky period soon passed. The possibility that infighting
might lead to electoral defeat drew the Congress together to cover over
its inner conflict and discontent.

By the beginning of April it was clear that the adoption of the
British parliamentary model with one-candidate constituencies meant
that only the big parties and coalitions would survive. Almost overnight
Nepal's voters were left with only three main political options. Out of
the forty-two political parties which had been registered by the Election
Commission on 23 January 1991, twenty-two were to take part in the
election. Out of these, only six were expected to capture seats in
parliament. Therefore the three options open to the Nepali people were:
the Nepali Congress as the biggest single party, the communist parties
with the United Marxist-Leninist Party to the forefront, and the pancha
parties, mainly the two National Democratic Parties, led by Surya
Bahadur Thapa and Lokendra Bahadur Chand. Members of the smaller
parties who had not yet given up the fight spent their time bargaining
with other parties and trying to clinch fruitless deals.

On 8 April 1991, Krishna Prasad Bhattarai officially opened the
election campaign of the Nepali Congress. Kathmandu had already
been covered in election slogans and party symbols for several weeks.
The main topic of conversation, from wayside teahouses in the capital
to remote mountain villages was the same—the country buzzed with

the party nominations and the elections. Just as during the last phase of the revolution, everyday concerns seemed to melt into the background and on street corners, in homes and in shops, the talk was only political.

After the official opening of the election campaign government policy seemed to be to postpone all action until after the election. Even the most minor decisions were frozen. In the new, heady atmosphere students demanded a one month holiday to travel back to their native villages to take part in the campaign. They were granted this immediately. The Election Commission seemed to take the place of government. Its decisions and achievements were announced daily over Radio Nepal. Election Day was declared a national holiday and special rules and regulations were issued to deal with the period around the election.

During the year which had passed since the revolution, every Nepali citizen had metamorphosed into an amateur politician. Everyone from children to old women discussed the rights and wrongs of democracy and the Panchayat system—were things better or worse— and what was the best solution to Nepal's manifold problems?

But how did the majority of the Nepali people view the coming election? Though many were excited, the thrill of the previous year's revolution had subsided. Initial celebration had given place to long months of rising prices and instability. The realization that turning out on to the streets would not alter everything at once had finally sunk in. Opinions differed. Some people said that if the communists came to power everyone would become rich immediately; others declared that if the communists won there would be civil war. Many whose main interest was whether the rain came on time in order to plant their maize saw the election as just another burden to bear. One old Newari women sighed: 'We Nepalis have to endure many hardships. First came the problem with India, then the revolution—and now the elections!' Rumours sprang up anew in Kathmandu saying that the curfew would be reimposed and that in the inevitable violence the streets would run with blood.

The politicians were hard-pressed to garner votes in this volatile situation. Party programmes and manifestos were published during February, but the politicians knew that these did not count for much in a society like Nepal. The foreign journalists and Nepali intellectuals who waded through these lengthy documents were struck mainly by the similarity of their contents. All the parties promised social equality, economic development and stability. The differences between the parties lay more in minor details. For example, the Nepali Congress promised free education up to tenth grade, while the Nepal Peasants' and Workers' Organization advocated free education up to degree level. The communist parties devoted many paragraphs to their ideological basis—something which appeared completely lacking in the Nepali Congress programme. The National Democratic Parties emphasized national integrity and independence more than the other parties and published a separate programme for agricultural and village development.

Both the National Democratic Parties and the communists made a great deal of Prime Minister Bhattarai's supposed sell-out to India. Both groups condemned the 'common rivers' policy which Bhattarai had advocated and made this an election issue, though it was an issue emphasized more by the National Democratic Parties than by the communists. What distinguished the parties were their methods of campaigning rather than their ideologies.

The conflicts which shook the Nepali Congress Party to its very roots were soon forgotten after the start of the four-week election campaign. Despite its organizational weaknesses, the Congress managed to field candidates for all 205 constituencies. The knowledge that theirs was the only party to cover the entire country gave the Nepali Congress leadership renewed self-confidence. Returning by helicopter from his election tour of the western-most parts of Nepal, Ganesh Man Singh said: 'The question is not whether we will get a clear majority. The question is whether we will be able to get the two-thirds majority in parliament which we think is necessary for us to be able to run the government.' This remarkable self-assurance stamped the Congress' entire campaign.

Congress' methods, however, were less innovative than the communists. The Nepali Congress concentrated mainly on mass meetings and door-to-door canvassing. Their message was the same everywhere: the Nepali Congress was the only true democratic option flanked by the Panchayat kind of dictatorship (represented by the National Democratic Parties) on the one side, and communist dictatorship (fast disappearing in the rest of the world) on the other. Congress referred continually to the party's history. Party workers stressed their democratic tradition and reminded the people that they had formed the only previously democratically-elected government in the country's history. They pointed to how they had fought against dictatorship and tyranny for forty years since the days of the Ranas.

The communists aimed a different message at their supporters. They called for equality and justice. They claimed that they and they alone were capable of clearing up the mess left by the previous regime and they and they alone could banish exploitation and oppression. Was it right that a few were rich and many were poor? Was it right that these few lived in ease and luxury while the masses suffered and toiled? The communists staged cultural programmes with political songs. These, mixed with vigorous political speeches, drew large numbers of people. The most active was the United Peoples' Front which was an electoral alliance of the most radical of the communist parties. Their intention was to use the elections to stage a people's revolution. Their group was the second-largest of the communist parties, fielding ninety candidates.

The largest of the communist parties, the United Marxist-Leninist Party, with 193 candidates, had departed from their conciliatory tone. Now they hammered home the faults of the Nepali Congress at every public meeting. They laid the blame for the shoddiness of the interim government solely on the Nepali Congress. Patrolling the crowds at their public meetings to keep order were the young party cadres with red headbands and stout sticks.

The only moderate communists now left seemed to be the three small parties of the Nepal Peasants' and Workers' Organization (Rohit), the Nepal Communist Party (Democratic), the Nepal

Communist Party (Verma), and a few individuals such as Tulsi Lal Amatya and Padma Ratna Tuladhar. They openly admitted the communists' weaknesses and commented on their differences and lack of unity. They declared: 'There are those communists who only want to exploit the elections as part of their own strategy. These aren't truly democratic. Our main aim must be to prove to the rest of the world that we are truly democratic and as communists we only intend to win power through elections and maintain democracy after we come to power.' This was said by Padma Ratna Tuladhar. He went on to admit that the communists would have a hard time even after they came to power: 'We don't only need to prove that we are democratic, we have to be very careful with economic reform as the rest of the world is very suspicious towards us.'

The third main option, the ex-panchas, had forgotten all fears of reprisals and openly took part in the campaign. They stressed national integrity and law and order. The leaders of the two National Democratic Parties said: 'True prosperity and stability can only come through us because we are the only ones experienced in running the government.'

The main attack from all sides on the Nepali Congress was its closeness to India. Though the National Democratic Parties made much of this, their main struggle was to appear truly democratic as, after all, they were old panchas campaigning under a new name. New features in Nepali politics during this election were the regional and ethnic parties which had sprung up, the Sadbhavana Party (the Nepal Goodwill Party), and the National People's Liberation Front (Jana Mukti Morcha). Of these, the former fought for the rights of the Terai population and had a strong following in certain districts. But following the Panchayat tradition, the constituencies under the new system had been so drawn up that people of Indian origin in the Terai would not be able to win seats and form a power bloc.

The nagging question still remained as to whether a multi-party system could really be established in Nepal. Thirty-one years had passed since the last, brief multi-party period had been brought to an end by the King. In the meantime, partylessness had been the main principle of Nepali politics. Though recognizable factions had developed inside the Rashtriya Panchayat, these were largely centred on personalities and not political programmes. The election symbol, so important in a country with a high percentage of illiterate people, had become connected to an individual. Now the symbol represented a party. Congress chose a tree while the communists used the sun as their symbol. These symbols appeared in profusion everywhere.

This major shift was not felt too strongly by the average Nepali on account of the electoral system adopted. In each constituency every party had only one candidate.

This meant that at a local level the party symbol was still only connected to an individual. There was no doubt, therefore, that even in the 1991 election, the individual would play a vital role, just as under the previous Panchayat system. Personality, not party, would dominate.

The National Democratic Parties hoped to gain seats because of this. They aimed to field tried and tested candidates who were well-known in their home districts. These candidates had all held positions in the Rashtriya Panchayat and had made their political careers through local patronage in their own constituencies. One such person was B.P. Shrestha in Dhulikhel, a small town thirty kilometres west of Kathmandu.

As an important merchant Shrestha had been able to use some of his resources for local development. He had also been able to attract foreign aid agencies to invest in the district. In this way he had built up a successful political career and had served for several terms in the Rashtriya Panchayat. His popularity was undisputed. Largely due to this popularity and Shrestha's own charisma, the demonstrations and protests which had disrupted daily life during the revolution never reached Dhulikhel. According to one citizen in Dhulikhel, Shrestha was a genuine liberal and democrat. Consequently, he became a member of the Nepali Congress immediately after the revolution. Unfortunately he was not chosen to represent his constituency and the only option left for him was to throw in his lot with the National Democratic

Party—although he did not agree at all with Surya Bahadur Thapa, its leader. The voters of Dhulikhel now had the choice of starting from scratch with a new Congress candidate or voting for Shrestha, even though he was representing a reactionary party.

This dilemma did not occur in Constituency No. 1 of Bhaktapur. Here the populist leader was Narayan Man Bijukche, Comrade Rohit, a towering symbol of freedom and social justice. His campaign was characterized by open dialogue with the citizens of his constituency. In the early morning, before the sun began to scorch the heads of his listeners, Rohit would be speaking on street corners in the centre of Bhaktapur. Carefully and straightforwardly he would tell the people how their grievances against local and central government would be solved. He would go on to urge that together they could create a society of prosperity and equality based on self-reliance without dependence on foreign aid. After he had finished speaking he would be ready to answer questions. The rest of the day would be spent in door-to-door canvassing and speaking at large meetings in the afternoons.

This personal interaction between candidates and voters typified the campaign. Large numbers, reminiscent of the final days of the revolution, turned out to hear the politicians' attempts to woo them. These large numbers did cause some anxiety as many feared that the election campaign would erupt into violence. The radio and TV, which had spent the previous months informing listeners and viewers as to the technicalities of the election and how to go about casting a vote now reassured the public that law and order was secure. The army has already been called out to supervise the election in certain areas of the Terai and in the strongholds of the extreme Communist Mashal Party in Gorkha and Piutan in western Nepal. Even this, however, did not make the election officers less nervous. Until the very end of the campaign there were few who believed that a totally fair and peaceful election would actually take place.

On the eve of the elections most people still found it impossible to predict who would win. There were no polls to give any indication as to who would form the new government. Most of the parties had never taken part in a democratic election before. As such they had no track record to show and persuade people to vote for them. Nepali society had changed so much in the thirty-two years since the last multi-party general election that what had happened then could give no guide to the course of present events.

Nepal TV and radio were faced with a flurry of parties competing for prime time. The way this was allocated was according to the number of candidates filed by each party. This, of course, gave no real indication of the party's support country-wide. It did seem, however, that the Congress would win. Yet nobody dared rule out the chances of a surprise communist victory. There was also the unknown factor of the National Democratic Parties—the old liberal panchas in a new guise—who might pull in a sizable number of votes and even compete with the communists.

Early on 12 May, election day, long queues began to form outside the polling stations all over the country. Some of the queues in the Kathmandu valley stretched for more than a kilometre. People wanted to make an early start before the heat made waiting difficult and the atmosphere on the streets suggested more a holiday than an important political event. There was an expectant hush throughout Kathmandu as the city was devoid of vehicles. Voters turned out in their best clothes. Now with their demands for democracy finally realized, the scene was the opposite from the tension and demonstrations of the previous year during the height of the revolution.

The predictions of a bloodbath were not fulfilled. There were reports of only six people being killed during the entire campaign. Apart from a few irregularities in the Terai and the need for some repolling, the election passed off peacefully. Foreign observers confirmed that the elections had been conducted in a free and fair manner.

During the evening, reports began to come in from the rest of the country. As many as sixty-five per cent had taken part in the election, an extraordinarily high figure for a country like Nepal with a literacy rate of less than forty per cent.

The first results came from the Kathmandu constituencies and came as something of a shock—especially to the Nepali Congress. The communists had swept the board in Kathmandu and even swept the interim Prime Minister, Krishna Prasad Bhattarai, out of his seat in Constituency No. 1 of Kathmandu. Madan Bhandari, the leader of the United Marxist-Leninist Party (UML) had won in both Constituencies 1 and 5, against all the odds. A few days later Bhattarai announced his resignation as Prime Minister.

These first shock-waves subsided as other results began to come in. Nepal's geography made a quick count impossible, but it gradually became clear that the Congress had in fact won a clear majority gaining 103 seats and could form a government. The Congress had not, however, gained the two-thirds majority that it had so proudly expected. Yet, even though the Nepali Congress could govern as a single party in the new parliament, the communists were able to form a strong opposition. The UML came behind the Congress with sixty-nine seats. There were also other communist parties who succeeded in having candidates elected. The most surprising communist victor was the United People's Front, the most radical of the parties standing, with nine seats. The other communist parties who gained entry into parliament in the election were: the Nepal Peasants' and Workers' Organization (Comrade Rohit) with two seats and the Nepal Communist Party (Democratic) which also gained only two seats.

The main surprise of the election, however, was the crushing defeat of the two National Democratic Parties who managed to secure only four seats. This result spelled a wholesale rejection of the old Panchayat system by the Nepali people. The only other party to succeed in being represented in parliament was the Nepal Sadbhavana Party, the communal party in the Terai.

When the votes were finally counted a map of the results showed that the Congress and the communists drew their support from different regions. The communists' stronghold turned out to be the Kathmandu valley and eastern Nepal—in other words, the most politicized parts of the country. The Nepali Congress was returned mainly from the western region and more remote areas.

The general election brought the revolution to a final end. The election was solid proof that a democratic system had at last been introduced into Nepal and that the revolution had been real. In the 1989 revolutions in the Eastern European countries, none of the parties representing the old regimes there had gained as little in their first elections as in Nepal. When all was said and done the two National Democratic Parties had received less than five per cent of the vote.

The strong communist support showed that the Nepali people did not only want to sweep away the Panchayat system—they wanted radical changes in their society.

The election results also showed that the ideals of democracy and the multi-party system had been embraced and supported by the population. For the first time the Nepali people had been able to send the clear message that they no longer wanted to accept monarchy—they wanted to rule themselves.

On 23 May 1991 the Nepali Congress chose Girija Prasad Koirala, leader of the Congress in the House of Representatives, to follow Bhattarai as Prime Minister. He was the third brother from the same family to be Prime Minister.

On 29 May the new government was sworn in. This government, under a conservative leader, promised to be more active than the interim government. Its freedom, however, would be limited by the watchful communists in the opposition. It would not be possible for the Congress government to sell any national resources to India, for example, without their approval.

The general election also brought a year of dramatic upheaval and change to a close. Now the Nepali people wanted stability and peace and looked to their newly-elected government to work towards this end.

Epilogue

With the general election, held on 12 May 1991 an important chapter in Nepal's modern history had come to an end. The demands which had been voiced at the Nepali Congress Convention in January 1990 had been achieved. The King had capitulated; the Panchayat system had been dissolved and a new constitution had been proclaimed.

When Girija Prasad Koirala was sworn in as Prime Minister on 29 May to head the newly-elected government he could feel relatively secure in his new position. He had the backing of a clear Congress majority in parliament and the backing of the majority of Nepalis for the new democratic system. This may help explain why this quiet, modest man was able to embark on a radical policy of liberal economic reform. He aimed to restructure the burdensome administration which was vastly overladen with civil servants. A commission was formed to investigate how their numbers could be reduced. Furthermore, in line with India's new Congress (I) government, headed by Prime Minister P.V. Narasimha Rao, Girija Prasad Koirala showed himself intent on privatizing businesses and changing the centrally-planned economy of the Panchayat era into a free market economy.

The new Prime Minister obviously had admirable intentions. The question uppermost in many people's minds was whether Girija Prasad Koirala would achieve more than just intentions. The problems and challenges facing the new government by the autumn of 1991 were so overwhelming as to appear quite insoluble.

Dirga Raj Koirala, a seasoned civil servant and main adviser to the new Prime Minister, pointed out that the new government had to deal with all the problems left over from the interim government period. During the last fifteen months almost all the day-to-day decisions had been postponed in order to concentrate on framing the new constitution and preparing for the coming general election. Promises had been freely given during that time which were clearly impossible to fulfil. The civil servants' agitation which greeted the new Congress government was a result of this.

Because of the civil servants' strikes and protests the business of the government was effectively paralyzed for the first two months of the new Prime Minister's tenure. The conflict became serious when the communists became involved in the dispute. The Congress government resorted to harsh measures to control the situation which were criticized by several of the Nepali Human Rights' organizations. Towards the end of August 1991, the government did gain the upper hand and the agitation fizzled out.

The Congress government was threatened more by the economic situation than by the civil servants, however. Price rise, a late monsoon and a partially-failed rice crop created a serious situation in the country. Furthermore, unemployment was a growing problem. Dirga Raj Koirala commented that more than seventy per cent of the crowd which gathered outside the Prime Minister's residence each morning to ask for favours were in search of a job. He added that unfortunately, 'we have no jobs to give them'.

Such a situation was obviously ripe for further unrest. The Nepali Congress found that they had to steer themselves carefully. In addition to the massive problems facing them they still had the communists criticizing them on the one hand and the party had to keep an eye on the Palace on the other. Rumours persisted in Kathmandu that the Palace was again playing an active role, though this was hotly and repeatedly denied by all politicians. Dirga Raj Koirala was cautious, though confident in his assessment of the situation: 'You must remember that legally speaking the King is still in the centre of power. In the constitution he does have emergency powers which he could use if he wanted. But at the present moment we are fairly certain that he will not do this.'

Corruption continued in public life in Nepal. Dirga Raj Koirala admitted that corruption within the government administration had increased rather than decreased since the revolution. He stated that checking corruption would be a long and tedious process, though the government was determined to succeed. This was not an easy task, he added, not least because the new members of parliament were inexperienced in the running of government. These politicians had to rely on secretaries and other officials who were not always trustworthy. Dirga Raj Koirala finished by saying that only after the government had gained complete control of the administration would there be any hope of imposing a new code of conduct on the civil service.

The Nepali people, however, wanted sudden change. They did not want to wait for a slow transformation of public life. Most people wanted members of the old regime punished for their misdemeanours under the Panchayat system.

It was also true that Dirga Raj Koirala's recipe for cleaning up the government administration necessitated politicians who were not corrupt themselves, but were people of stature and standing who enjoyed wide respect. Soon, however, rumours began to circulate that some of the new democratic politicians were corrupt, even up to the cabinet level.

Most people, however, believed that the new members of the parliament were largely honest. One Nepali historian said: 'The personalities of the leaders must develop so that people can believe that they are of another moral set from the former Panchayat politicians. Only when this trust between the people and the leaders has been established will it be possible for really good leaders to appear.'

People were also worried that they were not up to the task at hand. Even Dirga Raj Koirala expressed his frustration with the inexperience of the new members of parliament. Commenting on the first session of the new democratic parliament which had just finished, he said: 'Discipline and decorum in parliament have to be learned by our own members. Even ministers don't know how to behave. They all have to be trained in a lot of things.'

Padma Ratna Tuladhar, who had taken a seat as the only independent in parliament added a lack of will to the failings he had perceived in the new crop of politicians. In an interview in October 1991 he said: 'The main problem is a lack of seriousness among the leaders of the political parties. They could not follow the spirit that was there during the movement both in the Communist Party and also in the Congress Party. Everything was there up till the last days of the movement. But immediately after the restoration of the system I myself found that this spirit was not maintained by the leaders of the political parties. I think this is the main problem even now.'

Padma Ratna Tuladhar emphasized that the main problems facing Nepali society lay outside the jurisdiction of parliament: 'There are so many problems outside the political areas that cannot be analysed politically or by the government. Only politics cannot change all these things. You have to develop social movements. You have to develop religious, political and social activities. Only these can make a country prosperous. We have political leaders, but we lack leaders in religion and in cultural fields.' According to Padma Ratna Tuladhar this was the main concern facing Nepal, now that the 1990 revolution was over. Democracy had been established at an institutional level in Nepal, but it could not be said to have taken root. Tuladhar commented: 'Immediately after the change the people expected that they would get something better than the previous system—but they found nothing. This was not due just to the failure of the government or the parliament, but it is also due to the people's distraction from other activities and areas.'

Mentioning some of the features of Nepali society which in his opinion needed changing, Tuladhar said: 'The constitution and the law say that all Nepalis are equal, but we still have a racial system, a caste system. Even in Kathmandu there are some people who used to work as sweepers from generation to generation. They are still being treated as untouchables. Economically we Nepalis are very unequal. We have millionaires on the one hand and very poor people on the other. In the Terai there are still people who are being treated like slaves. Some races are not politically conscious or educated and they are exploited by other groups. The law has already disbanded all these things, but still in practice these things need to be changed.'

According to one influential member of the old regime, an increase in knowledge among the population was needed before any profound change could take place. 'The people of Nepal suffer from a poverty of ideas,' he said. Describing a general attitude to politics in Nepal, the interim Prime Minister, Krishna Prasad Bhattarai said in October 1991: 'Our society is a feudal society still. Feudalism means that you want to keep your power base in your own village or society. So what is the good of being a member of parliament if you can't be a minister? If you become a minister you can ride in a car with flags on and have all the advantages and prestige.' A close adviser to the King gave this opinion: 'We Nepalis worship power. It is not a question of a person's qualities, but whether he holds power or not.'

Many politicians seemed to be in agreement: what was needed after the political revolution of 1990 was a social and cultural one. In order to secure democracy as a stable governing system for the future people needed to learn more and alter some of their basic attitudes. Padma Ratna Tuladhar summed up this general conviction by saying: 'We cannot change all this politically—we need a change in the minds of the people.'

The long and difficult process of democratization which had been launched on 18 February 1990 had not come to an end therefore, it had barely started.

If the new democratic order in Nepal was faced with such momentous problems, what had the previous fifteen months of revolutionary change actually achieved? What had the 1990 revolution really meant for the people of Nepal?

First and foremost, the 1990 revolution in Nepal had meant that the process of democratization could at last begin. Nepal's society, which had been traditionally closed, had been forced open. Now people were allowed to express their opinions freely and take part in public life and politics.

At a deeper level the advent of democracy as an idea had begun in Greece and taken root first in Europe. As a philosophy, democracy demanded reliance on individual political consciousness and a sense of responsibility on the part of each citizen to participate in deciding who should govern. As such, democracy was at odds in its essence with the basis of a traditional Hindu society. Hinduism stressed the caste, sub-caste or group over and above the individual. In a Hindu society merit came through fate rather than achievement. It was little wonder that some intellectuals in Kathmandu were wary of democracy as being another western imposition. One man said: 'The West have forced their political system on us, not understanding that democracy cannot work in Nepal. In a society like ours with a caste system nothing else than Hindu monarchy can work.' Others, however, insisted that democracy would and could work in this part of the world. They pointed to India which, after all, was the largest democracy in the world.

One thing did emerge from the 1990 revolution in Nepal. Hinduism was no longer viable as a state ideology. On the one hand, the economic and cultural changes which had taken place since the 1951 revolution had begun to erode the old order. Moreover, Hinduism had lost credibility during the years of the Panchayat system when it was used to maintain an élite and suppress large sections of Nepali society. The 1990 revolution could be seen as completing this process. Even in 1989, before the revolution, a young Brahmin, speaking for his generation, said: 'I would like to see Hinduism in Nepal reform. A change is necessary or else religion will disappear.'

Change came in a surprising, almost shocking way when the ethnic groups and non-Hindus in Nepal took their new democratic freedoms seriously and began to demand legal rights. This move, which followed swiftly on the heels of the revolutions, was not just a reaction against the politics of the last thirty years, but against the traditional Hindu high caste élite.

Padma Ratna Tuladhar warned that the first stirrings of a religious and ethnic revolt in Nepal which were experienced in the summer of 1990 were just the beginning: 'There are so many reasons for them to strike against this unfair politics,' he said. Tuladhar was firm that the Brahmins had to give up their dominant position and insistence on Nepal as a Hindu State. 'Soon these groups will become politically conscious and educated. Then they will become aware of the historical past and how they have been suppressed for hundreds and hundreds of years. They will learn that they have been deprived of all kinds of rights: political, social and economic.' In Tuladhar's opinion it was imperative that the Brahmins learned to accommodate their interests with the interests of Nepal's other ethnic and religious groups. If not, Tuladhar's predictions were dire: 'If these groups demand something and this is not fulfilled, it could lead to the disintegration of the country.'

Yog Prasad Upadhyaya, Home Minister in the interim government, was more optimistic than Padma Ratna Tuladhar. He believed that Nepal's religious and ethnic diversity was actually a reason to believe in a strong democratic future for Nepal: 'Had it been a homogeneous group,' he stated, 'dictatorship would have a better chance here. Because it is a heterogeneous society, democracy has a better chance because small groups cannot be viable political units on their own. Therefore they must come together and talk it out. So I think democracy stands a good chance in Nepal.'

Opinions differed widely, therefore, as to whether democracy would survive in Nepal and whether the new freedom it brought would cause the country to cohere or to splinter.

The 1990 revolution in Nepal therefore achieved two ends. First of all, it opened the country to democracy and political freedom. Secondly, the revolution opened Nepal to the possibility of another revolt; this time of a religious and ethnic nature. Whether this second revolt could be contained within the new democratic structures or whether it would pull the country apart remained to be seen. What was clear was that, for the first time the Nepali people had woken up to demand their basic democratic rights. What was equally clear was that the turbulent fifteen months from February 1990 till May 1991 had not only changed the political institutions of Nepal—they had changed the Nepali people themselves.

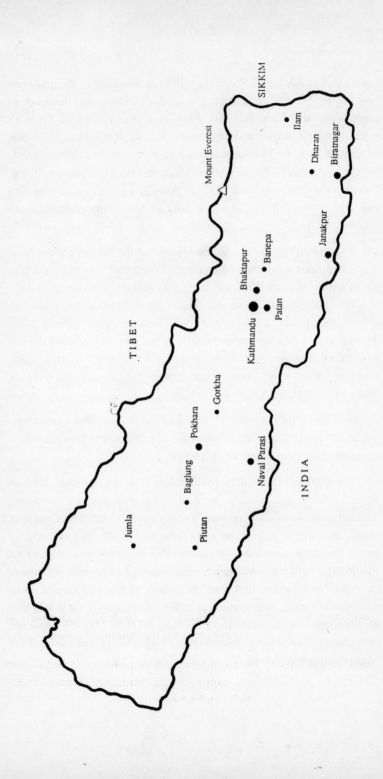

Appendix I

Chronology

1950, November 6:   King Tribhuvan seeks political asylum in the Indian embassy, the event which sparks off the 1950-51 revolution against the Rana regime.

1951, February 18:   The new Rana-Nepali Congress coalition is sworn in by King Tribhuvan.

1959, February 12:   King Mahendra promulgates his new democratic constitution.

1959, Feb.-March: Nepal's first multi-party elections are held.

1959, May 5:   The Nepali Congress ministry under the leadership of B.P. Koirala is sworn in.

1960, December 15:   King Mahendra takes power in his own hands and declares a state of emergency using article 55 of the constitution.

1962, December 16:   King Mahendra introduces the Panchayat constitution.

1979, May 24:   King Birendra announces a national referendum on the future of the Panchayat system.

1980, May 2:   The national referendum held which results in a slim victory for the Panchayat system.

1989, March 23:   India imposes a trade embargo on Nepal after the expiry of the Trade and Transit Treaty between the two countries.

1990, January 18:   The Nepali Congress opens its party convention in Kathmandu during which the plans for a pro-Democracy movement are announced.

1990, February 14:   Leaders of the pro-Democracy movement are arrested and telephone lines cut.

1990, February 18:   The official celebration of Democracy Day, and the first planned demonstration against the regime.

1990, Feb. 19 - 20: Several persons killed in major clashes between demonstrators and police in Bhaktapur.

1990, February 25:   The police successfully suppresses the demonstrations planned by the opposition for what they have called 'black day'.

1990, March 16:   The King fails to announce any political reforms in his speech at a major government rally in Pokhara.

1990, March 29:   The uprising in Patan begins.

1990, April 2:   Minister of Foreign Affairs, Shailendra Kumar Upadhyaya, resigns in protest.

1990, April 6:   King Birendra announces the dismissal of the Marich Man Singh Shrestha government. The biggest demonstration during the pro-Democracy movement leads to a massacre of civilians outside the Palace, and the beginning of a twenty-four hour curfew.

1990, April 8:   The King lifts the ban on political parties in the Panchayat constitution. The curfew is lifted.

1990, April 9: The success of the pro-Democracy movement is celebrated.

1990, April 15: The King announces the formation of an interim government under the leadership of Krishna Prasad Bhattarai.

1990, April 23: The return of violence in Kathmandu instigated by the Mandales.

1990, May 7: The King dissolves the remaining structures of the Panchayat system, and declares that all his powers have been transferred to the interim government.

1990, May 11: King announces the formation of a Constitutional Reform Recommendation Committee without consulting the interim cabinet.

1990, May 15: One person killed and several injured in Mandale instigated violence in Baglung.

1990, May 31: King announces the formation of a new Constitution Recommendation Committee on the recommendation of the cabinet.

1990, June 30: More than 20,000 walk through Kathmandu demanding a secular state in a demonstration organized by Nepal Buddhist Association.

1990, August 23: The Queen physically assaulted while visiting the Pashupatinath temple during the Hindu festival of Teej.

1990, August 31: The term of the Constitution Recommendation Committee expires, but no new constitution appears.

1990, September 10: A first draft of the new constitution is handed over to the King.

1990, October 19:	Leader of the United Left Front, Sahana Pradhan, declares that unless the new constitution appears before 24 October the interim government will resign and the mass movement would be resumed.
1990, October 22:	Draft of an alternative constitution allegedly originating from the palace is circulated in Kathmandu.
1990, November 6:	The population of Bhaktapur march into Kathmandu denouncing the royal conspiracy and demanding the announcement of the new constitution.
1990, November 9:	King Birendra promulgates Nepal's new democratic constitution.
1990, December:	The second civil servants' agitation.
1990, December 13:	One person killed in clashes in connection with a public meeting with Surya Bahadur Thapa (National Democratic Party) in Banepa.
1991, January 8:	Nepal Communist Party (Marxist) and Nepal Communist Party (Marxist-Leninist) merge and form Nepal Communist Party (United Marxist-Leninist).
1991, February 4:	Three people killed and several injured in a clash between police and landless people at Naval Parasi.
1991, April 25:	The announcement of the Nepali Congress nominations for the general elections causes a serious crisis in the party.
1991, May 12:	Nepal's second multi-party elections are held.
1991, May 29:	The new Nepali Congress government led by Girija Prasad Koirala is sworn in.

Appendix II

Interviews

1. Achut Raj Regmi – 15 September 1990
2. Babu Ram Bhattarai – 8 September 1990
3. Basudev Dhungana – 15 April 1991, 7 April 1991
4. Bikash Pandey – March 1989
5. Bijay Kumar Pandey – 16 April 1991
6. Chandra Bahadur Gurung – 1 March 1991
7. Dirga Raj Koirala – 2 November 1991
8. Dr Mathura Prasad Shrestha – 15 October 1990
9. Dr Mukundra Bahadur – 11 February 1990
10. Gajendra Narayan Singh – 4 November 1990
11. Ganesh Man Singh – 1 May 1990, May 1991
12. Ghore Bahadur Khapangi – 22 September 1990, 20 November 1990
13. Grishma Bahadur Devkota – 11 September 1990
14. Harihar Birahi – 17 April 1991
15. Harka Bahadur Gurung – May 1989
16. Kamala Pant – 15 April 1991
17. Keshar Bahadur Bista – 3 September 1990
18. Khagendra Jung Gurung – 19 September 1990
19. Krishna Prasad Bhatarai – May 1989, 1 February 1990, 3 December 1990, 10 October 1991
20. Madan Mani Dixit – 16 February 1990
21. Mangal Bir Byenjankar – 5 May 1991
22. Marich Man Singh Shrestha – 28 November 1990
23. Mohammad Mohsin – 1 December 1990

24. Narayan Man Bijukche (Comrade Rohit) – 8 May 1990,
    April 1991
25. Narayan Prasad Shrestha   –   28 April 1990, 18 October 1990,
    21 September 1991
26. Nava Raj Subhedi – 26 November 1990
27. Nirmal Lama – 12 September 1990
28. Nirmal Shrestha – 10 November 1990
29. Padam Thakurathi – 14 September 1990
30. Padma Ratna Tuladhar   –   29 August 1990, 2 April, 1991,
    21 October 1991
31. Prakash Kaphley & Sushil Pyakural – 8 October 1991
32. Prayog Raj Sharma – April 1989
33. Prem Krishna Pathak – 6 March 1991
34. Prof. Asha Ram Sakhya – 20 September 1990
35. P.L. Singh – April 1991
36. Radha Krishna Mainali – 19 September 1990
37. Rajeshwor Devkota – April 1991, 31 August 1990
38. Rishi Kumar Pandey – 19 November 1990
39. Risikesh Shaha – 30 August 1990
40. Sahana Pradhan – 22 September 1990
41. Shailendra Kumar Upadhyaya – 31 August 1990
42. Shanti Mishra – 19 March 1991
43. Shopkeeper Shrestha in Dhulikhel – 14 April 1991
44. Shree Bhadra Sharma – 3 March 1990, 29 April 1990
45. Surya Bahadur Thapa – 30 November 1990
45. Tanka Prasad Acharya – 14 November 1990
46. Tulsi Lal Amatya – 28 April 1990
47. Yog Prasad Upadhyaya – 9 April 1991

Appendix III

List of Political Parties in Nepal
(December 1990)

1. Bikash Dal (The Development Party)
2. Chutachut Mukti Sangathan
3. Conservative Party
4. Gorkha Bhumi Samrakshan Samaj
5. Green Democratic Party
6. Internationalist Democratic Party
7. Janata Dal Samajvadi Prajatantrik (Socialist Democratic)
8. Janavadi Morcha
9. Liberal Democratic Party
10. Limbuvan Mukti Morcha (Limbuvan Liberation Front)
11. Mongol National Organization
12. Nepal Rashtriya Jana Mukti Morcha (Nepal National People's Liberation Front)
13. Nepal Communist Party (Amatya)
14. Nepal Communist Party (Fourth Convention)
15. Nepal Communist Party (Janamukhi)
16. Nepal Communist Party (Manandhar)
17. Nepal Communist Party (Marxist)
18. Nepal Communist Party (Marxist-Leninist)
19. Nepal Communist Party (Mashal-majority)
20. Nepal Communist Party (Mashal-minority)
21. Nepal Communist Party (Sixth Convention)
22. Nepal Communist Sangathan
23. Nepal Communist Party (Varma)

24. Nepal Janahit Party
25. Nepal Janata Dal
26. Nepal Majdur Kisan Sangathan (Nepal Workers' and Peasants' Party)
27. Nepal Marxvadi Leninvadi Party
28. Nepal Panchayat Parishad
29. Nepal Praja Parishad
30. Nepal Rashtriya Congress
31. Nepal Rashtriya Loktantrik Dal
32. Nepal Sadbhavana Party (Nepal Goodwill Party)
33. Nepal Samajvadi Parishad
34. Nepal Sarvodaya Samajvadi Party
35. Nepal Terai Communist Party
36. Nepal Terai Muslim Congress Party
37. Nepali Communist League
38. Nepali Congress
39. Nepali Congress Party (38 group)
40. Nepali Janata Party
41. Panchayat Prajatantra Party
42. Prajantantrik Samajvadi Party
43. Rashtriya Jana Jati Party
44. Rashtriya Janata Party
45. Rashtriya Prajatantrik Samyukta Morcha
46. Rashtriya Prajatantra Party (National Democratic Party) (L)
47. Rashtriya Prajatantra Party (National Democratic Party) (S)
48. Rashtriya Pratantrik Ekta Panchayat Party
49. Rashtriya Svatantra Party
50. Samyukta Janata Morcha
51. Samyukta Prajantra Party
52. Sarvahara Vadi Shramik Sangathan
53. Svatantra Janata Dal
54. Utpidit Jatiya Manch

Appendix IV

Some of the Main Political Actors

Achut Raj Regmi: Minister in Lokendra Bahadur Chand's short-lived cabinet, again nominated by the King as a minister in the interim cabinet of Krishna Prasad Bhattarai, active member of the Hindu World Federation.

Dr Mathura Prasad Shrestha: Human rights activist, Minister of Health in the interim cabinet of Krishna Prasad Bhattarai.

Ganesh Man Singh: Veteran leader of the Nepali Congress, and supreme leader of the pro-Democracy movement. As the 'grand old man' of the revolution he functioned as a symbolic leader for the diverse political forces which toppled the Panchayat system.

Girija Prasad Koirala: Younger brother of the late B.P. Koirala and General Secretary of the Nepali Congress. As the third important member of the party leadership, Koirala became the Prime Minister of the Nepali Congress government after the 1991 elections.

Gore Bahadur Khapangi: General Secretary of the Nepal Rashtriya Jana Mukti Morcha (Nepal National People's Liberation Front), and activist in the religious and ethnic movement after the revolution.

Krishna Prasad Bhattarai: President of the Nepali Congress and Prime Minister of the interim government. As the second veteran leader after Ganesh Man Singh, Bhattarai played a crucial role during the pro-Democracy movement.

Lokendra Bahadur Chand: Prime Minister until 1986 and reappointed to the same position by the King on 6 April 1990, served during the dramatic turning point of the revolution, resigned on 15 April 1990, presently leader of the National Democratic Party (Chand).

Madhav Bhandari: President of the Nepal Communist Party (United Marxist-Leninist). Bhandari contested the 1992 elections from the same constituency as the interim Prime Minister, Krishna Prasad Bhattarai, and defeated the latter by a small margin.

Marich Man Singh Shrestha: Prime Minister from 1986 until 6 April 1990 and officially responsible for the suppression of the pro-Democracy movement.

Narayan Man Bijukche: Populist leader from Bhaktapur and founder of the Nepal Peasants' and Workers' Party.

Nirenjan Thapa: Home Minister in Marich Man Singh Shrestha's cabinet, popularly held responsible for the killings during the pro-Democracy movement.

Nava Raj Subedhi: Chairman of the old parliament, and chairman of the Panchayat Policy and Evaluation Committee, considered the most powerful man in the old regime, and together with Marich Man Singh Shrestha and Nirenjan Thapa blamed for the suppression of the pro-Democracy movement.

Padma Ratna Tuladhar: Populist leader from Kathmandu, Newari language activist, and independent member of the United Left Front.

Radha Krishna Mainali and Chandra Prakash Mainali: Leading members of Nepal Communist Party (Marxist-Leninist). Imprisoned for years for their involvement in the Naxalite movement in eastern Nepal in the early seventies.

Rajeshwor Devkota: Influential member of the old regime, and leader of the political opposition within the Panchayat system, presently leading member of the National Democratic Party (Chand).

Sahana Pradhan: Widow of the founder of the Nepal Communist Party, Pushpa Lal Shrestha. Was appointed president of the new United Left Front immediately before the revolution, and became Minister of Industry and Commerce in the interim government. She continued as a leading member of the new Nepal Communist Party (United Marxist-Leninist) after January 1991.

Shailendra Kumar Upadhyaya: Foreign Minister in Marich Man Singh Shrestha's government, active during the period of the Indian Embargo, resigned in protest on 2 April 1990.

Surya Bahadur Thapa: Several times Prime Minister, and influential member of the Panchayat system, presently president of the National Democratic Party (Thapa).

Tulsi Lal Amatya: Veteran leader of the communist movement and of his own party, Nepal Communist Party (Amatya).

Bibliography

Anderson, B.,	*Imagined Communities*, Verso Editions and NLB, 1983.
Baral, L.R.,	*Oppositional Politics in Nepal*, Columbia, Mo.: South Asia Books, 1978.
Beanett, L.,	*Dangerous Wives and Sacred Sisters.*
Blaike P., Cameron, J., Seddon, D.,	*Nepal in Crisis*, Delhi: Oxford University Press, 1980.
Burghart, R.,	"The Concept of Nation-State in Nepal" in the *Journal of Asian Studies*, Volume 44 No. 1 November, 1984.
Caplan L.,	*Land and Social Change in Nepal*, London: Routledge and Kegan Paul.
Caplan L.,	*Land and Social Change in East Nepal: A Study of Hindu-Tribal Relations*, Berkeley and Los Angeles: University of California Press, 1970.
Chatterji, Bhola,	*Portrait of a Revolutionary: B.P. Koirala*, 1982.
Chatterji, P.,	*Nationalist Thought and the Colonial World:, A Derivative Discourse*, The United Nations University, 1986.
Chauhan, R.S.,	*The Political Development in Nepal, 1950-70*, Delhi: 1971.
Gaige, F.H.,	*Regionalism and National Unity in Nepal*, Berkeley: University of California Press, 1975.
Gellner, E.,	*Nations and Nationalism*, Blackwells, 1983.
Gupta, A.,	*Politics in Nepal*, Bombay: Allied, 1964.
Hutt, M.J.,	"Nepali: The Emergence of a National Language ", Ph.D. Thesis, University of London, 1986.

Joshi, Bhuwan Lal and Leo, Rose E.,	*Democratic Innovations in Nepal*, 1966.
Khanal Y.,	*Reflections on Nepal-India Relations*, 1964.
Khanal Y.,	*Nepal: Transition from Isolationism*, Kathmandu: Sajha Prakashan, 1977.
Van Kooij, K.R.,	*Religion in Nepal*, Leiden: E.J. Brill, 1978.
Kramer, K.H.,	*Das Konigtum in Der Modernen Nepalischen Geschicte*, VGH Wissenschaftsverlag Sankt Augustin, 1981.
Ranad, K., Malla, P.S.J.B.,	*Nepal in Perspective*, Kathmandu: CEDA, 1973.
Muni, S.D.,	*Foreign Policy of Nepal*, Delhi: National Publishing House, 1973.
Muni, S.D., (ed.)	*Nepal; An Assertive Monarchy*, Delhi: Chetana, 1977.
Muni, S.D.,	*Political Change: A Framework Of Analysis.*
Jha, S.K.,	*Policy Towards India:Quest For Independence.*
Nath, T.,	*The Nepalese Dilemma*, Delhi: Sterling Publishers, 1975.
Paramanand,	*The Nepali Congress in Exile*, 1978.
Paramanand,	*The Nepali Congress Since its inception: A Critical Assessment*, 1982.
Pophur,	*Dawn of Democracy – People's Power in Nepal*, Kathmandu: 1990.
Poudyal,	*Public Administration and National-Building in Nepal*, Delhi: NBO Publishers and Distributors, 1984.
Ramakant,	*Nepal, China and India*, Delhi: Abhinav, 1976.
Rawat, P.C.,	*Indo-Nepal Economic Relations* Delhi: National, 1974.

Regmi, M.C.,   *Thatched Huts and Stucco Palaces* Delhi: Vikas Publishing House, 1978.

Regmi, M.C.,   *The State and Economic Surplus* Varanasi: Nath Publishing House, 1984.

Rose, Leo E.,   *Strategy For Survival*, 1966.

Rose, Leo E., and Scholz, John T.,   *Nepal: Profile of a Himalayan Kingdom* Boulder, Colorado: Westview Press, 1975.

Shaha, R.,   *Nepali Politics: Retrospect and Prospect* Delhi: Oxford University Press, 1975.

Shaha, R.,   *Essays in the Practice of Government in Nepal,* 1982.

Shrestha, P.P.,   *Nepal Rediscovered*, London: Serindia, 1986.

Slusser, M.S.,   *Nepal Mandala*, Princeton University Press, 1982.

Stiller, L.,   *Rise of the House of Gorkha*, Kathmandu: Patna Jesuit Society, 1973.

Stiller, L.,   *The Silent Cry: The People Of Nepal 1816-1837*, Kathmandu: Sahayogi Press, 1976.

Stiller, L.,   *The Kot Massacre*, Kathmandu: CENAS, 1981.

Subedi, A.,   *Nepali Literature: Background and History*, Kathmandu: Sahayogi Press, 1978.

Verma, R.S. (ed.)   *The Cultural Heritage of Nepal*, Allahabad: 1972.

Whelpton, J.,   *Jang Bahadur in Europe*, Kathmandu: Sahayogi Press, 1983.

INDEX

Printed at Rekha Printers Pvt Ltd, New Delhi 110020